Carlton Ware

Patterns and Shapes

Dr Czes & Yvonne Kosniowski

© Dr Czes & Yvonne Kosniowski 2014

This book provides a list of Carlton Ware Pattern Numbers and Shape Numbers. No pictures are included in this book. It consists purely of two lists (searchable on eBooks). For pictures of Carlton Ware you need to buy one of the following books by the authors:

A Pocket Guide to Carlton Ware

Carlton Ware Catalogue and Price Guide

Carlton Ware – The Complete Guide including a Price Guide

Contents

Pattern Numbers and Impressed Numbers	1
Carlton Ware Patterns	3
Patterns 1 – 999	4
Patterns 1000 – 1999	10
Patterns 2000 – 2999	16
Patterns 3000 – 3999	38
Patterns 4000 – 4999	79
Patterns 5000 – 5999	113
Patterns with unknown pattern numbers	114
List of pattern numbers by pattern name	116
Carlton Ware Shapes	136
Shapes 1 – 499	137
Shapes 500 – 999	140
Shapes 1000 – 1499	142
Shapes 1500 – 1999	159
Shapes 2000 – 2499	176
Shapes 2500 – 2999	194
Shapes 3000 – 3499	213
Shapes 3500 – 3999	232
List of shape numbers by shape name	234

Pattern Numbers and Impressed Numbers

There are two numbers that are important when looking at Carlton Ware; these are the Pattern and Impressed Numbers. Broadly speaking the Impressed (or Shape) number, which is applied before the firing process, indicates the "shape" of the item. On the other hand the Pattern number is usually hand painted on the base or on to a Carlton Ware sticker. This number represents the "pattern" and "colour" of the piece and is applied when the decorating takes place.

For example the impressed number **217** is a 6-inch tall vase. This shape has been used over a large number of years and came with many different patterns.

Often an impressed numbers is followed by a space or "/" followed by further numbers. These further numbers refer to the "size" of the Carlton Ware piece. For example the conical shape **111** usually came with an additional number 10, 8 or 6 that represented the size in inches.

In principle if you know the correct Pattern number, the Impressed number and the size then you should then be able to determine what the item looks like including its colour.

With the embossed range of Carlton Ware the Impressed number also characterises the pattern. For instance, Shape **2311** is a Jug with the Hazelnut pattern. It came in three sizes: large, medium and small. It was also available in three colours Matt Cream, Green and Blue. Each would have its own pattern number (in the 4000 number range). Thus, although the impressed

Carlton Ware Patterns and Shapes

number in this case would also identify the pattern, the pattern number would also tell you the pattern and the colour.

Of course life with Carlton Ware is not always that simple. Pattern numbers sometimes had an additional letter added and that produced a slightly different pattern. For example

3765 Red Devil

3765 Devil's Copse

Both are on a gloss turquoise ground. The second pattern is basically the same as the first but without the Red Devil on it.

Sometimes the same pattern numbers were produced with different colourways such as:

2907 Magpies on red ground

2907 Magpies on blue ground

Finally we have examples where the patterns are different and the colourways are different. For example:

3965 Heron and Magical Tree on cream ground.

3965 Plain Rouge Royale

We have received many examples of this particular pair from several different people. It is therefore unlikely to be just the case of one person misreading a number

In summary you can characterise Carlton Ware, almost uniquely, by the pattern number (with additional suffixes) and impressed number (with additional suffixes for size).

Dr Czes & Yvonne Kosniowski

Carlton Ware Patterns

Carlton Ware designed several thousands of different patterns; and these were produced in many different shapes and colours. Each design and associated colour was normally designated a pattern number. This number was usually either painted on the base or written on a paper sticker stuck to the bottom.

There is no complete list of patterns. The original pattern books have disappeared, although a few pages have surfaced recently. We have, over many years, been collating a list of patterns together with their associated pattern numbers. The list has been compiled from a number of sources – from our own purchases and from other collectors. We would like to thank everyone that has sent us pictures of their Carlton Ware.

Sometimes hand painted numbers are difficult to read and therefore we may attribute two different patterns to the same number. Sometimes Carlton Ware used the same number for different patterns which they distinguished by the addition of an extra letter.

The following is a list of the patterns that we are aware of. This list is not perfect and we apologise for any errors.

Patterns 1 - 999

52 Blush Ware - Cistus : *Colourful flowers.*
74 Blush Ware - Cistus : *Colourful flowers.*
110 Blush Ware : *Flowers.*
128 Chequered Border : *Border design on Red ground.*
142 Blush Ware - Sweet Violet : *Violet like flowers on pale pink and cream ground.*
184 Blush Ware - Camellia : *Camelia flowers on pale cream ground.*
186 Blush Ware - Peony : *Peony flowers.*
194 Blush Ware - Peony : *Peony flowers.*
206 Blush Ware - Poppy : *Flowers*
220 Flow Blue - Florida : *Flow blue, flowers and leaves in blue and gilt with gilt background.*
230 Flow Blue : *Flow Blue*
237 Blush Ware - Violet : *Violet like flowers.*
253 Blush Ware : *Flowers.*
303 Blush Ware - Poppy : *Poppies on White/Cream.*
305 Blush Ware - Poppy : *Poppies on pale Blue.*
306 Blush Ware - Poppy : *Poppies on Pink.*
307 Blush Ware - Poppy : *Poppies on Pink.*
347 Blush Ware - Azalea : *Flowers.*
348 Blush Ware - Rose Garland : *Flowers*
376 Blush Ware - Convolvulous : *Pinkish Convolvulous flowers.*
401 Blush Ware - Chrysanthemum : *Chrysanthemum flowers, pale cream ground.*
403 Blush Ware - Rose Bud : *Flowers.*

405 Blush Ware - Chrysanthemum : *Chrysanthemum flowers on pale Pink.*
406 Blush Ware - Chrysanthemum : *Chrysanthemum flowers on pale Pink.*
407 Blush Ware - Chrysanthemum : *Chrysanthemum flowers, pale cream ground.*
409 Blush Ware - Chrysanthemum : *Chrysanthemum flowers.*
418 Blush Ware - Heather : *Flowers*
421 Bird : *A bit like lovebirds*
425 Blush Ware - Camellia : *Flowers on pale cream ground.*
428 Blush Ware - Arvista : *Flowers.*
438 Blush Ware - Dianthus : *Carnation like flowers.*
438 Blush Ware - Rose Garland : *Flowers*
439 Blush Ware - Roses : *Roses on pale cream ground.*
458 Blush Ware - Dianthus : *Flowers.*
476 Blush Ware - Arvista : *Flowers.*
483 Blush Ware - Carnation : *Flowers.*
491 Blush Ware - Petunia : *Colourful flowers.*
504 Blush Ware - Chrysanthemum : *Flowers.*
508 Blush Ware - Royal May : *Flowers.*
509 Blush Ware - Royal May : *Flowers*
522 Chinese Quail : *Bird with plumed tail sitting on branch with foliage and flowers. Black ground.*
523 no name : *Long tailed bird.*
524 Blush Ware : *Flowers.*
528 Red Rose : *Red roses and leaves on matt black ground.*
534 Flow Blue - Petunia : *Flowers*
538 Blush Ware - Peony : *Flowers*
547 Flow Blue - Catalpa : *Flowers*

Carlton Ware Patterns and Shapes

561 Blush Ware - Arvista : *Colourful poppy like flowers on pale cream ground.*
561 Flow Blue - Arvista : *Poppy like flowers.*
566 Flow Blue : *Flowers on Flow Blue*
578 Blush Ware - Tulips : *Flowers.*
585 Blush Ware : *Flowers.*
586 Flow Blue - Flower Garland : *Flowers in blue.*
595 Bird & Tree Peony : *Small bird on Peony like blossoms. Matt black ground.*
596 Kang Hsi : *Variety of flowerheads, blossom and leaves on white ground within blue bordered cartouches.*
597 Kang Hsi Fish : *Beautiful realistic looking orange fish swimming amongst gilt seaweed. Blue ground with Kang Hsi backstamp.*
599 Kang Hsi : *Variety of flowerheads, blossom and leaves on white ground.*
601 Grecian Figures : *Frieze of white foliage and white Grecian style figures raised as in Wedgewood. Pink ground.*
601 Plain : *Plain pink with gilt.*
602 Grecian Figures : *Frieze of white foliage and white Grecian style figures raised as in Wedgewood. Grey ground.*
602 Blush Ware - Royal May : *Flowers.*
602 Grecian Figures with no Figures : *Normally with a frieze of white foliage and white Grecian style figures raised as in Wedgewood. Grey ground.*
603 no name : *Pale green ground with white perimeter band.*
604 Grecian Figures : *Frieze of white foliage and white Grecian style figures raised as in Wedgewood. Pale green ground.*

614 Dancing Figures : *Frieze of white foliage and white Grecian style dancing figures raised as in Wedgewood. Dark green matt ground.*
616 Flow Blue : *Flow Blue*
621 Blush Ware - Carnation Spray : *Carnation flowers*
624 Reproduction Swansea China : *Colourful posies of flowers in gilt cartouches with decorative gilt leaves and bands on black ground.*
624 Blush Ware - Picotees : *Carnation like flowers*
628 Pheasant Cartouche : *Cartouche of multi-coloured exotic birds, flowers and butterflies. Often has Kang Hsi back stamp.*
634 Blush Ware - Hibiscus : *Flowers.*
637 Blush Ware - Cornucopia : *Multi-coloured flowers.*
638 Blush Ware - Hibiscus : *Hibiscus floral cluster, rim edged in gold. Pale ground.*
639 Blush Ware - Hibiscus : *Flowers.*
641 Blush Ware - Daffodil : *Daffodil like flowers*
642 no name : *Flowers and foliage on cream ground.*
649 Blush Ware : *Flowers.*
653 Blush Ware - Cornucopia : *Multi-coloured flowers.*
659 Blush Ware - Wild Rose : *Flowers.*
661 Blush Ware - Catalpa : *Flowers.*
666 Blush Ware - Honfleur : *Flowers.*
670 Blush Ware : *Flowers.*
682 Blush Ware - Dahlia : *Flowers.*
683 Blush Ware - Dahlia : *Flowers.*
686 Blush Ware - Daisy : *Flowers*
694 Blush Ware - Petunia : *Flowers.*
695 Blush Ware - Petunia : *Flowers.*
698 Blush Ware - Petunia : *Flowers.*
708 Blush Ware : *Flowers.*
709 Blush Ware - Cornflower : *Flowers*

Carlton Ware Patterns and Shapes

722 Stork : *White Stork bird with insets of colourful flowers and leaves. Cloisonne Ware on matt green ground.*

723 Stork : *White Stork bird with insets of colourful flowers and leaves. Cloisonne Ware on matt black ground.*

732 Blush Ware : *Flowers.*

735 Blush Ware - Dahlia : *Flowers.*

739 Blush Ware - Cornucopia : *Blossom on pale cream ground.*

751 Flow Blue - Poppy : *Blue lined design of poppies on white gloss ground.*

752 Flow Blue - Poppy : *Blue lined design of poppies on white gloss ground.*

777 Flow Blue - Diadem : *Blue flowers on white ground.*

821 Blush Ware - Clematis : *Flowers.*

826 Blush Ware - Clematis : *Flowers.*

827 Pheasant Cartouche : *Cartouche of multi-coloured exotic birds, flowers and butterflies.*

832 Blush Ware - Cornucopia : *Multi-coloured flowers design.*

838 Blush Ware - Nouveau Poppies : *Poppies on pale cream ground.*

839 Blush Ware - Hibiscus : *Flowers.*

843 Blush Ware - Camellia : *Flowers and leaves*

848 Blush Ware - Camellia : *Flowers and leaves*

849 Blush Ware - Camellia : *Flowers and leaves*

850 Insects : *Insects and foliage on white ground.*

852 Plain : *Plain white with gilt on handles.*

856 Blush Ware - Queen Victoria : *Flowers with Queen Victoria.*

860 Blush Ware - Camellia : *Flowers and leaves*

876 Flow Blue - May : *Flowers*

878 Blush Ware - Dahlia : *Dahlia like flowers*
886 Blush Ware - Nouveau Poppies : *Poppies on white ground.*
888 Blush Ware - Nouveau Poppies : *Poppies on pale cream ground.*
913 Blush Ware - Roses : *Flowers.*
914 Blush Ware - Pansy : *Flowers*
921 Blush Ware - Honfleur : *Flowers.*
945 Blush Ware - Peony : *Peony flowers*
949 Blush Ware - Peony : *Peony flowers*
975 Blush Ware : *Flowers.*

Patterns 1000 - 1999

1002 Blush Ware - Honfleur : *Flowers.*
1006 Flow Blue - Poppy : *Blue lined design of poppies on white gloss ground.*
1015 Blush Ware - Poppy : *Poppies*
1031 Blush Ware - Arvista : *Flowers on pale cream ground.*
1031 Flow Blue - Poppy : *Blue lined design of poppies on white gloss ground.*
1034 Blush Ware - Peony : *Peonies*
1038 Blush Ware - Carnation : *Carnation like flowers*
1041 Blush Ware - Carnation : *Carnation like flowers*
1041 Flow Blue - Poppy : *Blue lined design of poppies on white gloss ground.*
1042 Blush Ware - Poppy Spray : *Flowers*
1057 Blush Ware - Arvista : *Flowers on pale cream ground.*
1075 Blush Ware : *Flowers.*
1089 Blush Ware - Chrysanthemum : *White to light cream ground with orange and beige chrysanthemums.*
1091 Blush Ware - Chrysanthemum : *White to light cream ground with pink and mauve chrysanthemums.*
1123 Blush Ware - Wild Rose : *Flowers.*
1125 Blush Ware - Wild Rose : *Flowers.*
1153 Blush Ware - Camellia : *Flowers on creamy background.*

1162 Blush Ware - Cornucopia : *Brownish ground, deep blue border, multi-coloured flowers.*
1166 Blush Ware - Heather : *Flowers.*
1172 Rose Bud : *Flowers*
1186 Blush Ware - Rose Garland : *Flowers*
1219 Blush Ware : *Flowers.*
1220 First Blush of Day : *Intricate design which appear to depict a bird and sun.*
1221 Blush Ware - Roses : *Flowers.*
1225 Flow Blue : *Flow Blue*
1229 Blush Ware - Royal May : *Flowers.*
1230 Blush Ware : *White ground with figures of grey and brown.*
1242 Blush Ware - Carnation Spray : *Flowers on pale ground.*
1246 Blush Ware : *Apple blossom & butterfly.*
1274 Flow Blue : *Flowers in blue and colours edged in gilt on pale cream ground.*
1283 Blush Ware - Violet : *Violets*
1304 no name : *Patterned flowers on green and red ground.*
1315 Blush Ware - Violet : *Violets*
1332 Blush Ware - Violet : *Violets*
1340 Blush Ware : *Flowers.*
1358 Blush Ware : *Flowers.*
1372 Blush Ware - Chrysanthemum : *Orange and beige chrysanthemums on white to light cream ground.*
1400 Blush Ware - Dog Rose : *Flowers.*
1406 Flow Blue : *Flowers in blue and gilt.*
1414 Blush Ware : *Flowers.*
1422 Flow Blue - Iris : *Iris like flowers.*
1451 Blush Ware - Petunia : *Flowers*
1453 Blush Ware - Petunia : *Flowers.*

Carlton Ware Patterns and Shapes

1467 Blush Ware - Petunia : *Flowers*
1474 Blush Ware - Cistus : *Colourful flowers.*
1509 Blush Ware : *Brownish ground, gilt feet and rim. Sprays of flowers.*
1518 Blush Ware : *Flowers.*
1524 Blush Ware - Dog Rose : *Flowers.*
1572 Blush Ware : *Flowers.*
1573 no name : *Blue transfer flowers, raised gilding.*
1582 Blush Ware - Carnation : *Flowers*
1601 Blush Ware - Honeysuckle : *Honeysuckle flowers*
1609 Blush Ware - Wild Rose : *Flowers.*
1619 Flow Blue : *Multi-flowered panels*
1621 Blush Ware : *Flowers.*
1624 Blush Ware : *Flowers.*
1630 Blush Ware - Arvista : *Flowers.*
1631 Flow Blue : *Flowers on pale ground.*
1635 Flow Blue - Chrysanthemum : *Blue Chrysanthemums edged in gilt and with heavy gold surrounding.*
1635 Blush Ware - Hibiscus : *Flowers.*
1639 Flow Blue - Honfleur : *Flowers.*
1646 Flow Blue - Daffodil : *Daffodil flowers on Flow Blue*
1650 Blush Ware - Diadem : *Thistle like flowers*
1652 Blush Ware - Arvista : *Flowers on pale cream ground.*
1653 Blush Ware - Dahlia : *Flowers*
1655 Blush Ware - Marguerite : *Patterns of flowers in cobalt blue outlined in gilt. Gold floral design on cream ground.*
1658 Blush Ware - Peony : *Peony flowers*
1661 Blush Ware - Peony : *Peony flowers on pale cream ground.*
1664 Blush Ware : *Flowers.*

1681 Blush Ware : *Deep blue like Doulton.*
1682 Blush Ware - Peony : *Peony flowers*
1683 Blush Ware - Peony : *Peony flowers*
1685 Blush Ware - Peony : *Peony flowers*
1693 Blush Ware - Carnation : *Carnations on pale cream ground with some blue.*
1713 Blush Ware - Heather : *Flowers.*
1728 no name : *Chinoiserie design, light blue ground and enamels.*
1732 Blush Ware - Carnation : *Floral sprays printed in colours.*
1733 Blush Ware - Carnation : *Carnations on pale cream ground.*
1739 Blush Ware : *Flowers.*
1741 Blush Ware - Dahlia : *Chrysanthemum flowers on pale cream ground.*
1742 Blush Ware - Heather : *Flowers.*
1747 Blush Ware : *Flowers.*
1749 Blush Ware : *Flowers.*
1750 Blush Ware - Gladioli : *Flowers.*
1752 Blush Ware : *Flowers.*
1757 no name : *Figures in garden, blue ground.*
1769 Blush Ware - Cistus : *Colourful flowers*
1770 Blush Ware - Poppy : *Multi-coloured poppies*
1775 Chrysanthemum : *Blue Chrysanthemum type flowers.*
1786 Blush Ware : *Flowers.*
1795 Blush Ware - Mixed Cottage : *Pansy like flowers.*
1799 Blush Ware : *Flowers.*
1804 Blush Ware - Cistus : *Colourful flowers*
1810 Blush Ware - Petunia : *Flowers.*
1832 Blush Ware - Peony : *Peony flowers*

Carlton Ware Patterns and Shapes

1839 Blush Ware - Peony : *Peony flowers on pale cream ground.*
1846 Chorisia :
1848 Blush Ware : *Flowers on pale cream ground.*
1853 Blush Ware - Peony : *Flowers.*
1863 Blush Ware : *Flowers.*
1865 Blush Ware - Peony : *Flowers.*
1869 Blush Ware - Peony : *Flowers.*
1878 Blush Ware - Dahlia : *Flowers.*
1879 Blush Ware - Arvista : *Flowers.*
1883 Mikado : *Chinoiserie design of pagodas, bridges, oriental ladies and usually a pair of kissing birds. Coral and black ground.*
1886 Mikado : *Chinoiserie design of pagodas, bridges, oriental ladies and usually a pair of kissing birds. Coral and black ground.*
1902 Blush Ware : *Flowers.*
1905 Almond Blossom : *White blossom on blue ground.*
1911 Flow Blue - Catalpa : *Flowers*
1918 Blush Ware - Wild Rose : *Sprays of flowers on pale cream ground.*
1919 Blush Ware - Wild Rose : *Sprays of flowers on pale cream ground.*
1928 Blush Ware : *Flowers.*
1935 Blush Ware : *Flowers.*
1939 Blush Ware - Wild Rose : *Flowers.*
1941 Flow Blue - Multi- Flowers : *Gilt outline of flowers with blue banding*
1942 Blush Ware : *Flowers with frieze.*
1946 Blush Ware - Arvista : *Flowers.*
1947 Blush Ware - Wild Rose : *Sprays of flowers with blue border.*

1950 Flow Blue : *Blue flowers and leaves on white ground.*
1960 Flow Blue - Poppy : *Poppy flowers.*
1966 Blush Ware - Petunia : *Flowers*
1974 Blush Ware - Wild Rose : *Flowers.*
1981 Carnation : *Sprays of carnations, enamels and gilt. Blue ground.*
1982 Blush Ware - Dahlia : *Flowers.*
1986 Blush Ware - Wild Rose : *Sprays of flowers on pale cream ground.*
1987 Blush Ware - Petunia : *Blue flowers on white ground.*
1990 Blush Ware - Arvista : *Flowers on pale cream ground.*
1996 Blush Ware - Peony : *Peony flowers*

Patterns 2000 - 2999

2006 Dragon : *Oriental dragons in gilt and colours. Black ground.*
2007 Blush Ware - Petunia : *Petunia flowers on pale cream ground.*
2021 Kang Hsi Chinoiserie : *Chinese design of Foliage and Pagodas, one has an ornamental wall and one has a post fence. A gold sun and a frieze of oriental motifs. Blue ground.*
2021 Blush Ware - Hibiscus : *Flowers.*
2030 Peach Blossom : *Pink and green blossom sprays on matt black ground.*
2031 Kien Lung : *Birds on prunus blossom and flowers within cartouches of good luck symbols. Pink ground.*
2033 Cartouche of Flowers : *Cartouche with flowers. Blue lustre ground.*
2040 Blush Ware : *Flowers.*
2041 Rockery & Pheasant : *Pheasant on a rockery of ornate flowers and foliage. Blue ground.*
2041 Willow : *Chinoiserie design of willow trees, pagodas, bridge and a fence. Also a pair of kissing birds in flight. Similar to Mikado. White ground with blue frieze.*
2044 Swansea Flowers : *Flowers on white ground with yellow border.*
2046 Chintz : *Vividly decorated with intensely packed (usually) multi-coloured flowers.*

2047 Chintz : *Vividly decorated with intensely packed multi-coloured flowers.*
2053 Kien Lung : *Small flowers on black good luck symbols. Terracotta and black ground.*
2053 Dragon : *Chinese Dragon on a yellow ground.*
2062 Dragon : *Chinese Dragon on a powder blue ground.*
2064 Dragon : *Chinese Dragon on a yellow ground.*
2066 Dragon : *Chinese Dragon in red on matt black ground.*
2067 Dragon : *Chinese Dragon on red ground.*
2069 Chintz : *Vividly decorated with intensely packed flowers in greens, yellow, blue, purple and orange.*
2071 Rockery & Pheasant : *Pheasant on a rockery of flowers and foliage, highly enamelled design. Blue ground.*
2080 Rose Trellis : *Realistic Roses on a white ground amidst black lines.*
2083 Blush Ware - Cornucopia : *Multi-coloured flowers.*
2086 Blush Ware - Cornucopia : *Flowers on pale cream ground.*
2089 Birds and Blossom : *Variety of birds, including swallows, and blossom on a white ground.*
2091 New Mikado : *Chinese Figures, Pagodas, Bridges and sometimes two crane like birds. Gloss olive green ground.*
2093 Flies : *Large and small butterflies or moths on deep red lustre ground.*
2095 Flies : *Large and small butterflies or moths on a pinky red lustre ground. Armand back stamp.*
2099 Flies : *Large or small butterflies or moths on pinky red lustre ground. Armand back stamp.*
2102 Dragon : *Chinese Dragon. Armand Lustre Ware.*
2103 Dragon : *Chinese Dragon. Armand Lustre Ware.*

2105 Flies : *Large and small butterflies or moths on green ground. Armand back stamp.*
2109 Flies : *Large and small butterflies or moths on blue ground. Armand back stamp.*
2112 Flies : *Large and small butterflies or moths on dark green lustre ground. Armand back stamp.*
2115 no name : *Five yellow cartouches of birds of paradise. Matt black ground.*
2121 Lovebirds : *Birds in tree, Armand backstamp. Pale Blue ground.*
2124 Basket of Flowers : *Ornate formal basket of flowers. Light blue ground.*
2126 no name : *Bird in flowers and foliage on a white ground.*
2131 Flies : *Large and small butterflies or moths on orange lustre ground.*
2133 Flies : *Large and small butterflies or moths on a pale pink ground.*
2134 Flies : *Large and small butterflies or moths on pale blue lustre. Armand backstamp.*
2143 Pink Carnation : *Pink Carnation like blossom on matt black ground.*
2145 Worcester Birds : *Enamelled bird design set in black decorative panels. Matt coral ground.*
2151 Basket of Flowers : *Ornate formal basket of flowers. Blue ground.*
2154 Blush Ware - Nasturtium : *Flowers*
2166 Blush Ware - Hibiscus : *Flowers.*
2174 Flies : *Butterflies or Moths on pale blue. Armand backstamp.*
2175 Worcester Birds : *Enamelled bird design set in black decorative panels. Matt coral ground.*

2175 Worcester Birds without Birds : *Enamelled design set in black decorative panels. Matt coral ground.*

2178 Dancing Figures : *Grecian style dancing figures. Dark green ground.*

2179 Blush Ware - Petunia : *Petunia flowers on pale cream ground.*

2184 Basket of Flowers : *Ornate formal basket of flowers. Blue ground.*

2185 Basket of Flowers : *Ornate formal basket of flowers. Black ground.*

2186 Rockery & Pheasant : *Pheasant on a rockery of flowers and foliage, highly enamelled design. White ground.*

2189 Basket of Flowers : *Ornate formal basket of flowers. Blue ground and white panels.*

2191 Old Wisteria : *Trailing wisteria design on matt black ground.*

2192 no name : *Peony flowers on Matt black ground.*

2193 no name : *Armand backstamp?*

2195 Worcester Birds : *Enamelled bird design set in black decorative panels. Blue lustre ground.*

2196 Worcester Birds : *Enamelled bird design set in black decorative panels. Yellow ground.*

2197 no name : *Plain matt black with orange interior.*

2199 Mikado : *Chinoiserie pagodas, bridges, oriental ladies and usually a pair of kissing birds. Blue ground.*

2212 Geometric Clouds : *Pale blue ground.*

2215 Blush Ware - Wild Rose : *Flowers*

2216 Cartouche of Flowers : *Cartouche with flowers with butterfly. Terracotta ground.*

2218 Bird & Chequered Border : *Cartouche with bird design. Yellow ground*

2221 Bird & Chequered Border : *Cartouche with bird design. Matt black ground.*
2224 Blush Ware - Daisies : *Flowers on pale cream ground.*
2227 Blush Ware - Daisies : *Flowers on pale cream ground.*
2234 no name : *Yellow ground with black pattern border.*
2238 Old Wisteria : *Vertical panels, decorated stripes, sprays of wisteria. Black ground.*
2240 Mikado : *Chinoiserie pagodas, bridges, oriental ladies and usually a pair of kissing birds. Matt black ground.*
2244 Rockery & Pheasant : *Pheasant on a rockery of flowers and foliage, highly enamelled design. Blue ground.*
2250 Cock & Peony : *Two cockerels standing amongst foliage. Also has a variety of beautifully enamelled flowers including peonies. Sometimes has a Cock & Peony backstamp. Powder Blue ground.*
2264 Mikado : *Chinoiserie pagodas, bridges, oriental ladies and usually a pair of kissing birds. Blue ground.*
2270 Mikado : *Chinoiserie pagodas, bridges, oriental ladies and usually a pair of kissing birds. Coloured enamels and Matt black ground.*
2280 Cock & Peony : *Two cockerels standing amongst foliage. Also has a variety of beautifully enamelled flowers including peonies. White ground.*
2281 Cock & Peony : *Two cockerels standing amongst foliage. Also has a variety of beautifully enamelled flowers including peonies. Sometimes has a Cock & Peony backstamp. Matt black ground.*
2282 Cock & Peony : *Two cockerels standing amongst foliage. Also has a variety of beautifully enamelled*

flowers including peonies. Sometimes has a Cock & Peony backstamp. White ground.

2284 Dancing Figures : *Green jasper finish with white Grecian style dancing ladies, similar to Wedgewood.*

2285 Cock & Peony : *Two cockerell standing amongst foliage. Also has a variety of beautifully enamelled flowers including peonies. Sometimes has a Cock & Peony backstamp.*

2286 Roses : *Roses on a black ground.*

2287 Cock & Peony : *Two cockerels standing amongst foliage. Also has a variety of beautifully enamelled flowers including peonies. Sometimes has a Cock & Peony backstamp. Yellow ground.*

2288 Cock & Peony : *Two cockerels standing amongst foliage. Also has a variety of beautifully enamelled flowers including peonies. Sometimes has a Cock & Peony backstamp. Bright Blue ground.*

2300 Blush Ware - Camellia : *Flowers.*

2301 Blush Ware - Marguerite : *Patterns of flowers in cobalt blue outlined in gilt. Gold floral design on cream ground.*

2308 Cock & Peony : *Two cockerels standing amongst foliage. Also has a variety of beautifully enamelled flowers including peonies. Sometimes has a Cock & Peony backstamp. Pale blue ground.*

2309 Blush Ware - Primula : *Flowers.*

2314 Mikado : *Chinoiserie pagodas, bridges, oriental ladies and usually a pair of kissing birds. Powder blue ground.*

2319 Flow Blue : *Flow Blue. Flower heads and petals.*

2326 Lovebirds : *Birds in tree, Armand backstamp. Pale Blue ground.*

2328 Lovebirds : *Birds in tree, Armand backstamp. Orange ground.*
2332 no name : *Pheasant on pale blue ground.*
2333 Lovebirds : *Birds in tree, Armand backstamp. Green ground.*
2334 Rose Medallion : *Roses and a chain of bells.*
2339 Blush Ware : *Flowers*
2340 Mikado : *Chinoiserie pagodas, bridges, oriental ladies and usually a pair of kissing birds. Black ground.*
2341 Willow : *Parts of Willow pattern in checkered border. Mauve ground.*
2351 Willow : *Chinoiserie pagodas, Willow tree, bridge, and a fence. Usually a pair of kissing birds in flight. Orange lustre ground.*
2352 Willow : *Chinoiserie pagodas, Willow tree, bridge, and a fence. Usually a pair of kissing birds in flight. Pale blue lustre ground.*
2355 Mikado : *Chinoiserie pagodas, bridges, oriental ladies and usually a pair of kissing birds. White mother of pearl lustre ground.*
2356 Mikado : *Chinoiserie pagodas, bridges, oriental ladies and usually a pair of kissing birds. Pale blue ground.*
2357 Mikado : *Chinoiserie pagodas, bridges, oriental ladies and usually a pair of kissing birds. Matt blue ground.*
2359 Chinoiserie design : *Figures, Pagodas, Bridges. Powder blue ground.*
2361 Mikado : *Chinoiserie pagodas, bridges, oriental ladies and usually a pair of kissing birds. Red ground.*
2363 Mikado : *Chinoiserie pagodas, bridges, oriental ladies and usually a pair of kissing birds. Black ground and colourful frieze.*

2364 Mikado : *Chinoiserie pagodas, bridges, oriental ladies and usually a pair of kissing birds. Powder blue ground.*

2366 Blush Ware : *Flowers.*

2367 Mikado in Cartouche : *Chinoiserie pagodas, bridges, oriental ladies and usually a pair of kissing birds. Orange ground.*

2368 Mikado in Cartouche : *Chinoiserie pagodas, bridges, oriental ladies and usually a pair of kissing birds. Yellow ground.*

2369 Fairy and Sunflower : *Fairies, sunflowers and butterflies on a pale blue ground. Armand backstamp.*

2370 Mikado : *Chinoiserie pagodas, bridges, oriental ladies and usually a pair of kissing birds. Matt black ground.*

2371 Peach Blossom : *Pink and green blossom sprays on matt black ground.*

2377 Blush Ware - Floral : *Flowers*

2385 Cornflower : *Cornflower like flowers on pale ground (see also 2392).*

2392 Cornflower : *Cornflower like flowers on pale ground (see also 2385).*

2393 no name : *Flowers on cream ground.*

2398 Cock & Peony : *Two cockerels standing amongst foliage. Also has a variety of beautifully enamelled flowers including peonies. Sometimes has a Cock & Peony backstamp. Light blue ground.*

2399 Mikado : *Chinoiserie pagodas, bridges, oriental ladies and usually a pair of kissing birds. Blue ground and gilt outlines.*

2405 Cock & Peony Spray :

2406 Blush Ware - Cherry Blossom : *Flowers*

2407 Blush Ware - Chrysanthemum : *Flowers.*

2410 Mikado : *Chinoiserie pagodas, bridges, oriental ladies and usually a pair of kissing birds. Black ground with green frieze.*

2410 Blush Ware - Chrysanthemum : *Flowers.*

2412 Quince : *Blossom spray on matt black ground.*

2412 Prunus and Bird : *Bird on prunus blossom spray. Pale yellow ground.*

2413 Prunus and Bird : *Bird on prunus blossom spray. Blue ground.*

2420 Flies : *Butterflies on powder blue ground - Armand backstamp.*

2421 Prunus and Bird : *Bird on prunus blossom spray. Lemon ground.*

2422 Mikado : *Chinoiserie pagodas, bridges, oriental ladies and usually a pair of kissing birds. Orange and red ground.*

2424 no name : *Flowers and foliage on peach ground.*

2428 New Mikado : *Chinese Figures, Pagodas, Bridges and two crane like birds. Blue lustre ground.*

2428 New Mikado without Mikado : *Normally with Chinese Figures, Pagodas, Bridges and two crane like birds. Blue lustre ground.*

2431 Prunus and Bird : *Bird on prunus blossom spray. Bright yellow ground.*

2436 Peach Blossom : *Pink and green blossom sprays on matt black ground.*

2437 River Fish : *Beautiful realistic looking fish swimming amongst gilt seaweed. Blue ground.*

2440 River Fish : *Beautiful realistic looking fish swimming amongst gilt seaweed. Lemon ground.*

2441 River Fish : *Beautiful realistic looking fish swimming amongst gilt seaweed. Pink ground.*

2442 Mikado : *Chinoiserie pagodas, bridges, oriental ladies and usually a pair of kissing birds. Red ground with greyish blue frieze.*

2445 Almond Blossom : *White flowers on dark pink ground.*

2446 Berries and Bands : *Multicoloured berries on multicoloured bands. Yellow ground.*

2454 Berries and Bands : *Multicoloured berries on multicoloured bands. Light purple ground.*

2455 Blush Ware - Heather : *Flowers.*

2456 Flies : *Butterflies or Moths on orange interior, blue exterior.*

2458 Blush Ware - Dahlia : *Flowers.*

2460 Berries and Bands : *Multicoloured berries on multicoloured bands. Purple ground - see 2446, 2454, 2931 for different colourways.*

2461 Berries and Bands : *Multicoloured berries on multicoloured bands. Yellow ground.*

2463 New Prunus Spray : *Sprays of white and pink prunus blossom on yellow ground.*

2466 Bird & Tree Peony : *Small bird on Peony like blossoms. White ground.*

2469 Flies : *Large and small butterflies or moths on a pink ground.*

2470 Mikado : *Chinoiserie pagodas, bridges, oriental ladies and usually a pair of kissing birds. Matt black ground.*

2473 Flies : *Butterflies or Moths on cream.*

2474 Blush Ware - Cornucopia : *Multi-coloured flowers.*

2477 Oriental Water Garden : *Oriental lady on bridge in garden.*

2480 Peach Blossom : *Pink and green blossom sprays on matt black ground.*

Carlton Ware Patterns and Shapes

2481 Temple : *Oriental scene of figures in temple with large circular doorway. Ornate trees and a golden sun. Blue ground with coloured enamels.*

2482 Temple : *Oriental scene of figures in temple with large circular doorway. Ornate trees and a golden sun. Blue ground (as 2481 but in gilt only).*

2486 Blush Ware - Carnation : *Flowers*

2494 Blush Ware - Cistus : *Colourful flowers.*

2497 Rainbow Portal : *Bird sitting on a bough and a cameo with multicoloured stripes. Yellow ground.*

2500 Rainbow Portal : *Bird sitting on a bough and a cameo with multicoloured stripes. Red/Purple ground.*

2510 Blush Ware - Hibiscus : *Flowers.*

2517 Kingfisher : *Kingfisher sitting or flying. Pale blue lustre ground.*

2518 no name : *Nursery Ware.*

2519 Barge : *Chinoiserie design with punt like boat. Blue ground.*

2530 Kingfisher : *Kingfisher sitting or flying. Cream lustre ground.*

2537 Kingfisher : *Kingfisher sitting or flying. Pale yellow lustre ground.*

2539 Basket of Fruit : *Colourful basket full of fruit including grapes, bananas, pineapple, etc. White ground with yellow band and black.*

2552 Temple : *Oriental scene of figures in temple with large circular doorway. Ornate trees and a golden sun. Pale blue ground with coloured enamels.*

2556 Basket of Fruit : *Colourful basket full of fruit including grapes, bananas, pineapple, etc. White ground with yellow band and black.*

2560 Fruit : *Fruit (pears, grapes etc) on pale blue ground.*

2560 Blush Ware - Impatiens : *Flowers*

2561 Blush Ware - Arvista : *Flowers.*
2562 Blush Ware - Arvista : *Flowers.*
2564 Fruit : *Fruit (pears, grapes etc) on lemon, orange ground.*
2565 Fruit : *Fruit (pears, grapes etc) on blue ground.*
2567 Fruit : *Fruit (pears, grapes etc) on black ground.*
2586 Brodsworth : *Odd looking colourful bird amongst flowers.*
2591 Italian Scenes : *Market scene in Italy (Genoa) in gilt. Powder blue ground.*
2621 Kingfisher : *Kingfisher sitting or flying. Pal blue ground.*
2630 Eighteenth Tee : *Playing Golf on the 18th tee on a lemon ground.*
2633 Eighteenth Tee : *Playing Golf on the 18th tee on a lemon ground.*
2634 Long Tailed Bird and Tree Peony : *A long tailed exotic bird sitting on a branch with Peony like flowers. White ground.*
2636 Eighteenth Tee : *Playing Golf on the 18th tee on a blue ground.*
2642 Flies Border : *Plain red with Butterflies and Moths on a black border.*
2644 no name : *Geometric pattern in colours.*
2654 Moderne Lady : *Moderne Lady in 18th/19th century dress.*
2659 Blush Ware : *Flowers.*
2662 Blush Ware - Convolvulous : *Flowers.*
2669 Blush Ware - Convolvulous : *Pink and blue Convolvulous flowers.*
2681 Temple : *Oriental scene of figures in temple with large circular doorway. Ornate trees and a golden sun. Blue ground with coloured enamels.*

Carlton Ware Patterns and Shapes

2686 Tutankhamen : *Egyptian figures and motifs in colours and gilt on pale blue ground.*
2687 Blush Ware - Hibiscus : *Flowers.*
2689 Tutankhamen : *Egyptian figures and motifs in colours and gilt on orange ground.*
2691 Blush Ware - Peony : *Flowers.*
2700 Blush Ware - Camellia : *Flowers.*
2706 Tutankhamen : *Egyptian figures and motifs in colours and gilt. Gloss mother of pearl ground.*
2708 Tutankhamen : *Egyptian figures, motifs and symbols in gilt. Matt black ground.*
2709 Tutankhamen : *Egyptian figures, motifs and symbols in colours and gilt. Matt black ground, colours and gilt detail.*
2710 Tutankhamen : *Egyptian figures, motifs and symbols in gilt. Powder blue ground.*
2711 Tutankhamen : *Egyptian figures, motifs and symbols in colours and gilt. Blue lustre ground.*
2711 Tutankhamen : *Egyptian figures, motifs and symbols. Orange or brown ground.*
2713 Blush Ware - Heather : *Flowers.*
2718 Blush Ware - Heather : *Flowers.*
2721 Orange Blossom : *Bird, butterflies and white Orange blossom tree. Pale lemon ground.*
2722 Orange Blossom : *Bird, butterflies and white Orange blossom tree. Orange ground.*
2723 Orange Blossom : *Bird, butterflies and white Orange blossom tree. Blue ground.*
2723 Pomander Pendant : *Enamelled design representing balloons with strings. Mauve ground.*
2724 Orange Blossom : *Bird, butterflies and white Orange blossom tree. Pale purple ground.*

2725 Orange Blossom : *Bird, butterflies and white Orange blossom tree. Red ground.*
2727 New Mikado : *Chinese figures, pagoda, bridge and trees. Sometimes has two cranes and punt like boat. Red ground.*
2728 New Mikado : *Chinese figures, pagoda, bridge and trees. Sometimes has two cranes and punt like boat. Blue ground.*
2729 New Mikado : *Chinese figures, pagoda, bridge and trees. Sometimes has two cranes and punt like boat. Blue ground with gilt only (no enamels).*
2731 no name : *Delicate border design on plain yellow.*
2740 New Mikado : *Chinese figures, pagoda, bridge and trees. Sometimes has two cranes and punt like boat. Pearl lustre ground.*
2749 Blush Ware - Nasturtium : *Flowers*
2752 Chinoiserie : *Chinese figures, pagoda, bridge and trees. Mother of Pearl ground, blue rim.*
2755 Chinoiserie : *Figures, Pagodas, Bridges (possibly Mikado). Pale blue ground.*
2757 Blush Ware - Heather : *Flowers.*
2779 Spray of Flowers : *Spray of flowers with yellow borders on pale ground.*
2780 Tutankhamen : *Egyptian figures and motifs in colours and gilt. White ground.*
2782 Lovebirds : *Birds in tree, Armand backstamp. Pale blue ground.*
2787 Flow Blue - Dragons & Unicorn : *Dragons and Unicorn in blue.*
2788 New Mikado : *Chinese figures, pagoda, bridge and trees. Sometimes has two cranes and punt like boat. Rouge ground.*

2794 Birds on Bough : *Yellow birds with long feathery tails in tree with blue foliage. Pale ground.*
2798 Blush Ware - Cistus : *Pansies*
2804 Gallant : *Lady and Dandy with gazebo in garden. Orange ground.*
2810 Chinoiserie : *Figures, Pagodas, Bridges. Matt black ground with green frieze with motifs.*
2814 New Mikado : *Chinese figures, pagoda, bridge and trees. Sometimes has two cranes and punt like boat. Blue lustre ground.*
2814 New Mikado with Lady : *Chinese figures, pagoda, bridge and trees. Sometimes has two cranes and punt like boat. Blue lustre ground. Also with a moderne Lady.*
2814 New Mikado without Mikado : *No Chinese figures, pagoda or bridge. Cranes, two flying and two wading. Blue lustre ground.*
2815 New Mikado : *Chinese figures, pagoda, bridge and trees. Sometimes has two cranes and punt like boat. Red lustre ground.*
2816 Cock & Peony : *Two cockerels standing amongst foliage. Also has a variety of beautifully enamelled flowers including peonies. White ground.*
2818 Dragon : *Chinese Dragons and symbols in gilt. Rouge ground.*
2820 Temple : *Oriental scene of figures in temple with large circular doorway. Ornate trees with black stems. Coral ground with black frieze.*
2822 Stork and Bamboo : *Two storks (one drinking) in pool next to bamboo. Deep blue ground.*
2822 no name : *Pheasant and blossom on pale blue ground.*

2825 New Mikado : *Chinese figures, pagoda, bridge and trees. Sometimes has two cranes and punt like boat. Orange, red ground with gilt.*

2830 New Mikado : *Chinese figures, pagoda, bridge and trees. Sometimes has two cranes and punt like boat. Orange, red ground with gilt.*

2831 Prunus and Bird : *Bird on prunus blossom spray with white background.*

2832 Long Tailed Bird and Tree Peony : *A long tailed exotic bird sitting on a branch with Peony like flowers. Pale blue ground.*

2833 Blush Ware - Iris : *Flowers*

2834 Long Tailed Bird and Tree Peony : *A long tailed exotic bird sitting on a branch with Peony like flowers. Ice blue ground.*

2837 New Flies : *Spiders web and butterfly. Dark blue ground.*

2839 Gallant : *Lady and Dandy with gazebo in garden. Red, orange ground.*

2841 Willow : *Chinoiserie pagodas, Willow tree, bridge, and a fence. Usually a pair of kissing birds in flight. Orange lustre ground.*

2843 Pomander Pendant : *Enamelled design representing balloons with strings. Blue lustre ground.*

2845 Pomander Pendant : *Enamelled design representing balloons with strings. Blue ground.*

2851 Willow : *Chinoiserie pagodas, Willow tree, bridge, and a fence. Usually a pair of kissing birds in flight. Red ground.*

2851 Willow : *Chinoiserie pagodas, Willow tree, bridge, and a fence. Usually a pair of kissing birds in flight. Orange ground.*

2852 Willow : *Chinoiserie pagodas, Willow tree, bridge, and a fence. Usually a pair of kissing birds in flight. Pale Blue ground.*
2853 Blush Ware - Peony : *Peony like flowers*
2854 Willow : *Chinoiserie pagodas, Willow tree, bridge, and a fence. Usually a pair of kissing birds in flight. Pale blue ground.*
2857 Pheasant and Rose : *Bird on rose tree. Blue ground.*
2858 Kingfisher : *Kingfishers, sitting and flying. Blue ground.*
2858 Willow : *Chinoiserie pagodas, Willow tree, bridge, and a fence. Usually a pair of kissing birds in flight. Pale blue ground.*
2863 Gallant : *Lady and Dandy with gazebo in garden. Pale yellow ground.*
2863 Blush Ware - Rose : *Flowers*
2864 Gallant : *Lady and Dandy with gazebo in garden. Red, orange ground.*
2866 Bird & Tree Peony : *Small bird on Peony like blossoms. White ground.*
2867 Gallant : *Lady and Dandy with gazebo in garden. Matt pale blue ground.*
2868 Gallant : *Lady and Dandy with gazebo in garden. Yellow ground.*
2869 Gallant : *Lady and Dandy with gazebo in garden. Matt orange ground.*
2872 Gallant : *Lady and Dandy with gazebo in garden. Yellow ground.*
2872 Gallant : *Lady and Dandy with gazebo in garden. Pink ground.*
2872 Blush Ware - Rose : *Flowers*
2872 Blush Ware - Tulips : *Flowers*

2880 Temple : *Oriental scene of figures in temple with large circular doorway. Ornate trees with black stems. Red ground with black frieze.*

2880 Temple without Temple : *Plain pattern with Temple frieze. Red ground with black frieze.*

2881 Mikado : *Chinoiserie pagodas, bridges, oriental ladies and usually a pair of kissing birds. Matt black ground with terracotta frieze.*

2882 Persian : *Persian design of figures in a temple, usually two white birds by water. Desert scene and palm trees. Persian back stamp. Powder blue ground.*

2883 Persian : *Persian design of figures in a temple, usually two white birds by water. Desert scene and palm trees. Persian back stamp. Blue lustre ground.*

2884 Persian : *Persian design of figures in a temple, usually two white birds by water. Desert scene and palm trees. Persian back stamp. Blue lustre ground.*

2885 Orchard : *Sprays of orchard fruits with blossom. Blue lustre ground.*

2886 Orchard : *Sprays of orchard fruits with blossom. Blue lustre ground.*

2887 Dragon : *Chinese dragons and symbols. Blue lustre ground.*

2893 Gallant : *Lady and Dandy with gazebo in garden. Matt black ground with mother of pearl interior.*

2896 Trailing : *Spays of blossom on creamy yellow ground.*

2903 Dragon : *Chinese dragons and symbols. Blue ground.*

2905 Dancers : *Figures dancing with pan pipes and small birds flying around. White ground and red frieze.*

2907 Magpies : *Magpie on tree branch and sometimes also others flying around. Blue ground.*

Carlton Ware Patterns and Shapes

2907 Magpies : *Magpie on tree branch and sometimes also others flying around. Matt red ground.*

2908 Magpies : *Magpie on tree branch and sometimes also others flying around. Yellow ground.*

2908 Magpies : *Magpie on tree branch and sometimes also others flying around. Orange ground.*

2909 Fruit Bough : *Peach like fruit and slender leaves on tree. Blue ground.*

2910 Mikado : *Chinoiserie pagodas, bridges, oriental ladies and usually a pair of kissing birds. Matt black ground with green frieze.*

2911 Magpies : *Magpie on tree branch and sometimes also others flying around. Orange lustre ground.*

2912 Magpies : *Magpie on tree branch and sometimes also others flying around. Orange ground.*

2913 Cretonne : *Oriental tree with red crested bird. Matt black ground and yellow band.*

2914 Mikado : *Chinoiserie pagodas, bridges, oriental ladies and usually a pair of kissing birds. Black ground with green frieze.*

2917 Plain : *Matt black with orange lustre interior to cup. Carlton China.*

2920 Fruit Branch : *Fruit and branch on Orange and White ground.*

2922 Sunrise : *Matt black and orange lustre exterior with fine enamelled border design.*

2923 Blush Ware - Heather : *Flowers.*

2924 no name : *Chinoiserie design on brown ground.*

2926 no name : *Flowers and foliage on cream ground.*

2927 Mikado : *Chinoiserie pagodas, bridges, oriental ladies and usually a pair of kissing birds. Also has a Temple pattern Frieze. Red ground with pinkish frieze.*

2927 Mikado without Mikado : *Temple pattern frieze but plain body. Red ground with pinkish frieze.*
2928 Temple : *Oriental scene of figures in temple with large circular doorway. Ornate trees some with black stems, sometimes a gold sun. Yellow ground.*
2929 Temple : *Oriental scene of figures in temple with large circular doorway. Ornate trees some with black stems, sometimes a gold sun. Gloss bright blue with matt black frieze.*
2930 Chrysanthemum : *Realistic Chrysanthemum flowers on a blue ground. Look at newsletter 8 Nov 2005.*
2931 Berries and Bands : *Multicoloured berries on multicoloured bands. Orange ground.*
2932 Stork and Bamboo : *Two storks (one drinking) in pool. Bamboo shoots with green leaves. Blue lustre ground.*
2933 Stork and Bamboo : *Two storks (one drinking) in pool. Bamboo shoots with green leaves. Matt orange ground.*
2934 Stork and Bamboo : *Two storks (one drinking) in pool. Bamboo shoots with green leaves. White gloss ground.*
2935 Scalloped Lace : *Black granite type border on yellow ground with black frieze.*
2936 Chinese Tea Garden : *Oriental scene of figures in pagoda garden. Blue ground.*
2939 Flies : *Brightly coloured butterflies on yellow ground.*
2940 no name : *Lustre orange and mother of pearl ground.*
2941 Temple : *Oriental scene of figures in temple with large circular doorway. Ornate trees some with black*

stems, sometimes a gold sun. Green ground with black lower frieze.
2944 Moonlight Cameo : *Orange medallion with figures playing with bubbles in the moonlight. Matt black ground.*
2944 Moonlight Cameo : *White medallion with figures playing with bubbles in the moonlight. Orange ground.*
2945 Moonlight Cameo : *Deep blue medallion with figures playing with bubbles in the moonlight. Dark orange ground.*
2946 Moonlight Cameo : *Pale blue medallion with figures playing with bubbles in the moonlight. Orange ground.*
2947 Moonlight Cameo : *Pale blue medallion with figures playing with bubbles in the moonlight. Black ground.*
2948 Chinaland : *Complex chinoiserie design with underglaze enamels. Pagoda, terraces, trees, figures and usually mountains. Coloured W&R backstamp. Orange lustre ground.*
2949 Chinaland : *Complex chinoiserie design with underglaze enamels. Pagoda, terraces, trees, figures and usually mountains. Mottled green lustre ground.*
2950 Chinaland : *Complex chinoiserie design with underglaze enamels. Pagoda, terraces, trees, figures and usually mountains. Dark blue lustre ground.*
2953 Gallant : *Lady & Dandy in garden. Blue ground.*
2954 Gallant : *Lady & Dandy in garden. Orange ground.*
2956 Gallant : *Lady & Dandy in garden. Yellow ground.*
2957 no name : *Chinese scene with figures, cloisonne.*
2960 Moonlight Cameo : *White medallion with figures playing with bubbles in the moonlight. Orange ground.*
2961 Citrus Fruit : *Oranges and other fruit on white ground.*
2962 The Hunt : *Hunting Scene on white ground.*

2964 Moonlight Cameo : *White medallion with figures playing with bubbles in the moonlight. Blue ground.*
2969 Moonlight Cameo : *Pale blue medallion with figures playing with bubbles in the moonlight. Green ground.*
2971 Temple : *Oriental scene of figures in temple with large circular doorway. Ornate trees some with black stems, sometimes a gold sun. Emerald green ground with black frieze.*
2972 Chinoiserie : *Chinese figures in pagodas. Deep blue ground.*
2975 Magpies : *Magpie on tree branch and sometimes also others flying around. Green ground.*
2976 Magpies : *Magpie on tree branch and sometimes also others flying around. Cream, yellow ground.*
2978 Mikado : *Chinoiserie pagodas, bridges, oriental ladies and usually a pair of kissing birds. Matt black ground with brown frieze.*
2979 Embellished Gilt : *Orange lustre or matt black ground, ornate gold border.*
2980 Moonlight Cameo : *White medallion with figures playing with bubbles in the moonlight. Brown, orange ground.*
2990 New Mikado : *Chinese figures, pagoda, bridge and trees. Sometimes has two cranes and punt like boat. Powder blue lustre ground with border.*
2993 Dragon : *Pink dragon on blue glazed ground.*

Patterns 3000 - 3999

3003 Temple : *Oriental scene of figures in temple with large circular doorway. Ornate trees some with black stems, sometimes a gold sun. Red lustre ground.*
3013 no name : *Orange lustre ground with wide white frieze.*
3014 Chinaland : *Complex chinoiserie design with underglaze enamels. Pagoda, terraces, trees, figures and usually mountains. Pale blue lustre ground.*
3015 Chinaland : *Complex chinoiserie design with underglaze enamels. Pagoda, terraces, trees, figures and usually mountains. Red lustre ground.*
3016 Parrots : *Multicoloured parrot and coloured friezes. Green ground.*
3017 Parrots : *Multicoloured parrot and coloured friezes. Matt black ground.*
3018 Parrots : *Multicoloured parrot and coloured friezes. Blue lustre ground.*
3019 Galleon : *Galleon ship sailing on waves. Blue ground.*
3020 Galleon : *Galleon ship sailing on waves. Green ground.*
3023 New Flies : *Spiders web and butterfly. Dark blue lustre ground.*
3024 New Flies : *Spiders web and butterfly. Mottled orange ground.*

3025 New Flies : *Spiders web and butterfly. Light blue lustre ground.*
3026 Temple : *Oriental scene of figures in temple with large circular doorway. Ornate trees some with black stems, sometimes a gold sun. White, cream ground with green frieze.*
3026 no name : *Birds, trees on vellum ground.*
3027 Temple : *Oriental scene of figures in temple with large circular doorway. Ornate trees some with black stems, sometimes a gold sun. Cream ground with black frieze.*
3028 New Flies : *Spiders web and butterfly. Rouge ground.*
3033 Almond Blossom : *White blossom on blue ground.*
3033 Shagreen : *Black band with gold speckles above green ground.*
3037 Parrots : *Brightly coloured parrots and coloured friezes. Orange lustre ground.*
3041 Apple and Blossom : *Apple and blossom on blue lustre ground.*
3042 Orange Embossed : *Oranges and leaves on dark blue lustre ground.*
3043 Violets : *Gilt design on dark blue lustre ground.*
3046 Bird & Pine Cone : *Coloured birds in pine trees with pine cones. Dark blue lustre ground.*
3047 Temple : *Oriental scene of figures in temple with large circular doorway. Ornate trees some with black stems, sometimes a gold sun. Off white ground with terracotta frieze.*
3048 Mikado : *Chinoiserie pagodas, bridges, oriental ladies and usually a pair of kissing birds. Pale cream ground with blue frieze.*

Carlton Ware Patterns and Shapes

3048 Temple : *Oriental scene of figures in temple with large circular doorway. Ornate trees some with black stems, sometimes a gold sun. Pale cream ground with pale blue frieze.*

3049 Mayflower : *Flower heads and foliage on mottled blue ground with pale yellow border.*

3050 Persian Flowers or Turkish : *Persian stylised floral heads and leaves. Enamelled flower design. Blue lustre ground.*

3052 Orange Embossed : *Oranges and leaves on white lustre ground.*

3053 Shagreen : *Gold band with blue speckles above orange ground.*

3054 Shagreen : *Matt black with yellow and gilt honeycomb like band.*

3056 Shagreen : *Grey band with dark grey speckles above blue, grey ground.*

3057 Shagreen : *Black band with gold speckles above jade green ground or rouge ground.*

3063 Embellished Gilt : *Plain yellow with intricate gilt border.*

3064 Orchard : *Sprays of oranges, cherries and other fruits with blossom and leaves. Orange ground.*

3065 Plain : *Plain Pink.*

3065 Persian : *Persian design of figures in a temple, usually two white birds by water. Desert scene and palm trees. Terracotta ground with black frieze.*

3067 Persian : *Persian design of figures in a temple, usually two white birds by water. Desert scene and palm trees. Ivory ground with black frieze.*

3068 Persian : *Persian design of figures in a temple, usually two white birds by water. Desert scene and palm trees. Pale cream ground with blue frieze.*

3069 Shagreen : *Orange and gilt speckles on red ground.*
3069 Persian : *Persian design of figures in a temple, usually two white birds by water. Desert scene and palm trees. Yellow ground..*
3071 Persian Flowers or Turkish : *Enamelled flower design. Powder Blue ground.*
3073 Swallow & Cloud : *Swallow or swallows in flight with gold ornate cloud. Blue lustre ground.*
3074 Swallow & Cloud : *Swallow or swallows in flight with gold ornate cloud. Red lustre ground.*
3075 Moonlight : *Figures playing with bubbles in the moonlight. Pale ground.*
3075 Swallow & Cloud : *Swallow or swallows in flight with gold ornate cloud. Mottled matt orange ground.*
3076 Moonlight : *Figures playing with bubbles in the moonlight. Orange lustre ground.*
3077 Meadow : *Orange ground and enamelled floral border.*
3078 Meadow : *Yellow ground and enamelled floral border.*
3078 Embellished Gilt : *Plain with intricate gilt border.*
3087 Temple : *Oriental scene of figures in temple with large circular doorway. Ornate trees some with black stems, sometimes a gold sun. Cream ground with dark frieze.*
3093 Temple Flowers :
3095 Parrots : *Brightly coloured parrots and coloured friezes. Purple ground.*
3115 Cameo Wren : *Wren on branch set in cameo. Orange ground.*
3116 Persian Flowers or Turkish : *Gilt and enamelled flower design. Blue ground.*

Carlton Ware Patterns and Shapes

3118 Moonlight : *Figures playing with bubbles in the moonlight. Dark Orange ground.*

3127 Moonlight : *Figures playing with bubbles in the moonlight. Green ground.*

3129 Temple : *Oriental scene of figures in temple with large circular doorway. Ornate trees some with black stems, sometimes a gold sun. Orange lustre ground with black frieze.*

3130 Temple : *Oriental scene of figures in temple with large circular doorway. Ornate trees some with black stems, sometimes a gold sun. Light green ground with black frieze.*

3130 Temple : *Oriental scene of figures in temple with large circular doorway. Ornate trees some with black stems, sometimes a gold sun. Powder blue ground.*

3131 Persian : *Persian design of figures in a temple, usually two white birds by water. Desert scene and palm trees. Persian back stamp. Red ground.*

3134 Swallow & Cloud : *Swallow or swallows in flight with gold ornate cloud. Blue Lustre ground.*

3134 Swallow & Cloud : *Swallow or swallows in flight with gold ornate cloud. Green ground.*

3137 New Mikado : *Chinese figures, pagoda, bridge and trees. Sometimes has two cranes and punt like boat. Green ground.*

3141 Landscape Tree : *Blossom, birds and umbrella shaped trees with green foliage. Light ground.*

3142 Landscape Tree : *Blossom, birds and umbrella shaped trees with orange foliage. Light ground.*

3143 Paradise Bird & Tree with Cloud : *Bird of Paradise with long plumed tail flying across clouds and among oriental trees. Red ground.*

3144 Paradise Bird & Tree with Cloud : *Bird of Paradise with long plumed tail flying across clouds and among oriental trees. Mottled pale blue ground.*

3145 Dragon in Cartouche : *Dragon in black panel on red ground plus decorative frieze.*

3146 Dragon in Cartouche : *Dragon in black panel on mottled dark red ground plus decorative frieze.*

3147 Paradise Bird & Tree : *Bird of Paradise with long plumed tail flying among oriental trees. Matt black ground.*

3149 Paradise Bird & Tree with Cloud : *Bird of Paradise with long plumed tail flying across clouds and among oriental trees. Red ground.*

3150 Paradise Bird & Tree : *Bird of Paradise with long plumed tail flying among oriental trees. Red ground with black frieze.*

3151 Paradise Bird & Tree : *Bird of Paradise with long plumed tail flying among oriental trees. Gloss yellow ground.*

3154 Paradise Bird & Tree with Cloud : *Bird of Paradise with long plumed tail flying across clouds and among oriental trees. Orange ground.*

3155 Paradise Bird & Tree : *Bird of Paradise with long plumed tail flying among oriental trees. Gloss blue ground.*

3155 no name : *Good Luck motif on coral ground.*

3157 Paradise Bird & Tree : *Bird of Paradise with long plumed tail flying among oriental trees. Gloss orange ground.*

3158 Mikado : *Chinoiserie pagodas, bridges, oriental ladies and usually a pair of kissing birds. Matt black ground.*

3159 Paradise Bird & Tree : *Bird of Paradise with long plumed tail flying among oriental trees. Pale blue ground.*
3161 Mayflower : *Flower heads and foliage on blue ground with yellow border.*
3165 Mayflower : *Flower heads and foliage on mottled blue ground with yellow border.*
3173 Lace Frieze : *Yellow, black with ornate border.*
3174 Swallow & Cloud : *Swallow or swallows in flight with gold ornate cloud. Red ground.*
3178 Mikado in Cartouche : *Chinoiserie pagodas, bridges, oriental ladies and usually a pair of kissing birds. Orange ground.*
3179 no name : *Chines figures and pagodas with frieze on rust ground.*
3185 Temple : *Oriental scene of figures in temple with large circular doorway. Ornate trees some with black stems, sometimes a gold sun. Red ground.*
3188 no name : *Stylised flowers and trees. Mottled red ground.*
3190 Cubist Butterfly : *Bold stylised flowers, berries and butterflies. Matt red ground.*
3191 Bird of Paradise : *Bird of Paradise with long plumed tail flying among oriental trees. Blue, pink lustre ground.*
3193 Prunus : *Spays of prunus blossom on pale blue ground.*
3194 Cubist Butterfly : *Bold stylised flowers, berries and butterflies. Blue ground.*
3195 Cubist Butterfly : *Bold stylised flowers, berries and butterflies. Orange ground.*
3196 Chinese Bird : *Exotic bird with curly tail, flower and cloud motifs. Blue lustre ground.*

3197 Chinese Bird : *Exotic bird with curly tail, flower and cloud motifs. Blue ground.*

3198 Chinese Bird : *Exotic bird with curly tail, flower and cloud motifs. Rouge ground.*

3199 Chinese Figures : *Oriental scene of figures, tree and sometimes pagodas. Blue ground.*

3201 Mikado : *Chinoiserie pagodas, bridges, oriental ladies and usually a pair of kissing birds. Green ground and black frieze.*

3202 Paradise Bird & Tree : *Bird of Paradise with long plumed tail flying among oriental trees. Pale green ground plus enamels.*

3222 Chinoiserie : *Figures, Pagodas, Bridges. Pale lemon ground and border.*

3223 Cubist Butterfly : *Bold stylised flowers, berries and butterflies. Green ground.*

3225 Corolla : *White flower heads on dark blue gloss ground.*

3226 Corolla : *White flower heads on red, orange ground.*

3227 Corolla : *White flower heads on blue ground.*

3228 Corolla : *White flower heads on yellow ground.*

3229 Spots : *White spots on blue.*

3231 Spots : *White spots on green.*

3233 Cubist Butterfly : *Bold stylised flowers, berries and butterflies. Green ground.*

3234 Floral Scallops : *Overlapping scallop shapes containing five coloured petals of a flower, handcraft. Cream ground.*

3235 Shamrock : *Three petalled large blue flowers, handcraft. White ground with blue borders.*

3236 Floribunda : *Orange flowers and leaves on blue and white ground.*

3237 Dragon and Cloud : *Oriental dragon amongst stylised ornate clouds. Deep blue ground and gilt.*
3238 Forest Tree : *Exotic birch like trees. Slender tree rising to a wide pendulous canopy of foliage. Deep blue lustre ground.*
3239 Forest Tree : *Exotic birch like tree. Slender tree rising to a wide pendulous canopy of foliage. Glazed yellow ground.*
3240 Forest Tree : *Exotic birch like trees. Slender Tree rising to a wide pendulous canopy of foliage. Matt terracotta ground.*
3241 Paradise Bird & Tree : *Bird of Paradise with long plumed tail flying among oriental trees. Mottled red ground.*
3242 Flowering Papyrus : *Geometric handcraft design in blue, yellow, mauve and black on white ground.*
3243 Swallow & Cloud : *Swallow or swallows in flight with gold ornate cloud. Matt blue ground.*
3244 Forest Tree : *Exotic birch like trees. Slender tree rising to a wide pendulous canopy of foliage. Matt blue ground with mauve foliage.*
3244 Forest Tree : *Exotic birch like trees. Slender tree rising to a wide pendulous canopy of foliage. Green ground with mauve foliage.*
3248 Forest Tree : *Exotic birch like trees. Slender tree rising to a wide pendulous canopy of foliage. Grey ground with dark green foliage.*
3249 Flower and Fruit : *Large Fruit on a branch together with Petal design.*
3250 Forest Tree : *Exotic birch like trees. Slender tree rising to a wide pendulous canopy of foliage. Mottled blue ground with orange foliage.*

3250 Dutch : *Handcraft with windmill like pattern, blue, yellow, mauve and black on white ground.*
3251 Dragon : *Red dragons with symbols and shapes. Blue ground.*
3252 Paradise Bird & Tree with Cloud : *Bird of Paradise with long plumed tail flying across clouds and among oriental trees. Matt cream and mauve ground.*
3253 Forest Tree : *Exotic birch like trees. Slender tree rising to a wide pendulous canopy of foliage. Blue ground.*
3254 Forest Tree : *Exotic birch like trees. Slender tree rising to a wide pendulous canopy of foliage. Red lustre ground.*
3255 Orchid : *Central floral medallion with star containing Orchid. Mauve Blue, Green Yellow and Black stripes, handcraft. Blue gloss ground.*
3259 no name : *Similar to Flowering Papyrus.*
3265 Forest Tree : *Exotic birch like trees. Slender tree rising to a wide pendulous canopy of foliage. Matt cream and mauve ground.*
3270 Diaper : *Matt white ground.*
3271 Marigold : *Blue, cream and mauve flowers outlined in blue (Asters?). Handcraft.*
3272 Cherry : *Crude stems and leaves behind yellow and red cherries. Flowers and leaves on blue ground.*
3273 Delphinium : *Blue delphinium flowers and leaves, handcraft. White or pinky white ground.*
3274 Chinese Bird & Cloud : *Exotic bird with curly tail, flower and cloud motifs. Matt blue mosaic ground.*
3275 Chinese Bird & Cloud : *Exotic bird with curly tail, flower and cloud motifs. Matt orange ground.*
3275 Chinese Bird & Cloud : *Exotic bird with curly tail, flower and cloud motifs. Matt green ground.*

Carlton Ware Patterns and Shapes

3276 no name : *Cream ground similar to 3498 Iris.*
3278 Honesty : *Stylised Honesty branches. Royal Blue ground.*
3279 Tree & Swallow : *Swallows flying past slender stemmed tree with wide canopy of pendulous foliage. Matt pale blue ground with blue and green foliage.*
3280 Tree & Swallow : *Swallows flying past slender stemmed tree with wide canopy of pendulous foliage. Matt blue ground with orange foliage.*
3281 Tree & Swallow : *Swallows flying past slender stemmed tree with wide canopy of pendulous foliage. Matt cream and mauve ground.*
3282 Tree & Swallow : *Swallows flying past slender stemmed tree with wide canopy of pendulous foliage. Light blue ground with green, blue and orange foliage.*
3283 Forest Tree : *Exotic birch like trees. Slender tree rising to a wide pendulous canopy of foliage. Matt blue ground with orange foliage.*
3283 Tree & Swallow : *Swallows flying past slender stemmed tree with wide canopy of pendulous foliage. Matt blue ground with lilac foliage.*
3284 no name : *Matt blue/orange/yellow, diamonds. Handcraft.*
3285 Tree & Swallow : *Swallows flying past slender stemmed tree with wide canopy of pendulous foliage. Matt blue ground.*
3289 Marrakesh : *Marrakesh Handcraft design in blue, yellow and black.*
3290 Butterfly : *Handcraft pattern depicting a butterfly.*
3291 Stellata or Wild Cherry : *Cherry blossom star shaped flowers with leaves and brightly coloured berries. Leaves of blues and greens in star shaped pattern.*

3294 Bluebells : *Bluebell flowers and usually with snowdrops, primulas and autumn leaves. Light blue/grey ground.*

3296 Chinese Bird : *Exotic bird with curly tail, flower and cloud motifs. Black ground.*

3297 Farrago : *Handcraft. Flowers and chevrons, geometric pattern. Pink ground.*

3299 Zig Zag : *Lightning like, zig zag patterns. Matt buff ground.*

3304 New Chinese Bird : *Exotic bird looking back angrily, on pale grey or pale pink ground.*

3305 Carnival : *Brightly coloured geometric design with butterfly. Matt pale ground.*

3313 Sunflower Geometric : *Sprays of stylised geometric foliage and sunflower heads on blue ground.*

3314 Swallow & Cloud : *Swallow or swallows in flight with gold ornate cloud. Orange ground.*

3320 New Chinese Bird & Cloud : *Exotic bird looking back angrily, flying past stylised cloud and flowerheads. Matt blue ground .*

3321 New Chinese Bird & Cloud : *Exotic bird looking back angrily, flying past stylised cloud and flowerheads. Matt chocolate brown ground.*

3322 New Chinese Bird & Cloud : *Exotic bird looking back angrily, flying past stylised cloud and flowerheads. Blue lustre ground.*

3324 Pomona : *Citrus type fruit and leaves on a blue ground.*

3325 Orchid : *Central floral medallion with star containing Orchid. Yellow Beige, Green Yellow and Black stripes. Matt yellow ground.*

Carlton Ware Patterns and Shapes

3326 Stellata or Wild Cherry : *Cherry blossom star shaped flowers with leaves and brightly coloured berries. Blue ground.*

3327 Chinese Bird & Cloud : *Exotic bird with curly tail, flower and cloud motifs. Blue lustre ground.*

3328 Pomona : *Citrus type fruit and coloured leaves on a blue ground.*

3331 Dragon and Cloud : *Oriental dragon amongst stylised ornate clouds. Matt green ground.*

3332 Dragon and Cloud : *Oriental dragon amongst stylised ornate clouds. Gloss red ground.*

3333 Dragon and Cloud : *Oriental dragon amongst stylised ornate clouds. Matt blue ground.*

3333 Sunflower Geometric : *Sprays of stylised geometric foliage and sunflower heads on blue lustre ground.*

3334 Sunflower Geometric : *Sprays of stylised geometric foliage and sunflower heads on orange ground.*

3337 Bookends - Two Tone : *Bookends in two colours, brown and black.*

3339 Sunflower Geometric : *Sprays of stylised geometric foliage and sunflower heads on pale grey/blue ground.*

3341 Daisy & Stripe :

3350 Paradise Bird & Tree : *Bird of Paradise with long plumed tail flying among oriental trees. Matt mottled blue ground.*

3351 Dragon and Cloud : *Oriental dragon amongst stylised ornate clouds. Red ground.*

3352 Jazz : *Geometric design with brightly coloured lightning flashes, bands and small bubbles. Red lustre ground.*

3353 Jazz : *Geometric design with brightly coloured lightning flashes, bands and small bubbles. Orange lustre ground.*

3354 Feathertailed Bird and Flower : *Bird of paradise on stylised blossom bough. Matt pale blue ground.*
3355 Feathertailed Bird and Flower : *Bird of paradise on stylised blossom bough. Matt green ground.*
3356 Lightning : *Lightning like, zig zag patterns in two tone blue. Blue ground.*
3357 Lightning : *Lightning like, zig zag patterns in matt tan, black, orange with silver strip.*
3358 Gentian : *Large blue flower heads with black stamens, handcraft. Blue ground.*
3359 Stag : *Handcraft with realistic animal leaping in front of the Sun. Brown ground.*
3360 River Fish : *Beautiful realistic looking fish swimming amongst gilt seaweed. Powder blue ground.*
3361 Jazz : *Geometric design with brightly coloured lightning flashes, bands and small bubbles. Blue lustre ground.*
3362 Farrago : *Handcraft. Flowers and chevrons, geometric pattern. Pink ground.*
3384 Tree & Swallow : *Swallows flying past slender stemmed tree with wide canopy of pendulous foliage. Grey ground.*
3385 Floral Comets : *Stylised flowerheads and triple banded comets tails on matt pale green ground.*
3387 Floral Comets : *Stylised flowerheads and triple banded comets tails on matt green ground.*
3388 Fantasia : *Exotic bird with swallow like tail amongst exotic flowers and foliage. Matt pale blue ground.*
3389 Fantasia : *Exotic bird with swallow like tail amongst exotic flowers and foliage. Matt mauve ground.*
3390 Garden : *Spires of Daisy like flowers in many colours. Matt green ground.*

Carlton Ware Patterns and Shapes

3392 Moonlight Cameo : *Blue medallion with figures playing with bubbles in the moonlight. Light Orange ground.*

3394 Birds on Bough : *Birds with plumed tail sitting on branch with foliage. Pale blue ground.*

3396 Garden : *Spires of Daisy like flowers in many colours. Gloss green ground.*

3397 no name : *Small flowers, leaves, petals and triangle shapes on cream ground.*

3400 Fantasia : *Exotic bird with swallow like tail amongst exotic flowers and foliage. Blue matt ground.*

3401 Floral Comets : *Stylised flowerheads and triple banded comets tails. Pale blue ground.*

3404 Tutankhamen : *Egyptian figures and motifs in colours and gilt. Gloss Light & Dark Blue.*

3405 Floral Comets : *Stylised flowerheads and triple banded comets tails. Matt blue ground.*

3406 Fantasia : *Exotic bird with swallow like tail amongst exotic flowers and foliage. Blue gloss ground.*

3408 Rudolf's Posy : *Pattern of large and small flowerheads with leaves.*

3411 Scroll : *Swirling patterns of shapes and curves, multi-coloured. Blue ground.*

3412 Aurora : *Multi-coloured bold, bulbous cloud like shapes outlined in gilt on blue ground. Handcraft.*

3413 Garden : *Spires of Daisy like flowers in many colours. Matt pale blue ground.*

3414 Lazy - Daisy : *Simple flower heads large and small. Orange ground.*

3415 Sagitta : *Cloud shaped flowers and blue stylised trees. Matt pinky brown.*

3416 Arrowhead : *Abstract design of feathery leaves and flowers. Matt pale blue ground.*

3417 Cherry : *Crude stems and leaves behind yellow and red cherries. Flowers and leaves on yellow ground.*
3418 Holly : *Multi colour (orange and brown etc) abstract design.*
3420 Metropolis : *Stylised city skyline with mauve and pink details. Matt pale blue ground.*
3421 Fantasia : *Exotic bird with swallow like tail amongst exotic flowers and foliage. Dark blue ground.*
3422 Floral Comets : *Stylised flowerheads and triple banded comets tails. Oven blue ground.*
3423 Parkland : *Bold simple tree with enamelled dense foliage of autumn colours on matt blue ground.*
3424 Prickly Pansy : *Stylised landscape, trees and pansy like flowers in matt finish. Pale brown ground.*
3427 Fantasia : *Exotic bird with swallow like tail amongst exotic flowers and foliage. Blue matt ground.*
3428 Floral Comets : *Stylised flowerheads and triple banded comets tails. Blue gloss ground.*
3431 Jigsaw : *Stylised flower heads with spikey leaves and a patchwork of patterns. Matt green ground.*
3433 Garden : *Spires of daisy like flowers in many colours. Blue lustre ground.*
3438 Garden : *Spires of daisy like flowers in many colours. Blue lustre ground.*
3439 Jaggered Bouquet : *Bouquet of stylised flowers and spikey leaves. Rouge ground.*
3440 Camouflage : *Yellow, green & grey squiggles.*
3445 Neapolitan : *Circles of rims with variety of colours. Pale pink ground.*
3446 no name : *Matt pink ground with large flower heads. Handcraft.*
3447 Explosion : *Extravagant starburst design in blue, black, silver, gold. Matt grey ground.*

3448 Peach Melba : *Large orange flower heads, with blue foliage. Pale blue ground.*
3449 Prickly Pansy : *Stylised landscape, trees and Pansy like flowers on lustre orange ground.*
3450 Awakening : *Stylised sunrise design, cloud with jagged centres and ornate sun. Matt light brown ground.*
3451 Victorian Lady : *Crinoline lady with parasol in garden.*
3452 Explosion & Butterfly : *Star shaped colourful exploding flower heads and butterfly. Powder blue ground.*
3452 Awakening : *Stylised sunrise design, cloud with jagged centres and ornate sun. Matt green ground.*
3453 Awakening : *Stylised sunrise design, cloud with jagged centres and ornate sun. Matt light blue ground.*
3454 Explosion : *Extravagant starburst design in blue, black, silver, gold. Matt grey ground.*
3455 Prickly Pansy : *Stylised landscape, trees and Pansy like flowers. Lustre red mottled ground.*
3456 Awakening : *Stylised sunrise design, cloud with jagged centres and ornate sun. Mottled red ground.*
3457 Jaggered Bouquet : *Bouquet of stylised flowers and spikey leaves. Matt green ground.*
3458 Towering Castle : *Fantasy Castle with trees and rocks in the foreground in white, brown, blue, and yellow colours.*
3459 Peach Melba : *Large orange flower heads, with blue foliage. Orange ground*
3462 Humming Bird : *Elaborately decorated exotic bird and floral decoration with enamels. Pale blue ground.*
3462 Humming Bird without Bird : *Elaborately decorated with enamels as in 3462.*
3463 no name : *Abstract flower and clouds design.*

3465 Shadow Imprint : *Primula like flowers on mauve or lilac ground.*

3469 Cubist Butterfly : *Bold stylised flowers, berries and butterflies. Semi-matt blue ground.*

3470 Stork and Bamboo : *Two storks (one drinking) in pool. Bamboo shoots with green leaves. Matt orange ground.*

3471 Garden : *Spires of Daisy like flowers in many colours. Mottled cork coloured ground.*

3474 Garden : *Spires of Daisy like flowers in many colours. Mottled grey coloured ground.*

3475 Garden : *Spires of Daisy like flowers in many colours. Orange ground.*

3476 Garden : *Spires of Daisy like flowers in many colours. Mottled orange ground.*

3477 Garden : *Spires of Daisy like flowers in many colours. Glazed yellow/pink ground.*

3478 Garden : *Spires of Daisy like flowers in many colours. Glazed orange ground.*

3479 Garden : *Spires of Daisy like flowers in many colours. Glazed orange ground.*

3487 Delphinium : *Blue delphinium flowers and leaves, handcraft. Light mottled blue ground.*

3489 Jaggered Bouquet : *Bouquet of stylised flowers and spikey leaves.*

3491 Victorian Lady : *Crinoline lady with parasol in garden. Blue ground.*

3494 Awakening : *Stylised sunrise design, cloud with jagged centres and ornate sun. Orange lustre ground.*

3495 New Mikado : *Chinese figures, pagoda, bridge and trees. Sometimes has two cranes and punt like boat. Vivid green ground.*

Carlton Ware Patterns and Shapes

3496 Awakening : *Stylised sunrise design, cloud with jagged centres and ornate sun. Matt green ground.*
3497 Awakening : *Stylised sunrise design, cloud with jagged centres and ornate sun.*
3498 Iris : *Iris like flower design. Blue and white ground.*
3499 Prickly Pansy : *Stylised landscape, trees and pansy like flowers. Orange ground.*
3500 Sylvan Glade : *Simple trees in glade design, red border to edge of piece. Cream ground.*
3501 Garden : *Spires of Daisy like flowers in many colours. Matt brown ground.*
3502 Seagulls : *Handcraft with realistic seagulls.*
3503 Jazz Poppy : *Sprays of flowers and foliage in blue and pink, handcraft. Yellow ground.*
3504 Rose Marie : *Large flower head design in enamels. Matt green ground.*
3505 Magical Tree (Rosetta) : *Design of stylised trees with spangled trunk and large flowerheads by a lily pond. Orange ground.*
3506 Gypsy : *Gypsy like lady dancing. Dark blue ground.*
3507 Iceland Poppy : *Design of ornamental grasses, poppies and leaves. Matt green ground.*
3508 Wind & Flower : *Large stylised flowers in variety of bright colours, handcraft. Cream and blue ground.*
3509 no name : *Leaf green ground with underglaze tree in green and black.*
3510 Ensign : *Blue lustre ground with ornate border.*
3517 Autumn Trees & Ferns : *Stylised trees and ferns. White, cream ground.*
3519 Freehand Red Sunflower : *Pattern with multi-coloured diagonal swirl and large flower heads below. Pale ground.*

3522 Apple Blossom : *Black and grey branches with pink Apple blossom like flowers, handcraft. Matt pale blue ground.*

3523 Parkland : *Bold simple tree with enamelled dense foliage of autumn colours. Matt pale blue ground.*

3524 Parkland : *Bold simple tree with enamelled dense foliage of autumn colours. Matt green ground.*

3525 Clematis : *Large multi-coloured Clematis flower heads, handcraft. Mottled light ground.*

3526 New Delphinium : *Spires of Delphiniums in blue, pink, green and black. Blue matt ground.*

3527 Chinese Bird : *Exotic bird with curly tail, flower and cloud motifs. Mottled pale orange ground.*

3528 Oranges : *Oranges on black ground.*

3529 Crested Bird and Water Lily : *Exotic oriental crested bird perched on a water lily. Blue lustre ground.*

3530 Crested Bird and Water Lily : *Exotic oriental crested bird perched on a water lily. Red lustre ground.*

3532 Bookends - Fan : *Bookends in fan shape design coloured purple, yellow and green.*

3533 Bookends - Fan : *Bookends in fan shaped design in black, brown, orange and green.*

3535 Bookends - Asymmetric Flower : *Bookends with flower heads in brown with green and yellow petal heads.*

3536 Crested Bird and Water Lily : *Exotic oriental crested bird perched on a water lily. Mottled red ground.*

3537 Bookends - Saddleback : *Bookends in Saddleback design in blue and grey.*

3542 no name : *Apple Blossom.*

3544 Chinese Bird : *Exotic bird with curly tail, flower and cloud motifs. Orange ground.*

3545 Clematis : *Large multi-coloured Clematis flower heads, handcraft. Beige / brown ground.*
3546 Diamond : *Diamond shape and design in gilt on pale blue and ivory.*
3547 Diamond : *Diamond shape and design in gilt on green and black.*
3549 Diamond : *Diamond shape and design in green and gilt on cream ground.*
3550 Diamond : *Diamond shape and design in gilt on black and cream.*
3551 Eclipse : *Geometric design on red ground.*
3552 Deco Fan : *Brightly coloured fan design with pink rim and bottom border. Terracotta ground.*
3553 Strata : *Diagonal wavy stripes in gilt, beige, green and white. Matt black ground.*
3554 Ziggarette : *Vertical stripes of green yellow blue gold, descending from top rim. Black ground.*
3555 Entangled Droplets : *Brightly coloured enamelled beads on a gloss blue ground. Handcraft.*
3557 Fan : *Fan of brightly coloured and ornately decorated panels with clouds of dots. Ascending above exotic circular flowerheads. Blue ground.*
3558 Fan : *Fan of brightly coloured and ornately decorated panels with clouds of dots. Ascending above exotic circular flowerheads. Red ground.*
3562 Nightingale : *Singing Nightingale bird perched on a stem with a variety of colourful stylised flowers in red, yellow and blue. Dark green ground.*
3563 Tree & Cottage : *Cottage with smoking chimney in glade below stylised tree. Matt blue ground.*
3564 Fairy Shadow : *Motif of Fairy with delicate wings playing and casting shadows, also bands containing colourful flowerheads. Blue lustre ground.*

3565 Kaleidescopic : *Geometric shapes of patterns, stars and circles in profusion of brightly coloured enamels. Rouge ground.*
3566 Geometrica : *Modern Art design with geometric right-angle shapes, overlapping squares and patterns with wavy lines. Blue ground.*
3567 Russian : *Vibrant pattern of concentric circles in many colours. Stylised sun and bands of colour with leaves. Border has geometric pattern like saw teeth.*
3568 Nightingale Garden : *Large stylised brightly coloured flower heads. Black ground.*
3569 Green Trees : *Trees and foliage in shades of green. Green ground.*
3570 Mondrian : *Coloured squares and chevrons. Matt turquoise ground.*
3571 Fruit : *Fruit (pears, grapes etc) on blue ground.*
3574 Fairy Shadow : *Geometric shapes of patterns, stars and circles in profusion of brightly coloured enamels. Mustard ground.*
3576 Fairy Shadow : *Motif of Fairy with delicate wings playing and casting shadows, also bands containing colourful flowerheads. Red lustre ground.*
3581 Garden : *Spires of Daisy like flowers in many colours. Matt orange/brown ground.*
3587 Medley : *Bands of bright colours, blue, green, yellow, orange, red and purple.*
3588 Flower Medley : *Bands of bright colours, blue, green, yellow, orange, red and purple plus a simplistic pattern of shapes.*
3589 Hiawatha : *Large simplistic flowerheads in bold bright colours with feathers. Black ground.*
3590 Hiawatha : *Large simplistic flowerheads in bold bright colours with feathers. Black ground.*

Carlton Ware Patterns and Shapes

3591 Medley : *Bands of colours, yellow, orange and terracotta.*
3592 Gazania : *Large simplistic flower heads and leaves.*
3593 Medley : *Bands of bright colours, blue, green, yellow, orange, red and purple plus a simplistic pattern of shapes.*
3594 Dragon & Traveller : *Dragon & traveller. Oriental Dragon confronting a chinese traveller. Terracotta ground.*
3594 Dragon & Traveller : *Dragon & traveller. Oriental Dragon confronting a chinese traveller. Mustardy yellow ground.*
3595 Dragon & Traveller : *Dragon & traveller. Oriental Dragon confronting a chinese traveller. Turquoise ground.*
3596 Flower Medley : *Bands of bright colours plus a simplistic pattern of shapes.*
3597 Dragon & Traveller : *Dragon & traveller. Oriental Dragon confronting a chinese traveller. Blue lustre ground.*
3598 Nightingale : *Singing Nightingale bird perched on a stem with a variety of colourful stylised flowers in red, yellow and blue. Blue lustre ground.*
3599 Medley : *Bands of colours, yellow, orange, green, purple, blue and black.*
3600 Medley : *Bands of colours, purple, blue, grey and black.*
3601 Melange : *Large stylised flowerheads ornately decorated with leaves. Blue ground.*
3601 Melange : *Large stylised flowerheads ornately decorated with leaves. Pink ground.*
3603 no name : *Daisies, colours on blue ground.*

3606 Dahlia & Butterfly : *Bright yellow flower heads and butterflies with mottled green over blue ground.*

3609 Garden : *Spires of Daisy like flowers in many colours. Matt red ground.*

3639 Lace Cap Hydrangea : *Decorative Lace type design with Hydrangea flower heads and leaves. Light ground.*

3641 Forest Tree : *Exotic birch like trees. Slender tree rising to a wide pendulous canopy of foliage. Matt cream ground.*

3643 Victorian Garden : *Garden scene - similar to 3451 (Crinoline lady with parasol in garden) but without lady.*

3645 Rosetta : *Stylised flowers on trees with black and white bark. Orange ground.*

3645 Fairy Dell : *Scene with trees, snow and rabbits.*

3646 Iceland Poppy : *Designs of grasses, ornamental poppies and leaves.*

3648 Forest Tree : *Exotic birch like trees. Slender tree rising to a wide pendulous canopy of foliage. Mauve, cream ground, with green and yellow foliage.*

3650 Sylvan : *Stippled effect painted in green and blue.*

3651 Scimitar : *Geometric design of arches, bands and semi-circular shapes containing colourful patterns and flowers on mottled blue, green, pink background. Blue ground.*

3652 Scimitar : *Geometric design of arches, bands and semi-circular shapes containing colourful patterns and flowers on mottled blue, green, pink background. Blue ground.*

3653 Mandarins Chatting : *Two Chinese figures talking under Mandarin tree with beautiful coloured enamels and flowers. Second tree with detailed foliage and spikey leaves. Red frieze. Gloss black ground.*

Carlton Ware Patterns and Shapes

3654 Mandarins Chatting : *Two Chinese figures talking under Mandarin tree with beautiful coloured enamels and flowers. Second tree with detailed foliage and spikey leaves. Green frieze. Gloss black ground.*
3655 Jazz Stitch : *Geometric design of shapes some containing a stitch effect in orange, black and yellow. Light ground.*
3656 Dragon & Traveller : *Dragon & traveller. Fierce dragon decorated in many beautiful enamels, confronting chinese traveller also nearby is a pretty weeping tree. Dark blue ground.*
3657 Chevrons : *Geometric design in green, black and silver.*
3658 Carre : *Abstract design of black squares with silver borders. Green lustre ground.*
3659 Carre : *Abstract design of black squares. Orange lustre ground.*
3660 Dragon & Traveller : *Dragon & traveller. Fierce dragon decorated in many beautiful enamels, confronting chinese traveller also nearby is a pretty weeping tree. Yellow ground.*
3661 Norwegian Flowers : *Simplistic variety of flowers growing from green base. Matt blue ground.*
3662 Liberty Stripe : *Mauve, grey and pale blue separated by gold band.*
3663 Summer Medley : *Variety of brightly coloured flowers, some with spikey petals. Handcraft on black reserve.*
3665 Norwegian Lady : *Multicoloured simple flower heads. Blue ground.*
3665 Fairy Dell : *Scene with trees, snow and rabbits.*

3667 Tiger Lily : *Large stylised lily flowers design in blue, orange, yellow, pink and black colours. Frieze with tooth shaped pattern.*
3668 Norwegian Miss : *Image of a Norwegian girl surrounded by flowers. Blue ground.*
3669 Candy Flowers : *Anemone type flowerheads on mottled pale blue ground.*
3671 Chevrons : *Geometric design on orange lustre ground.*
3672 Mandarin Tree : *Mandarin tree in beautiful coloured enamels and flowers. Second tree with detailed foliage and spikey leaves. Blue ground and blue frieze.*
3672 Mandarins Chatting : *Two Chinese figures talking under Mandarin tree with beautiful coloured enamels and flowers. Second tree with detailed foliage and spikey leaves. Gloss blue ground.*
3673 Daisy : *Daisies on a blue ground.*
3675 Mandarins Chatting : *Two Chinese figures talking under Mandarin tree with beautiful coloured enamels and flowers. Second tree with detailed foliage and spikey leaves. White/Cream ground, red frieze.*
3678 Diamond : *Diamond shape and design in gilt on black and yellow.*
3680 Mandarins Chatting : *Two Chinese figures talking under Mandarin tree with beautiful coloured enamels and flowers. Second tree with detailed foliage and spikey leaves. Green and yellow ground.*
3681 Bathing Belle : *Handle formed as arched near naked female figure. White and dark blue.*
3684 Bathing Belle : *Handle formed as arched near naked female figure. White, red, gold and black.*
3688 Bathing Belle : *Handle formed as arched near naked female figure. Green and black*

Carlton Ware Patterns and Shapes

3690 Intersection : *Red, black, gilt stripe on cream ground.*
3691 Daisy : *Daisies on gloss green ground.*
3692 Lightning : *Lightning flashes of zig-zag lines. Orange, black and gilt.*
3693 Daisy : *Daisies on matt dark blue, light green ground.*
3694 Anemone : *Large stylised flower heads with spikey shaped petals and leaves. Mottled orange ground.*
3695 Egyptian Fan : *Elaborate geometric flower heads arranged in fan shapes and spires of brightly coloured flowers. Red lustre ground.*
3696 Egyptian Fan : *Elaborate geometric flower heads arranged in fan shapes and spires of brightly coloured flowers. Blue lustre.*
3696 Egyptian Fan : *Elaborate geometric flower heads arranged in fan shapes and spires of brightly coloured flowers. Green ground.*
3697 Egyptian Fan : *Elaborate geometric flower heads arranged in fan shapes and spires of brightly coloured flowers. Matt light blue ground.*
3698 Egyptian Fan : *Elaborate geometric flower heads arranged in fan shapes and spires of brightly coloured flowers. Gloss light blue ground.*
3699 Rainbow Fans : *Semi circular open fan shapes containing wavy patterns and exotic flower heads. Bands of colours as a rainbow. Orange ground.*
3700 Rainbow Fans : *Semi circular open fan shapes containing wavy patterns and exotic flower heads. Bands of colours as a rainbow. Gloss turquoise ground.*
3701 Mandarin Tree : *Mandarin tree in beautiful coloured enamels and flowers. Second tree with detailed foliage and spikey leaves. Red frieze and black ground.*

3702 Mandarin Tree : *Mandarin tree in beautiful coloured enamels and flowers. Second tree with detailed foliage and spikey leaves. Green frieze and black ground.*
3703 Mandarin Tree : *Mandarin tree in beautiful coloured enamels and flowers. Second tree with detailed foliage and spikey leaves. Red frieze and cream ground.*
3713 Rainbow Fans : *Semi circular open fan shapes containing wavy patterns and exotic flower heads. Bands of colours as a rainbow. Gloss blue ground.*
3714 Daisy : *Daisies on dark blue / mottled pale blue ground.*
3715 Sylvan : *Terracotta marks on dark cream ground.*
3716 Lightning : *Lightning flashes.*
3718 Sylvan : *Yellow, brown ground, vertical brush strokes with mottled effect.*
3719 Mandarin Tree : *Mandarin tree in beautiful coloured enamels and flowers. Second tree with detailed foliage and spikey leaves. Green Frieze and cream, yellow ground.*
3720 Bands : *Two tone green bands.*
3721 Rainbow Fans : *Semi circular open fan shapes containing wavy patterns and exotic flower heads. Bands of colours as a rainbow. Pale blue ground.*
3729 Christmas Tree : *Stylistic design of a Christmas Tree together with an ornate border. Orange ground.*
3742 Primula : *Primula flowers in pale mauve & pink.*
3745 Primula : *Primula flowers on pink, mauve ground.*
3746 Primula : *Primula flowers on pale peach ground.*
3753 Galleon : *Large Galleon like sailing ship. Pale blue, grey ground.*
3765 Red Devil : *Red devil (Mephistopheles) beneath a spangled tree with pendant foliage and blossoms like eye*

motifs. Large brightly coloured exotic flowers with spear shaped leaves. Gloss turquoise ground.
3765 Devils Copse : *Mottled exotic tree with pendant foliage and blossoms like eye motifs. Large brightly coloured exotic flowers with spear shaped leaves. Gloss turquoise ground.*
3766 Autumn Leaf : *Spray of leaves in Autumn hues of pink, green and orange. Pink mauve ground.*
3767 Red Devil : *Red devil (Mephistopheles) beneath a spangled tree with pendant foliage and blossoms like eye motifs. Large brightly coloured exotic flowers with spear shaped leaves. Wedgewood blue ground.*
3767 Devils Copse : *Mottled exotic tree with pendant foliage and blossoms like eye motifs. Large brightly coloured exotic flowers with spear shaped leaves. Wedgewood blue ground.*
3768 Gum Tree : *Flowers, spikey leaves and seed pods hanging from a tree. Pale blue ground.*
3769 Red Devil : *Red devil (Mephistopheles) beneath a spangled tree with pendant foliage and blossoms like eye motifs. Large brightly coloured exotic flowers with spear shaped leaves. Pale yellow ground.*
3769 Devils Copse : *Mottled exotic tree with pendant foliage and blossoms like eye motifs. Large brightly coloured exotic flowers with spear shaped leaves. Pale yellow ground.*
3770 Old Stone Ware : *Ribbed vase, blue, green.*
3770 Old Stone Ware : *Book ends, blue.*
3771 Drip Ware : *Running paint pattern. Ribbed vase, blue, brown, cream.*
3772 Drip Ware : *Running paint pattern. Ribbed vase, brown, cream.*

3773 Drip Ware : *Running paint pattern. Ribbed running yellow, green.*
3774 Bell : *Large stylised flower heads in multicoloured enamels and patterns with harebells curving out. One flowerhead contains a Bluebell. Detailed lace like triangular panels of pretty flowers. Cream gloss ground.*
3775 Old Stone Ware : *Ribbed light blue.*
3776 Old Stone Ware : *Running blue matt.*
3777 Old Stone Ware : *Matt stone.*
3778 Old Stone Ware : *Greenish grey.*
3779 Old Stone Ware : *Dark Pink.*
3780 Old Stone Ware : *Matt mauve.*
3781 Old Stone Ware : *Blue Matt.*
3782 Old Stone Ware : *Running design light and dark blue matt ground.*
3783 Old Stone Ware : *Matt stone*
3784 Old Stone Ware : *Running design blue grey matt ground design.*
3785 Bell : *Large stylised flower heads in multicoloured enamels and patterns with harebells curving out. One flowerhead contains a Bluebell. Detailed lace like triangular panels of pretty flowers. Matt pale blue ground.*
3786 Bell : *Large stylised flower heads in multicoloured enamels and patterns with harebells curving out. One flowerhead contains a Bluebell. Detailed lace like triangular panels of pretty flowers. Matt pale green ground.*
3787 Devils Copse : *Mottled exotic tree with pendant foliage and blossoms like eye motifs. Large brightly coloured exotic flowers with spear shaped leaves. Dark blue ground.*

Carlton Ware Patterns and Shapes

3788 Bell : *Large stylised flower heads in multicoloured enamels and patterns with harebells curving out. One flowerhead contains a Bluebell. Detailed lace like triangular panels of pretty flowers. Red Lustre ground.*
3789 Gum Tree : *Flowers, spikey leaves and seed pods hanging from a tree. Matt blue ground.*
3790 Gum Tree : *Flowers, spikey leaves and seed pods hanging from a tree. Green, yellow ground.*
3791 Mandarin Tree : *Mandarin tree in beautiful coloured enamels and flowers. Second tree with detailed foliage and spikey leaves. Grey ground.*
3792 Bell : *Large stylised flower heads in multicoloured enamels and patterns with harebells curving out. One flowerhead contains a Bluebell. Detailed lace like triangular panels of pretty flowers. Blue ground.*
3793 Mandarin Tree : *Mandarin tree in beautiful coloured enamels and flowers. Second tree with detailed foliage and spikey leaves. Ivory ground.*
3794 Gum Tree : *Flowers, spikey leaves and seed pods hanging from a tree. Matt pale green.*
3795 Gilt Scallop : *Rouge and black with border of scalloped edging in gilt of enamelled drops.*
3796 Bathing Belle : *Handle formed as arched near naked female figure. Blue ground with green handles and borders.*
3801 Herbaceous Border : *Spires of hollyhocks, foxgloves and pansy like flowers in a flowerbed. Multi-coloured on black and white ground.*
3802 Autumn Daisy : *Daisy flowerheads and leaves with a pattern of brushstrokes. Yellow ground.*
3803 Modern Crocus : *Medley of bright coloured bands and black border. Flowerheads of slender crocus shaped*

petals arranged in a circle with coloured leaves. Mauve brushstoke pattern. Pale green ground.
3804 Old Stone Ware : *Matt pale green.*
3809 Devils Copse : *Mottled exotic tree with pendant foliage and blossoms like eye motifs. Large brightly coloured exotic flowers with spear shaped leaves. Turquoise blue ground.*
3810 Embossed - Oak Tree : *Oak Tree with leaves and old gnarled trunk on concentric circles. Blue ground.*
3811 Embossed - Oak Tree : *Oak Tree with acorns and an old gnarled trunk on concentric circles. Fawn ground.*
3812 Wagon Wheels : *Exotic circular flower heads ornately decorated with enamels and leaves on stems. Pale green ground.*
3813 Wagon Wheels : *Exotic circular flower heads ornately decorated with enamels and leaves on stems. Mottled pink ground.*
3814 Wagon Wheels : *Exotic circular flower heads ornately decorated with enamels and leaves on stems. Red lustre ground.*
3815 Needlepoint : *Flower heads enamelled in embroidery like patterns. Bands and crescents of enamelled colours like lace. Dark blue ground.*
3816 Needlepoint : *Flower heads enamelled in embroidery like patterns. Bands and crescents of enamelled colours like lace. Maroon ground.*
3817 Devils Copse : *Mottled exotic tree with pendant foliage and blossoms like eye motifs. Large brightly coloured exotic flowers with spear shaped leaves. Matt turquoise ground.*
3818 Hollyhocks : *Spires of brightly coloured Hollyhocks, Pale green ground.*

Carlton Ware Patterns and Shapes

3819 Hollyhocks : *Spires of brightly coloured Hollyhocks. Pale blue ground.*
3820 Hollyhocks : *Spires of brightly coloured Hollyhocks. Black ground.*
3827 Hollyhocks : *Spires of brightly coloured Hollyhocks. Pale green ground.*
3829 Old Stone Ware : *Ribbed design in pink.*
3830 Old Stone Ware : *Ribbed design, semi-glazed in blue.*
3837 Delphinium : *Blue delphinium flowers and leaves, handcraft. Beige ground.*
3838 Gum Tree : *Flowers, spikey leaves and seed pods hanging from a tree. Matt light brown.*
3839 Autumn Breeze : *Stoneware design, flowers heads on pink and beige ground.*
3840 Autumn Breeze : *Stoneware design, flower heads on pale bluish pink with green edge.*
3841 Neapolitan : *Light green, light brown and light violet.*
3842 Neapolitan : *Stoneware, purple, mauve, green, pink.*
3843 Plain : *Green with gold band.*
3843 New Mikado : *Plain green but with New Mikado pattern. Chinese figures, pagoda, bridge and trees. Sometimes has two cranes and punt like boat. Green ground.*
3844 Plain : *Plain pale blue with gilt.*
3845 Medley : *Pink, green, blue and brown bands.*
3846 Plain : *Black lustre ground with wide band of gilding to borders.*
3847 Old Stone Ware : *Ribbed style in matt brown.*
3848 no name : *Pale green ground, flowers yellow orange green purple blue.*

3849 Plain : *Black gloss ground with wide band of gilding to borders.*
3852 Sketching Bird : *Exotic tree with pendant foliage and decoratively enamelled kingfisher like bird flying by. Pale blue lustre ground.*
3854 Hollyhocks : *Spires of Hollyhocks in enamels. Powder blue ground.*
3855 Bell : *Large stylised flower heads in multicoloured enamels and patterns with harebells curving out. One flowerhead contains a Bluebell. Detailed lace like triangular panels of pretty flowers. Gloss blue green.*
3857 Leaf : *Design of Leaves and small flower heads decorated in enamels. Powder blue ground.*
3858 Tendrillon : *Design of swirling patterns with leaves and tendrils in white and gilt. Black gloss ground.*
3859 Devils Copse : *Mottled exotic tree with pendant foliage and blossoms like eye motifs. Large brightly coloured exotic flowers with spear shaped leaves. Red ground.*
3860 New Mikado : *Chinese figures, pagoda, bridge and trees. Sometimes has two cranes and punt like boat. Blue ground.*
3861 Leaf : *Design of Leaves and small flower heads decorated in enamels. Red ground.*
3862 Bluebells : *Bluebell flowers with snowdrops, primulas and autumn leaves. Ruby Lustre.*
3863 Garden Gate : *Deco tree, bushes and flowers with path leading to garden gate. Pale green ground.*
3865 Spring : *Spring flowers depicted on a tree in many bright colours, handcraft. Grey ground.*
3866 Wisteria : *Wisteria like flowers trailing from tree with leaves. Pale blue ground.*

3867 New Laburnam : *Laburnham like flowers trailing from tree with leaves. Pale turquoise ground, yellow flowers.*
3867 New Laburnam : *Laburnham like flowers trailing from tree with leaves. Pale turquoise ground, lilac flowers.*
3868 Vogue : *Design of simple primula and hydrangea flowers. Pale matt green ground.*
3872 Bluebells : *Bluebell flowers with snowdrops, primulas and autumn leaves. Pink, blue glazed.*
3873 Leaf : *Design of Leaves and small flower heads decorated in enamels. Matt pale blue ground.*
3874 Bluebells : *Bluebell flowers with snowdrops, primulas and autumn leaves. Mottled grey ground.*
3875 Bluebells : *Bluebell flowers with snowdrops, primulas and autumn leaves. Light blue matt ground.*
3876 Embossed - Rock Garden : *Simple embossed primula like flowers heads. Spires of flowers with stone shaped patterns. Grey ground.*
3877 Old Stone Ware : *Ribbed style on blue ground.*
3878 Old Stone Ware : *Ribbed style on matt jade green ground slightly mottled.*
3879 Old Stone Ware : *Ribbed style on brown ground.*
3883 Beehives : *Mottled grey ground.*
3884 Humming Bird with Tree : *Elaborately decorated exotic bird hovering under weeping tree with floral decoration. Rouge ground.*
3884 Beehives : *Ivory matt ground.*
3885 Spring : *Flowering tree on mottled stone glaze ground.*
3886 Moderne : *Moderne set - Matt light & dark blue ground.*
3886 Dancing Deer : *Embossed Deer.*

3887 Moderne : *Moderne set - Matt blue with dark blue or Matt grey with gold or Matt blue with fawn or Matt grey with pink.*

3888 Moderne : *Moderne set - Matt blue with or without gold.*

3889 Sketching Bird : *Exotic tree with pendant foliage and decoratively enamelled kingfisher like bird flying by. Rouge ground.*

3890 Sketching Bird : *Exotic tree with pendant foliage and decoratively enamelled kingfisher like bird flying by. Matt Cream ground.*

3891 Sketching Bird : *Exotic tree with pendant foliage and decoratively enamelled kingfisher like bird flying by. Cream ground.*

3891 Sketching Bird with no Bird : *Exotic tree with pendant foliage. No bird. Cream ground.*

3892 Persian Garden : *Sprays of exotic enamel flowers and foliage, some in spires with star like heads. Sometimes a magical tree with a variety of flowerheads. Blue ground.*

3893 Persian Garden : *Sprays of exotic enamel flowers and foliage, some in spires with star like heads. Sometimes a magical tree with a variety of flowerheads. Black ground.*

3894 Persian Garden : *Sprays of exotic enamel flowers and foliage, some in spires with star like heads. Sometimes a magical tree with a variety of flowerheads. Matt green ground.*

3895 Chinaland : *Complex chinoiserie design with underglaze enamels. Pagoda, terraces, trees, figures and usually mountains. Green lustre ground.*

3896 Old Stone Ware : *Yellow/Cream ribbed*

Carlton Ware Patterns and Shapes

3897 Spring : *Deco tree and small flower heads. Peach ground.*

3900 Incised Square : *Incised geometric simplistic flower patterns, some flowerheads are square shaped. Also has some wavy lines. Beige ground.*

3901 Incised Diamond : *Incised geometric simplistic flower patterns, some flowerheads are diamond shaped. Also has some wavy lines. Pale blue ground.*

3902 Hammered Pewter : *Dimpled, turquoise, green, yellow ground.*

3904 Old Stone Ware : *Grey Ribbed.*

3905 Incised Diamond : *Incised geometric simplistic flower patterns, some flowerheads are diamond shaped. Also has some wavy lines. Beige ground.*

3907 Sketching Bird : *Exotic tree with pendant foliage and decoratively enamelled kingfisher like bird flying by. Pale ice blue lustre ground.*

3908 Crab & Lobster Ware : *Aero green.*

3909 Ring Posy Bowls : *Powder blue.*

3910 Mikado : *Chinoiserie pagodas, bridges, oriental ladies and usually a pair of kissing birds. Matt black with green frieze.*

3910 Crab & Lobster Ware : *Straw.*

3911 Plain : *Plain cream with black or gold edging.*

3912 Spots : *Turquoise polka dots on cream ground.*

3913 Floral Mist : *Floral wispy flower design in blue, yellow and green. Light ground.*

3915 Mirage : *Simplistic abstract pattern on cream ground.*

3916 Spots : *Yellow polka dots on beige ground.*

3917 Drip Ware : *Running paint pattern in green, yellow and blue on cream ground.*

3918 Leaf and Catkin : *Leaf and Catkin on white ground.*

3919 Leaf and Catkin : *Leaf and Catkin on matt pale green.*
3920 Old Stone Ware : *Splashes of blue and brown on grey.*
3922 Wild Duck : *Duck with shadow flying over wild grasses and shrubs. Rouge ground.*
3923 Wild Duck : *Duck with shadow flying over wild grasses and shrubs. Cream ground.*
3924 Wild Duck : *Duck with shadow flying over wild grasses and shrubs. Pale blue ground.*
3925 Summer Flowers : *Array of summer flowers and leaves. Matt blue ground.*
3926 Summer Flowers : *Array of summer flowers and leaves. Yellow ground with green frieze.*
3927 Summer Flowers : *Array of summer flowers and leaves. Cream ground.*
3927 Wild Duck : *Duck with shadow flying over wild grasses and shrubs. Pale green ground.*
3929 Will o'wisp : *Wavy pattern in mauve with wisps of paint in pale green and brown. Cream ground.*
3933 Plain : *Plain rouge deepening to brown with gilt.*
3939 Will o'wisp : *Wavy pattern in mauve with wisps of paint in pale green and brown. Yellow green ground.*
3943 Tube Lined Tree : *Tube lined tree with hanging foliage in yellow, mauve and green. Cream ground.*
3944 Tube Lined Tree : *Tube lined tree with hanging foliage in yellow, mauve and green. Pale matt green ground.*
3945 Tube Lined Flower : *Tube lined flower in blue and green with thistle like flower in yellow. Cream ground.*
3946 Hazelnut : *Hazelnuts and leaves. Pale mauve, grey ground.*

Carlton Ware Patterns and Shapes

3947 Wild Duck : *Duck with shadow flying over wild grasses and shrubs. Stippled green lustre ground.*
3948 Flower & Falling Leaf : *Exotic complex geometric flower heads with leaves swirling and falling over. Matt pale turquoise ground.*
3949 Flower & Falling Leaf : *Exotic complex geometric flower heads with leaves swirling and falling over. Rouge ground.*
3950 Flower & Falling Leaf : *Exotic complex geometric flower heads with leaves swirling and falling over. Pale cream ground.*
3951 Sketching Bird : *Exotic tree with pendant foliage and decoratively enamelled kingfisher bird flying by. Gloss pale green ground.*
3952 Flower & Falling Leaf : *Exotic complex geometric flower heads with leaves swirling and falling over. Blue ground.*
3952 Sketching Bird : *Exotic tree with pendant foliage and decoratively enamelled kingfisher like bird flying by. Powder blue ground.*
3953 Galleon : *Large Galleon sailing ship on waves. Blue, cream ground.*
3955 Rayure : *Black circular stripes on Moderne shape. Pale green ground.*
3956 Jacobean Figures : *Beautiful design containing Jacobean Figures with shadows. Gloss green ground*
3956 Jacobean Figures : *Beautiful design containing Jacobean Figures with shadows. Pale blue ground*
3957 Galleon : *Large Galleon sailing ship on waves. Pale blue, mauve ground.*
3957 Jacobean Figures : *Beautiful design containing Jacobean Figures with shadows. Ruby red ground*

3958 Summer Flowers : *Array of summer flowers and leaves. Cream ground.*
3959 Triple Band : *Wash bands in satin, yellow and brown.*
3960 Sketching Bird : *Exotic tree with pendant foliage and decoratively enamelled kingfisher bird flying by. Green ground.*
3965 Heron & Magical Tree : *Heron flying past large ornamental tree. Cream Lustre ground.*
3965 Plain : *Rouge Royale.*
3966 Lace Cap Hydrangea : *Lace type design with Hydrangea flower heads and leaves. Green ground.*
3967 Lace Cap Hydrangea : *Lace type design with Hydrangea flower heads and leaves. Red ground.*
3968 Blossom & Spray : *Blossom spray and small enamelled flower heads with gilt leaves. Powder blue ground.*
3969 Lace Cap Hydrangea : *Lace type design with Hydrangea flower heads and leaves. Pink lustre ground.*
3970 Shabunkin : *Ornamental brightly enamelled fish with flowing fins amongst exotic seabed plants. Pale blue or grey ground.*
3971 Shabunkin : *Ornamental brightly enamelled fish with flowing fins amongst exotic seabed plants. Green and Ivory ground.*
3972 Hollyhocks : *Spires of hollyhocks in enamels. Orange ground.*
3973 Hollyhocks : *Spires of brightly coloured hollyhocks. Green ground.*
3974 Tube Lined Poppy & Bell : *Tube lined poppies and bell flowers. Matt blue ground.*
3975 Persian Rose : *Gilt tube lining of flower heads and bell flowers. Mushroom ground.*

Carlton Ware Patterns and Shapes

3976 Banded and Crosstitch : *Moderne design with bands of circles and wavy patterns. Pale cream ground.*
3977 Engine Turned Ware : *Ribbed style in gloss pink ground.*
3978 Engine Turned Ware : *Ribbed style in gloss green ground.*
3979 Engine Turned Ware : *Ribbed style in matt green ground.*
3980 Engine Turned Ware : *Ribbed style in matt yellow ground.*
3981 Engine Turned Ware : *Ribbed style in matt blue ground.*
3982 Engine Turned Ware : *Ribbed style in matt white or cream ground.*
3982 Sunflower : *Large Sunflower heads. Black ground.*
3986 no name : *Stylised flowers on cream ground.*
3989 Eden (Tiger Tree) : *Exotic tree with gnarled trunk and lobes and pendulous hanging foliage with pretty flowers. The foliage also rises from the base in spires. Blue lustre ground.*
3990 no name : *Seedheads, flowers on cream ground.*
3993 Embossed - Buttercup : *Design in shape of Yellow Buttercup in embossed style. Cream, yellow ground.*
3994 Embossed - Buttercup : *Design in shape of Pink Buttercup and embossed style. Pink ground.*
3996 Sunflower : *Large Sunflower heads. Black ground.*
3997 Forest Night : *Large trees with pendulous hanging leaves. Dark blue ground.*
3998 Old Stone Ware : *Dark Green.*
3999 Engine Turned Ware : *Ribbed style in matt grey ground.*

Patterns 4000 - 4999

4000 Plain : *Burnt Orange with Gold*
4001 Plain : *Almond with Gold*
4002 Cherry Blossom : *Cherry Blossom. Burnt Orange ground*
4003 Cherry Blossom : *Cherry Blossom. Almond ground*
4009 Plain : *Plain lustre, Rouge Royale.*
4011 Plain : *Plain cobalt blue with gilt edging.*
4011 Spots : *Spots on cobalt blue ground.*
4012 Tube Lined Marigold : *Tubular raised edge flowerheads in red, orange and green with dark leaves. Mottled cream ground.*
4013 Plain : *Plain Vert Royale with gilt.*
4014 Harebells : *Harebell flowers edged with gilt. Green ground.*
4015 Harebells : *Harebell flowers edged with gilt. Pale green ground.*
4016 Harebells : *Harebell flowers edged with gilt. Pink ground.*
4017 Secretary Bird : *Exotic bird with fan shaped tail feathers and long legs similar to a road runner, under a decorative tree in enamels. Orange ground.*
4018 Secretary Bird : *Exotic bird with fan shaped tail feathers and long legs similar to a road runner, under a decorative tree in enamels. Red ground.*

Carlton Ware Patterns and Shapes

4019 Animal (Squirrel, Deer or Fox) : *Decorative landscape with woodland animals either a Squirrel, Deer or Fox. Green ground.*

4021 Plain : *Plain blue and mauve lustre ground in mottled effect with gilt.*

4030 Carlton China - Peony : *Flower design.*

4037 Plain : *Plain jade green with gilt.*

4040 Leaves : *Design of pale coloured leaves. Pale blue ground.*

4042 Wild Duck : *Duck with shadow flying over wild grasses and shrubs. Pale pink ground.*

4045 Blossom & Spray : *Blossom spray and small enamelled flower heads with gilt leaves. Red lustre ground.*

4047 Blossom & Spray : *Blossom spray and small enamelled flower heads with gilt leaves. Blue mottled ground.*

4060 no name : *Black bands and pink glaze.*

4076 Tyrolean Bands : *Multi-coloured circular bands in various sizes and wavy lines.*

4077 Vertical Stripes : *Large vertical stripes and sometimes smaller horizontal stripes on base in gilt. Cream ground.*

4078 Vertical Stripes : *Large vertical stripes and sometimes smaller horizontal stripes on base in gilt. Yellow ground.*

4079 Vertical Stripes : *Large vertical stripes and sometimes smaller horizontal stripes on base in gilt. Green ground.*

4080 Vertical Stripes : *Large vertical stripes and sometimes smaller horizontal stripes on base in gilt. Gloss pink ground with black and gold.*

4081 Beanstalk : *Plant with large leaves like a beanstalk. Pale blue ground.*
4083 Vertical Stripes : *Large vertical stripes and sometimes smaller horizontal stripes on base in russet brown stripe. Cream ground.*
4084 Vertical Stripes : *Large vertical stripes and sometimes smaller horizontal stripes on base in green. Cream ground.*
4092 Heatwave : *Diagonal bands of colours in orange and yellow and many fine wavy lines.*
4100 Plain : *Plain pale green with gold.*
4103 Spider's Web : *Cobwebs with fruiting berries on branch, also flowers (harebells) and dragonflies. Pale green ground.*
4104 New Mikado : *Chinese figures, pagoda, bridge and trees. Sometimes has two cranes and punt like boat. Pale green ground.*
4105 Black Crow : *Colourful scene with black crows.*
4106 Secretary Bird : *Exotic bird with fan shaped tail feathers and long legs similar to a road runner, under a decorative tree in enamels. Pale blue ground.*
4107 Secretary Bird : *Exotic bird with fan shaped tail feathers and long legs similar to a road runner, under a decorative tree in enamels. Green ground.*
4108 Heron & Magical Tree : *Heron flying past large ornamental tree. Pale green ground.*
4108 Plain : *Plain pale green with gilt.*
4108 Temple : *Oriental scene of figures in temple with large circular doorway. Ornate trees some with black stems, sometimes a gold sun. Pale green ground.*
4109 Plain : *Plain cream with gold highlight.*

Carlton Ware Patterns and Shapes

4109 New Mikado : *Chinese figures, pagoda, bridge and trees. Sometimes has two cranes and punt like boat. Cream ground with gilt.*

4109 Spider's Web : *Cobwebs with fruiting berries on branch, also flowers (harebells) and dragonflies. Matt white ground.*

4110 Plain : *Plain pale blue with gilt.*

4117 Bird of Paradise : *Bird of Paradise with long plumed tail flying among oriental trees. Red ground.*

4118 Bird of Paradise : *Bird of Paradise with long plumed tail flying among oriental trees. Powder Blue ground.*

4119 Primula and Leaf : *Primula flowers in bright colours and a butterfly. Rouge ground.*

4120 Primula and Leaf : *Primula flowers in bright colours and a butterfly. Pale yellow ground.*

4121 Primula and Leaf : *Primula flowers in bright colours and a butterfly. Pale green ground.*

4122 Butterfly : *Butterfly and grasses. Cream ground.*

4123 Butterfly : *Butterfly and grasses. Vibrant green ground.*

4125 Babylon : *Profusion of foliage and leaves cascading down with pretty bell and star flowers. Large star shaped flowerhead ornately decorated in enamels. Yellow, green ground.*

4125 Heron & Magical Tree : *Heron flying past large ornamental tree. Blue & green lustre ground.*

4126 Babylon : *Profusion of foliage and leaves cascading down with pretty bell and star flowers. Large star shaped flowerhead ornately decorated in enamels. Rouge red ground.*

4128 Banded : *Circles and plain green.*

4130 Banded : *Yellow highlights on white ground.*

4136 Harebells : *Harebell flowers edged with gilt. Pale green ground.*
4137 Babylon : *Profusion of foliage and leaves cascading down with pretty bell and star flowers. Large star shaped flowerhead ornately decorated in enamels. Matt Orange ground.*
4138 Tube Lined Fields and Trees : *Tube lined landscape scene with curving and bulbous fields, trees and hills. Blue ground.*
4139 Daisies : *Large and small blue flower heads. Pale blue, green ground.*
4140 Azealea : *Large design of Azalea flowerheads. Pale green ground.*
4141 Plain : *Plain pink ground with gilt.*
4142 Plain : *Plain pink ground with gilt.*
4146 Plain : *Plain pale yellow ground with gilt.*
4149 Plain : *Plain cream.*
4150 Heron & Magical Tree : *Heron flying past large ornamental tree. Red ground.*
4153 Heron & Magical Tree : *Heron flying past large ornamental tree. Pale yellow ground.*
4154 Harebells : *Harebell flowers edged with gilt. Orange ground.*
4155 Primula and Leaf : *Primula flowers in bright colours and a butterfly. Pale green ground.*
4156 Crocus and Cloud : *Realistic crocuses with clouds on a cream ground.*
4157 Plain : *Pale pink with gold handles.*
4157 Plain with Leaves : *Pale pink with white leaves.*
4158 Babylon : *Profusion of foliage and leaves cascading down with pretty bell and star flowers. Large star shaped flowerhead ornately decorated in enamels. Plain pale yellow ground.*

Carlton Ware Patterns and Shapes

4158 Plain : *Plain pale yellow ground with gilt.*
4159 Heron & Magical Tree : *Heron flying past ornamental tree. Rouge ground.*
4160 Heron & Magical Tree : *Heron flying past ornamental tree. Blue, green ground.*
4161 Fighting Cocks : *Two cockerels displaying in the fighting position amongst a beautiful display of flowers. Orange lustre ground.*
4162 Tube Lined Tulip : *Tube lined tulip flowers and leaves. Green ground.*
4163 Spangle Tree or Tiger Tree : *Stylised tree with black shadow and hanging green foliage with small flower heads. Yellow ground.*
4166 Plain : *Plain green with gilt.*
4168 Babylon : *Profusion of foliage and leaves cascading down with pretty bell and star flowers. Large star shaped flowerhead ornately decorated in enamels. Powder blue ground.*
4168 Carlton China - Greek Keys : *Simple gilt border design.*
4178 Plain : *Gilt on grey ground.*
4179 Plain : *Plain mauve with gilt.*
4181 Plain : *Plain rouge with gilt.*
4182 Heron & Magical Tree : *Heron flying past ornamental tree. Salmon ground.*
4183 Plain : *Plain pale green, gilt handles.*
4184 Fighting Glade : *Fighting Cocks pattern with no Cocks. Display of flower heads. Bluish, pink ground.*
4185 Pastoral : *Slender tree with orange and blue flowerheads also has large leaves. Pale green ground.*
4186 Fighting Cocks : *Two cockerels displaying in the fighting position amongst a beautiful display of flowers. Pale blue lustre ground.*

4188 Plain : *Plain pale grey ground with gilt.*

4189 Babylon : *Profusion of foliage and leaves cascading down with pretty bell and star flowers. Large star shaped flowerhead ornately decorated in enamels. Pink ground.*

4190 no name : *Pink flowers, yellow green foliage. Pale green ground.*

4191 Cinquefoil : *Yellow and purple flowers, green foliage. Pale green ground.*

4192 Iceland Poppy : *Designs of grasses, ornamental poppies and leaves. Pale gloss yellow ground.*

4192 Cinquefoil : *Yellow and purple flowers, green foliage. Pale yellow ground.*

4193 Iceland Poppy : *Designs of grasses, ornamental poppies and leaves. Pale gloss green ground.*

4194 Iceland Poppy : *Designs of grasses, ornamental poppies and leaves. Pale lemon ground.*

4198 Fighting Glade : *Fighting Cocks pattern with no Cocks. Display of flowers heads. Pale green ground.*

4199 Fighting Cocks : *Two cockerels displaying in the fighting position amongst a beautiful display of flowers. Deep blue lustre ground.*

4201 Primula and Leaf : *Primula flowers in bright colours and a butterfly. Blue lustre ground*

4202 Fighting Cocks : *Two cockerels displaying in the fighting position amongst a beautiful display of flowers. Ruby lustre ground.*

4204 Temple : *Oriental scene of figures in temple with large circular doorway. Ornate trees some with black stems, sometimes a gold sun. Cream gloss ground.*

4205 Temple : *Oriental scene of figures in temple with large circular doorway. Ornate trees some with black stems, sometimes a gold sun. Pale green ground.*

4208 Temple : *Oriental scene of figures in temple with large circular doorway. Ornate trees some with black stems, sometimes a gold sun. Dark red ground.*
4211 Sketching Bird : *Exotic tree with pendant foliage and decoratively enamelled kingfisher bird flying by. Gloss light green ground.*
4212 Fighting Glade : *Fighting Cocks pattern with no Cocks. Display of flowers heads. Rouge ground.*
4213 New Anemone : *Anemone flowers in bright colours and leaves. Pale yellow ground.*
4214 Temple : *Oriental scene of figures in temple with large circular doorway. Ornate trees some with black stems, sometimes a gold sun. Deep pink ground.*
4215 Starflower : *Flowers with geometric spires like stars and smaller flowers like stars cascading down. Rouge ground.*
4216 Starflower : *Flowers with geometric spires like stars and smaller flowers like stars cascading down. Light blue ground.*
4217 Tree & Clouds : *Stylised tree with gnarled trunk and pendulous foliage trailing down and clouds in the background. Red ground.*
4218 Leaf & Dots : *Dots and posies of leaves. Deep pink ground.*
4219 New Anemone : *Anemone flowers in bright colours and leaves. Pale green ground.*
4220 Iceland Poppy : *Designs of grasses, ornamental poppies and leaves. Pale green ground.*
4221 Iceland Poppy : *Designs of grasses, ornamental poppies and leaves. Yellow ground.*
4223 Spots : *Pale with orange spots.*
4224 Spots : *Royal blue with light blue spots.*
4225 Spots : *Rouge Royale with spots.*

4226 Spots : *Pale pink with green spots.*
4227 Spots : *Pale yellow with spots.*
4228 Iceland Poppy : *Designs of grasses, ornamental poppies and leaves. Green ground.*
4231 New Anemone : *Anemone flowers in bright colours and leaves. Yellow ground.*
4232 Spots : *Pale yellow with orange spots.*
4234 Bird of Paradise : *Bird of Paradise with long plumed tail flying among oriental trees. Mottled blue and orange lustre ground.*
4235 Embossed - Water Lily : *Embossed Water Lily. Pale yellow and pink.*
4235 Carlton China - no name : *Blue Flowers.*
4239 Bird of Paradise : *Bird of Paradise with long plumed tail flying among oriental trees. Pale blue ground.*
4241 Eden (Tiger Tree) : *Exotic tree with gnarled trunk and lobes and pendulous hanging foliage with pretty flowers. The foliage also rises from the base in spires. Rouge ground.*
4242 Eden (Tiger Tree) : *Exotic tree with gnarled trunk and lobes and pendulous hanging foliage with pretty flowers. The foliage also rises from the base in spires. Purple ground.*
4242 Spider's Web : *Cobwebs with fruiting berries on branch, flowers (harebells) and dragonflies. Pale blue lustre ground.*
4243 Spider's Web : *Cobwebs with fruiting berries on branch, flowers (harebells) and dragonflies. Blue, grey ground.*
4243 Rabbits at Dusk : *Rabbits playing amongst grasses shown in silhouette, under tall trees with green foliage. Orange ground.*

4244 Spider's Web : *Cobwebs with fruiting berries on branch, flowers (harebells) and dragonflies. Powder blue ground.*

4245 New Anemone : *Anemone flowers in bright colours and leaves. Mauve / pink / blue.*

4246 Daydream : *Large flower heads in blue with yellow centre also has a frieze of blue scrolls, handcraft. White ground.*

4247 Rabbits at Dusk : *Rabbits playing amongst grasses shown in silhouette, under tall trees with green foliage. Mottled orange ground.*

4247 Rabbits at Dusk : *Rabbits playing amongst grasses shown in silhouette, under tall trees with green foliage. Mottled pink ground.*

4248 Eden Canopy : *Pendulous hanging foliage with pretty flowers from an exotic tree. Rouge ground.*

4249 Rabbits at Dusk : *Rabbits playing amongst grasses shown in silhouette, under tall trees with green foliage. Orange ground.*

4249 Eden Canopy : *Pendulous hanging foliage with pretty flowers from an exotic tree. Blue ground.*

4252 Spider's Web : *Cobwebs with fruiting berries on branch, flowers (harebells) and dragonflies. Rouge ground.*

4254 Spider's Web : *Cobwebs with fruiting berries on branch, flowers (harebells) and dragonflies. Rouge Royale ground.*

4257 Rabbits at Dusk : *Rabbits playing amongst grasses shown in silhouette, under tall trees with green foliage. Pale green ground.*

4258 Plain : *Stiff strong pink and gold.*

4259 Spider's Web : *Cobwebs with fruiting berries on branch, flowers (harebells) and dragonflies. Pale pink ground.*
4260 Figurine - Monica : *Carlton China Figurine.*
4261 Figurine - Monica : *Carlton China Figurine.*
4262 Figurine - Curtsy : *Carlton China Figurine.*
4264 Figurine - Nan : *Grandmother figurine with shawl, bonnet and basket of flowers.*
4268 Figurine - Nell : *Carlton China Figurine.*
4269 Figurine - Nell : *Carlton China Figurine.*
4270 Figurine - Peggy : *Carlton China Figurine.*
4271 Figurine - Peggy : *Carlton China Figurine.*
4273 Figurine - Joan : *Carlton China Figurine in pink and green carrying a fan.*
4273 Heron & Magical Tree : *Heron flying past large ornamental tree. Pink ground.*
4274 Plain : *Plain dark blue lustre.*
4275 Figurine - Grandma : *Carlton China Figurine.*
4276 Figurine - Grandma : *Carlton China Figurine.*
4277 Marguerite Daisy : *Yellow daisy like flowers with green serrated leaves like nettle leaves. Yellow ground.*
4278 Palm Blossom : *Flower heads.*
4279 Lilac : *Realistic Lilac flowers and leaves. Pale green ground.*
4280 New Storks : *Two crane like birds wading in a lake under trees with pendulous hanging foliage. Rouge ground.*
4281 Beech Nut : *Leaves & nuts, cream ground.*
4282 Beech Nut : *Leaves & nuts, pale brown ground.*
4283 New Storks : *Two crane like birds wading in a lake under trees with pendulous hanging foliage. Green, pink, purple lustre ground.*
4284 Plain : *Purple Lustre plain.*

4285 Embossed - Foxglove : *Embossed Foxglove on Yellow*
4286 Silk Sands : *Contour lines as in a silk pattern or left by the sea on the sands. Light green ground with gilt.*
4286 Embossed - Foxglove : *Embossed Foxglove on Green*
4287 Silk Sands : *Contour lines as in a silk pattern or left by the sea on the sands. Light yellow ground with gilt.*
4289 Silk Sands : *Contour lines as in a silk pattern or left by the sea on the sands. Light cream ground with gilt.*
4291 Contours : *Pale blue ground with darker dashes and gilt.*
4292 Tree & Clouds : *Cream/pink ground, stylised gnarled tree and clouds.*
4293 Heron & Magical Tree : *Heron flying past ornamental tree. Pale blue or pale pink ground.*
4294 Carlton China - Arrow Border : *Simple arrows around edge design on either Blue or Dark Pink.*
4297 Palm Blossom : *Flower heads on mottled red ground.*
4298 Palm Blossom : *Flower heads on orange ground.*
4301 Figurine - Joan : *Carlton China Figurine.*
4302 Figurine - Grandma : *Carlton China Figurine.*
4303 Tree & Clouds : *Stylised gnarled tree and clouds on blue ground.*
4304 New Storks : *Two crane like birds wading in a lake under trees with pendulous hanging foliage. Green ground.*
4305 Harvest Fruit : *Fruit on a white ground with a net type background and a black border. Also found under Carlton China.*
4310 Lilac : *Realistic Lilac flowers and leaves. Pale green ground.*

4313 Heron & Magical Tree : *Heron flying past ornamental tree. Blue ground.*

4314 Figurine - Jean : *Carlton China Figurine in blue dress and pink shawl.*

4320 New Mikado : *Chinese figures, pagoda, bridge and trees. Sometimes has two cranes and punt like boat. Pale yellow ground.*

4321 Heron & Magical Tree : *Heron flying past large ornamental tree. Yellow ground.*

4322 Spots : *White spots on Noire Royale.*

4323 Spots : *White spots on pink.*

4324 Spots : *White spots on French green ground.*

4325 Heron & Magical Tree : *Heron flying past ornamental tree. Blue Royale ground.*

4326 Heron & Magical Tree : *Heron flying past ornamental tree. Rouge Royal ground.*

4327 Spider's Web : *Cobwebs with fruiting berries on branch, flowers (harebells) and dragonflies. Pale yellow ground.*

4328 New Mikado : *Chinese figures, pagoda, bridge and trees. Sometimes has two cranes and punt like boat. Pale green ground.*

4329 New Mikado : *Chinese figures, pagoda, bridge and trees. Sometimes has two cranes and punt like boat. Pale Ice blue ground.*

4330 Spider's Web : *Cobwebs with fruiting berries on branch, flowers (harebells) and dragonflies. Pale pink ground.*

4331 Spider's Web : *Cobwebs with fruiting berries on branch, flowers (harebells) and dragonflies. Pale green ground.*

4332 Heron & Magical Tree : *Heron flying past ornamental tree. Pink ground.*

4339 New Storks : *Two crane like birds wading in a lake under trees with pendulous hanging foliage. Powder blue ground.*
4340 New Storks : *Two crane like birds wading in a lake under trees with pendulous hanging foliage. Rouge Royale ground.*
4341 Plain : *Plain Cobalt blue with gilt.*
4342 New Storks : *Two crane like birds wading in a lake under trees with pendulous hanging foliage. Pale yellow ground.*
4343 New Storks : *Two crane like birds wading in a lake under trees with pendulous hanging foliage. Pale green ground.*
4344 New Storks : *Two crane like birds wading in a lake under trees with pendulous hanging foliage. Pale pink ground.*
4346 New Mikado : *Chinese figures, pagoda, bridge and trees. Sometimes has two cranes and punt like boat. Noir Royale ground.*
4347 Spider's Web : *Cobwebs with fruiting berries on branch, flowers (harebells) and dragonflies. Noire Royale ground.*
4348 New Storks : *Two crane like birds wading in a lake under trees with pendulous hanging foliage. Noire Royale ground.*
4350 Plain : *Plain green with gilt.*
4352 Plain : *Blue grey.*
4353 Plain : *Matt fawn.*
4354 Sketching Bird : *Exotic tree with pendant foliage and decoratively enamelled kingfisher like bird flying by. Ruby Lustre ground.*
4355 Humming Bird with Tree : *Elaborately decorated exotic bird and floral decoration. Powder blue ground.*

4355 Sketching Bird : *Exotic tree with pendant foliage and decoratively enamelled kingfisher like bird flying by. Powder Blue ground.*
4356 Plain : *Plain Vert Royale with gilt.*
4357 Plain : *Plain ribbed Bleu Royale.*
4358 no name : *Powder blue with border (raised enamel).*
4359 no name : *Rouge Royale with border.*
4360 Carlton China - Canterbury Border or New Bluebells : *Bluebells and other flowers design on edge.*
4362 New Mikado : *Chinese figures, pagoda, bridge and trees. Sometimes has two cranes and punt like boat. Vert Royale ground.*
4363 Spider's Web : *Cobwebs with fruiting berries on branch, also flowers (harebells) and dragonflies. Mottled green ground.*
4366 Spider's Web : *Cobwebs with fruiting berries on branch, flowers (harebells) and dragonflies. Mottled pale blue lustre ground.*
4367 New Storks : *Two crane like birds wading in a lake under trees with pendulous hanging foliage. Bleu Royale.*
4368 Embossed - Primula : *Embossed primula on yellow ground.*
4369 Embossed - Primula : *Embossed primula on green ground.*
4372 Spots : *Powder blue with spots.*
4373 Mikado : *Chinoiserie pagodas, bridges, oriental ladies and usually a pair of kissing birds. Vert Royale ground.*
4374 New Violets : *Violets on pale violet ground.*
4375 Snowdrops : *Snowdrops flowers on pale blue ground.*
4376 New Violets : *Violets on pale violet ground.*

4376 Sketching Bird : *Exotic tree with pendant foliage and decoratively enamelled kingfisher like bird flying by. Bleu Royale ground.*
4377 Fighting Glade : *Fighting Cocks pattern with no Cocks. Display of flowers heads. Rouge Royale.*
4379 Spots : *Lilac ground with white spots.*
4380 Fighting Cocks : *Two cockerels displaying in the fighting position amongst a beautiful display of flowers. Powder blue ground.*
4385 Vine : *Vine with leaves and grapes on rouge ground.*
4387 Vine : *Vine with leaves and grapes on pale yellow.*
4388 Embossed - Poppy & Daisy : *Embossed poppies and daisies. Pale green ground.*
4389 Embossed - Poppy & Daisy : *Embossed poppies and daisies. Pale blue ground.*
4391 Kingfisher & Water Lily : *Kingfisher perched on the stem of a climbing plant over water lilies. Rouge Royale.*
4393 Sketching Bird : *Exotic tree with pendant foliage and decoratively enamelled kingfisher like bird flying by. Vert Royale ground.*
4395 Vine : *Vine with leaves and grapes on pale green.*
4397 Plain : *Bleu Royale plain with gilt.*
4398 New Mikado : *Chinese figures, pagoda, bridge and trees. Sometimes has two cranes and punt like boat. Bleu Royale.*
4399 Spider's Web : *Cobwebs with fruiting berries on branch, flowers (harebells) and dragonflies. Bleu Royale ground.*
4400 New Storks : *Two crane like birds wading in a lake under trees with pendulous hanging foliage. Bleu Royale.*

4401 Fighting Cocks : *Two cockerels displaying in the fighting position amongst a beautiful display of flowers. Bleu Royale.*
4402 Vine : *Vine with leaves and grapes on Blue Royale.*
4402 Carlton China - Trellis Border : *Simple Frieze pattern on Blue.*
4403 no name : *Bleu Royale with border.*
4404 Spots : *Pale yellow/green ground with mauve spots.*
4405 Vine : *Vine with leaves and grapes on powder blue.*
4406 Spots : *Bleu Royale with spots.*
4408 Spots : *Green with red spots.*
4411 Vine : *Vine with leaves and grapes on pale pink.*
4414 no name : *Rouge Royale with bird & tree border (tea & coffee ware only).*
4415 no name : *Chinese on Rouge Royale - no enamels.*
4416 New Mikado : *Chinese figures, pagoda, bridge and trees. Sometimes has two cranes and punt like boat. Powder blue ground.*
4417 Plain : *Vert Royale plain.*
4417 Fighting Cocks : *Two cockerels displaying in the fighting position amongst a beautiful display of flowers. Rouge Royale.*
4418 Spots : *Vert Royale with white spots.*
4418 Bird of Paradise : *Bird of Paradise with long plumed tail flying among oriental trees. Powder Blue ground.*
4419 New Mikado : *Chinese figures, pagoda, bridge and trees. Sometimes has two cranes and punt like boat. Vert Royale.*
4419 Carlton China - Reproduction Swansea : *Colourful posies of flowers in gilt cartouches with decorative gilt leaves and bands.*

Carlton Ware Patterns and Shapes

4420 Spider's Web : *Cobwebs with fruiting berries on branch, flowers (harebells) and dragonflies. Vert Royale ground.*
4421 New Storks : *Two crane like birds wading in a lake under trees with pendulous hanging foliage. Vert Royale ground.*
4421 Carlton China - Bird Cartouche : *Birds in a Cartouche pattern.*
4422 Mikado : *Chinoiserie pagodas, bridges, oriental ladies and usually a pair of kissing birds. Rouge ground.*
4422 Fighting Cocks : *Two cockerels displaying in the fighting position amongst a beautiful display of flowers. Vert Royale.*
4423 Vine : *Vine with leaves and grapes on Vert Royale.*
4426 Forest Tree : *Exotic birch like trees. Slender tree rising to a wide pendulous canopy of foliage. Mottled blue ground, with mauve, orange and white foliage.*
4427 Embossed - Wild Rose : *Embossed Wild Rose on Yellow*
4428 Embossed - Wild Rose : *Embossed Wild Rose on Green*
4433 Mikado : *Chinoiserie pagodas, bridges, oriental ladies and usually a pair of kissing birds. Rouge ground.*
4434 Mikado : *Chinoiserie pagodas, bridges, oriental ladies and usually a pair of kissing birds. Blue ground.*
4435 Water Lily : *Water Lily with bullrushes and a dragonfly. Rouge Royale.*
4435 Sketching Bird : *Exotic tree with pendant foliage and decoratively enamelled kingfisher like bird flying by. Vert Royale ground.*
4436 Water Lily : *Water Lily with bullrushes and a dragonfly. Vert Royale.*
4437 Plain : *Cobalt blue.*

4438 no name : *Chinese on cobalt blue.*
4439 Spider's Web : *Cobwebs with fruiting berries on branch, flowers (harebells) and dragonflies. Cobalt blue ground.*
4440 New Storks : *Two crane like birds wading in a lake under trees with pendulous hanging foliage. Cobalt blue ground.*
4441 Vine : *Vine with leaves and grapes on cobalt blue.*
4442 Spots : *Powder blue with white spots.*
4443 New Storks : *Two crane like birds wading in a lake under trees with pendulous hanging foliage. Powder blue ground.*
4444 Vine : *Vine with leaves and grapes, no enamels. Vert Royale ground.*
4445 no name : *Rouge Royale with chinese border on edge only - no enamels.*
4446 no name : *Chinese on powder blue - no enamels.*
4448 Embossed - Hydrangea : *Embossed pink Hydrangea flowers on green.*
4449 Embossed - Hydrangea : *Embossed dark blue, mauve and pink Hydrangea flowers on blue.*
4450 no name : *Chinese on Vert Royale - no enamels.*
4451 Carlton China - Gothic Border or Gilt Crosses : *Simple border pattern on Green.*
4452 no name : *Cobalt blue with border (raised enamel red).*
4454 no name : *Cobalt blue with border (no raised enamel).*
4455 Duck : *Realistic Mallard type ducks flying above Irises and wild grasses. Rouge ground.*
4457 Lily of the Valley : *Lily of the valley on Rouge Royale.*
4458 Lily of the Valley : *Lily of the valley on Vert Royale.*

4459 Duck : *Realistic Mallard type ducks flying above Irises and wild grasses. Vert Royale ground.*
4460 Plain : *Vert Royale with gold border.*
4461 Canadian Views : *Variety of Canadian views printed in brown and finished in green.*
4461 Carlton China - no name : *Simple gilt border pattern on White.*
4462 Canadian Views : *Variety of Canadian views printed in black.*
4463 Embossed - Grape : *Embossed Grapes, bright green on beige.*
4464 Embossed - Grape : *Embossed Grapes, sandy brown on beige.*
4472 no name : *Vert Royale with chinese border - no enamel.*
4475 Stars : *Gold stars on Bleu Royale.*
4479 no name : *Powder blue with chinese border.*
4480 Vine : *Vine with leaves and grapes on Rouge Royale.*
4481 Vine : *Vine with leaves and grapes on cobalt blue.*
4482 Carlton China - Tidal Border : *Simple gilt border pattern on Blue.*
4484 Plain : *Noire Royale.*
4487 no name : *Bleu Royale with chinese border - no enamels.*
4488 Lily of the Valley : *Lily of the valley on Noire Royale.*
4489 Nosegay : *Pretty gilded and enamelled border design Rouge Royale.*
4490 Duck : *Realistic Mallard type ducks flying above Irises and wild grasses. Black ground.*
4491 Kingfisher & Water Lily : *Kingfisher perched on the stem of a climbing plant over water lilies. Noire Royale.*

4492 Water Lily : *Water Lily with bullrushes and a dragonfly on Noire Royale.*
4499 Duck : *Realistic Mallard type ducks flying above Irises and wild grasses. Cobalt blue ground.*
4500 Duck : *Realistic Mallard type ducks flying above Irises and wild grasses. Pale pink ground.*
4501 Duck : *Realistic Mallard type ducks flying above Irises and wild grasses. Pale yellow ground.*
4502 Duck : *Realistic Mallard type ducks flying above Irises and wild grasses. Pale green ground.*
4503 Duck : *Realistic Mallard type ducks flying above Irises and wild grasses. Powder blue ground.*
4503 Carlton China - Orange Tree or Coppice : *Tree with orange coloured fruit.*
4504 Embossed - Hazel Nut : *Embossed Hazel Nut on Matt Cream*
4505 Embossed - Hazel Nut : *Embossed Hazel Nut on Green*
4506 Plain : *Plain Jade green.*
4507 New Storks : *Two crane like birds wading in a lake under trees with pendulous hanging foliage. Jade green ground.*
4508 New Mikado (Part) : *Chinese figures, pagoda, bridge and trees. Sometimes has two cranes and punt like boat. Jade Green.*
4509 Spider's Web : *Cobwebs with fruiting berries on branch, flowers (harebells) and dragonflies. Jade green ground.*
4510 Carlton China - no name : *Simple border pattern on Blue.*
4511 Spots : *Jade green with spots.*
4512 Vine : *Vine with leaves and grapes on Noire Royale.*

4513 no name : *Turquoise & pink, gold edge & foot only - shell ware only.*
4514 Nosegay : *Pretty gilded and enamelled border design on Vert Royale.*
4514 Carlton China - Gothic Border or Gilt Crosses : *Simple but pretty border pattern on blue.*
4515 Nosegay : *Pretty gilded and enamelled border design on Noire Royale.*
4515 Crepes : *Speckled blue with gold frieze design.*
4515 Carlton China - Vine Border : *Bunches of grapes in border on Blue.*
4516 Carlton China - Nosegay : *Pretty gilded and enamelled border design on Blue.*
4517 Nosegay : *Pretty gilded and enamelled border design on Pale pink.*
4517 Carlton China - Gothic Border or Gilt Crosses : *Simple but pretty border pattern on blue.*
4518 Nosegay : *Pretty gilded and enamelled border design on pale yellow.*
4519 Nosegay : *Pretty gilded and enamelled border design on pale green.*
4520 Twin Tone : *Twin-tone jade green, salmon pink interior.*
4520 no name : *Gold edge & foot only, shellware only.*
4521 Twin Tone : *Twin-tone jade green, salmon pink interior.*
4521 no name : *Full Gold, shellware only.*
4522 Twin Tone : *Twin-tone jade green, yellow interior.*
4522 no name : *Gold edge & foot only, shellware only.*
4523 Twin Tone : *Twin-tone jade green, yellow interior.*
4523 no name : *Full gold, shellware only.*
4525 Twin Tone : *Pink and grey edged in gilt.*

4526 Carlton China - Crocus or Spring Border : *Crocuses on white ground.*
4527 Nosegay : *Pretty gilded and enamelled border design on jade green.*
4527 Carlton China - Summer Border or Cottage Flowers : *Summer or Cottage flowers on edge.*
4528 Nosegay : *Pretty gilded and enamelled border design on powder blue.*
4532 Twin Tone : *Black and yellow.*
4534 Carlton China - Dragons : *Blue Dragons on White.*
4536 Carlton China - Canterbury Border or New Bluebells : *Bluebells and other flowers design on edge.*
4539 Fish & Seaweed : *Fish swimming by coral on greyish ground.*
4544 Carlton China - no name : *Fruit design.*
4550 Carlton China - New Mikado : *Chinese figures, pagoda, bridge and trees. Sometimes has two cranes and punt like boat.*
4551 Twin Tone : *Twin-tone Green*
4552 Twin Tone : *Twin-tone Grey*
4553 Twin Tone : *Brown and Cream*
4556 no name : *Gold leaf on jade green.*
4557 no name : *Gold leaf on Noire Royale.*
4558 no name : *Gold leaf on Rouge Royale.*
4559 Twin Tone : *Twin-tone jade green, yellow interior.*
4560 Kingfisher & Water Lily : *Kingfisher perched on the stem of a climbing plant over water lilies. Pale yellow ground.*
4561 Kingfisher & Water Lily : *Kingfisher perched on the stem of a climbing plant over water lilies. Pale green ground.*

4562 Kingfisher & Water Lily : *Kingfisher perched on the stem of a climbing plant over water lilies. Jade green ground.*
4563 Water Lily : *Water Lily with bullrushes and a dragonfly. Pale yellow ground.*
4564 Water Lily : *Water Lily with bullrushes and a dragonfly. Pale green ground.*
4565 Water Lily : *Water Lily with bullrushes and a dragonfly. Jade green ground.*
4566 Water Lily : *Water Lily with bullrushes and a dragonfly. Powder blue ground.*
4574 Carlton China - Pendant Bubbles : *Enamelled pendant design.*
4576 Carlton China - Gothic Band : *Simple band design between blue and cream.*
4577 Carlton China - Blue & Gold : *Blue and gold bands.*
4578 Carlton China - Springtime : *Garden flowers and bluebirds on pale ground.*
4580 Kingfisher & Water Lily : *Kingfisher perched on the stem of a climbing plant over water lilies. Powder blue ground.*
4581 Windswept : *Leaves on matt cream and brown.*
4581 Carlton China - no name : *Simple double gold band design on blue.*
4582 Windswept : *Leaves on matt cream and sage green.*
4583 Windswept : *Leaves on glossy pale blue and bottle green.*
4592 no name : *Mutli-coloured flower heads, green leaves.*
4599 Plain : *Turquoise*
4601 Twin Tone : *Twin-tone Chartreuse*

4603 Kingfisher & Water Lily : *Kingfisher perched on the stem of a climbing plant over water lilies. Vert Royale ground.*

4603 Carlton China - no name : *Swirled gold pattern on blue and white.*

4604 Water Lily : *Water Lily with bullrushes and a dragonfly. Bleu Royale ground.*

4605 Duck : *Realistic Mallard type ducks flying above Irises and wild grasses. Bleu Royale ground.*

4605 Carlton China - Enchanted Garden : *Trees and birds design.*

4606 Kingfisher & Water Lily : *Kingfisher perched on the stem of a climbing plant over water lilies. Bleu Royale ground.*

4607 Kingfisher & Water Lily : *Kingfisher perched on the stem of a climbing plant over water lilies. Pale pink.*

4608 Duck : *Realistic Mallard type ducks flying above Irises and wild grasses. Pastel blue ground.*

4608 Carlton China - Playing Cards or Bridge Set : *Images of playing cards and symbols.*

4609 Pin Stripe : *Pin Stripe on Lime Green*

4609 Carlton China - Orchard Walk : *Crinoline lady surrounded by flowers.*

4610 Pin Stripe : *Pin Stripe on brown*

4611 Pin Stripe : *Pin Stripe on sand colour*

4611 Carlton China - Gallant : *Lady and Gent.*

4614 Carlton China - English Rose : *Design with roses.*

4614 Twin Tone : *Black and orange*

4614 Carlton China - Spider Flower or Cornflower : *Design with thistle like flowers.*

4615 Twin Tone : *Grey and pink.*

4616 Twin Tone : *Green and stripe*

4617 Twin Tone : *Orange and yellow with spots*

Carlton Ware Patterns and Shapes

4618 Twin Tone : *Brown and cream.*
4618 Carlton China - English Rose : *Design with roses.*
4620 Embossed - Hazel Nut : *Embossed Hazel Nut on Blue*
4621 Embossed - Foxglove : *Embossed Foxglove on Peach/Chartreuse*
4622 Windswept : *Leaves on dusky pink and pale blue.*
4623 Plain : *Leaf Green*
4624 Plain : *Blue*
4625 Plain : *Leaf Brown*
4626 Plain : *Black*
4627 Plain : *Chartreuse*
4628 Plain : *Lavender*
4629 no name : *Pagoda on Noire Royale.*
4632 Carlton China - no name : *Flowers in the border design.*
4633 Langouste : *Lobster design on Cream ground.*
4634 Langouste : *Lobster design on Chartreuse (green) ground.*
4636 Allium : *White design on brownish red ground.*
4636 Carlton China - Trailing Lobelia : *Red flowers with gold swirls.*
4637 Carlton China - Trailing Lobelia : *Blue flowers with gold swirls.*
4639 Carlton China - New Wisteria : *Wisteria design.*
4641 Eastern Splendour : *Figure in turban with castle and or slave under tree with hanging foliage. Rouge Royale ground.*
4642 Eastern Splendour : *Figure in turban with castle and or slave under tree with hanging foliage. Noire Royale ground.*

4643 Eastern Splendour : *Figure in turban with castle and or slave under tree with hanging foliage. Vert Royale ground.*

4644 Eastern Splendour : *Figure in turban with castle and or slave under tree with hanging foliage. Powder blue ground.*

4644 Carlton China - Spider Flower or Cornflower : *Design with thistle like flowers.*

4645 Eastern Splendour : *Figure in turban with castle and or slave under tree with hanging foliage. Bleu Royale ground.*

4645 Carlton China - Spider Flower or Cornflower : *Design with thistle like flowers.*

4646 Eastern Splendour : *Figure in turban with castle and or slave under tree with hanging foliage. Pale yellow ground.*

4647 Eastern Splendour : *Figure in turban with castle and or slave under tree with hanging foliage. Pale green ground.*

4648 Carlton China - Honeysuckle : *Orange Honeysuckle flowers.*

4649 Carlton China - Cherries : *Design with bunches of Cherries.*

4650 Carlton China - no name : *Colourful Harebell like flowers.*

4651 Carlton China - no name : *Simple colourful design.*

4653 Carlton China - Hibiscus : *Enamelled red flowers.*

4654 Carlton China - no name : *Blue flower swag design.*

4655 Carlton China - Target : *Design that looks like three arrows shot into a target.*

4657 Carlton China - no name : *Blue and orange petals.*

4658 Carlton China - Imari : *Aztec like symmetric design in blue and red on white.*

4660 Carlton China - Floral Band : *Colourful flowers and a blue band.*
4664 Carlton China - Field Scabious : *Flowers.*
4665 Carlton China - no name : *Blue and white with gilt edges.*
4668 Carlton China - Love-in-a-Mist : *Blue and pink flowers.*
4671 Carlton China - Bordered Baubles : *Design with baubles in border.*
4672 Plain : *Matt While*
4675 Carlton China - Orchard : *Enamelled trees and flowers.*
4676 Bamboo : *Bamboo and hanging foliage on white ground.*
4676 Carlton China - Strawberry Tree : *Tree resembling a strawberry on a white ground.*
4678 Mikado : *Chinoiserie pagodas, bridges, oriental ladies and usually a pair of kissing birds. Vert Royale ground.*
4683 Carlton China - Butterfly : *Pretty abstract Butterfly design.*
4693 Carlton China - Sunshine : *White gloss ground with groups of small flowers.*
4710 Plain : *Matt Black*
4710 Carlton China - no name : *Pale green band and gold swirls.*
4717 Dragon : *Golden dragons on a white ground.*
4722 Carlton China - Chintz Tulip : *Flowers in gilt design.*
4723 Carlton China - Lace : *Lace pattern on white ground.*
4727 Carlton China - Gilt Festoon : *Gilt design on white and yellow.*
4733 Pearl Insignia : *Symmetric design of circles (beads), curved triangles and flower heads. White ground.*

4734 Pearl Insignia : *Symmetric design of circles (beads), curved triangles and flower heads. Brownish ground.*
4734 Carlton China - Gothic Border or Gilt Crosses : *Simple but pretty border pattern on yellow.*
4735 Carlton China - Gothic Border or Gilt Crosses : *Simple but pretty border pattern on pale green.*
4741 Carlton China - Blue & Gold : *Blue and gold.*
4744 Carlton China - Bright Sunshine : *Flower design.*
4753 Carlton China - New Delphinium : *Delphinium flowers.*
4754 Carlton China - Springtime : *Garden flowers and bluebirds on pale ground.*
4758 Carlton China - Swags of Flowers : *Gilt design.*
4761 Carlton China - Spring Medley : *Garden flowers, similar to Sunshine.*
4762 Carlton China - Diamond Band : *Diamonds in border design.*
4763 Carlton China - Strawberry Tree : *Tree resembling a strawberry on a white ground.*
4764 Carlton China - Weeping Willow : *Stylized design with flowers, tree and bird.*
4769 Bamboo : *Bamboo and hanging foliage on blue ground.*
4769 Carlton China - Strawberry Tree : *Tree resembling a strawberry on a blue ground.*
4775 Carlton China - Springtime : *Garden flowers and bluebirds on pale ground.*
4777 Carlton China - Pimpernel or Lilac Posy : *Pretty flower design on pale mauve ground.*
4783 Plain with Floral : *Floral patterns on white insets on blue with gold highlights. Powder blue ground.*
4785 no name : *Printed floral design on pale green ground.*

4794 New Bird of Paradise : *Buds, blossom, birds of paradise and butterflies. Rouge ground.*
4794 Carlton China - no name : *Garden scene with flowers, bush and tree.*
4795 New Bird of Paradise : *Buds, blossom, birds of paradise and butterflies. Mottled blue ground.*
4799 Carlton China - Carlton China - Chinese Figures : *Oriental scene of figures, tree and sometimes pagodas.*
4801 Malvern : *Medallion with bird and fruit on a yellow ground.*
4801 Carlton China - River Fish : *Beautiful realistic looking fish swimming amongst gilt seaweed. Blue ground.*
4805 Pheasant : *Pheasant like bird and flowers with gilt and enamels. Black ground.*
4805 Mikado : *Chinoiserie pagodas, bridges, oriental ladies and usually a pair of kissing birds. Black ground*
4805 New Bird of Paradise : *Buds, blossom, birds of paradise and butterflies. Black ground.*
4805 Carlton China - Canterbury Border or New Bluebells : *Bluebells and other flowers design on edge.*
4808 Thistle Heads : *Thistle heads on red ground.*
4809 Thistle Heads : *Thistle heads on powder blue ground.*
4812 Carlton China - Floral Spray : *Sprigs of flowers.*
4813 Carlton China - Butterflies & Seaweed : *Butterflies and foliage.*
4818 Carlton China - Floral Trumpet : *Flowers in trumpet shape.*
4821 Carlton China - Enamelled Berries or Berry Cluster : *Berries with floral design on a cobalt blue ground.*
4823 Carlton China - Tulip Garden : *Tulips.*
4824 Carlton China - Posies : *Posies of flowers.*

4838 Carlton China - Festive Border : *Garland of flowers that resemble festive lights.*
4841 Plain : *Mottled grey with gilt.*
4861 Carlton China - Meadow Tree : *Stylized tree in blue grass meadow.*
4864 Carlton China - Fantail Birds on Branch : *Birds on foliage on white ground.*
4865 Carlton China - Enamelled Berries or Berry Cluster : *Berries with floral design on a yellow border.*
4870 Carlton China - Enamelled Berries or Berry Cluster : *Berries with floral design on a green border.*
4876 Carlton China - Meadow Tree : *Stylized tree in grey grass meadow.*
4878 Carlton China - Afternoon Stroll : *Lady and hanging leaf design.*
4879 Carlton China - Bouquet : *Stylised flowers.*
4880 Carlton China - New Garden : *Spires of Daisy like flowers in many colours. Powder blue ground.*
4881 Carlton China - New Garden : *Spires of Daisy like flowers in many colours.*
4885 Carlton China - New Garden : *Spires of Daisy like flowers in many colours.*
4886 Carlton China - Enamelled Berries or Berry Cluster : *Berries with floral decorations on blue and cream.*
4888 Carlton China - Spider Flower or Cornflower : *Design with thistle like flowers.*
4889 Carlton China - Zig-Zag Tree : *Stylized trees with angled trunks.*
4894 Carlton China - Vine Border : *Bunches of grapes in border.*
4897 Carlton China - Bouquet : *Bouquet of flowers.*
4900 Carlton China - Fantail Birds on Branch : *Birds on foliage on white ground.*

Carlton Ware Patterns and Shapes

4901 Malvern : *Medallion with bird and fruit on a blue ground.*
4903 Carlton China - Sylvan Trees : *Topiary trees.*
4904 Carlton China - Cottage Garden or Hollyhocks : *Flower beds of cottage flowers.*
4905 Carlton China - no name : *Deco angular shapes.*
4906 Carlton China - Chinese Lanterns : *Bold angular shapes with tiny flower heads.*
4907 Enchantment Medallion : *Medallions of romantic scenes. Rouge Royale ground.*
4907 Carlton China - Starburst Tree & Birds : *Stylized star shaped trees with fantailed birds on a white ground.*
4908 Enchantment Medallion : *Lady and Dandy in Garden with Gazebo. Powder blue ground.*
4908 Carlton China - Spring Flower : *Floral design with a display that looks like a Christmas Tree.*
4909 Malvern : *Medallion with bird and fruit. White medallions on black ground.*
4909 Carlton China - Celebration or Technicolour Posies : *Colourful posies.*
4910 Carlton China - Canterbury Border or New Bluebells : *Bluebells and other flowers design on edge.*
4911 Carlton China - Summer Border or Cottage Flowers : *Summer or Cottage flowers on edge.*
4912 Carlton China - Zig-Zag Tree : *Stylized trees with angled trunks.*
4913 Carlton China - Starburst Tree & Birds : *Stylized star shaped trees with fantailed birds on a blue ground.*
4914 Dragon : *Green Dragon on white ground.*
4916 Carlton China - no name : *Gilt decoration on blue ground over white.*
4923 Aquilegia : *Flowers, including Aquilegia type flowers on a white ground.*

4923 Carlton China - Summer Posy : *Flowers.*
4925 Carlton China - New Delphinium : *Delphinium flowers.*
4927 Carlton China - Wild Garden : *Flowers and trees.*
4928 Carlton China - Hanging Baubles : *Baubles hanging design.*
4929 Carlton China - Charleston : *Deco emblems.*
4934 Pheasant : *Pheasant like bird and flowers with gilt and enamels. Red ground.*
4935 Pheasant : *Pheasant like bird and flowers on blue ground with a matt sheen plus enamelled and gilded decoration.*
4940 Carlton China - Rainbow : *Deco rainbow like pattern on a cream ground.*
4942 Carlton China - Bud Eye : *Floral display with buds.*
4943 Carlton China - Rainbow : *Deco rainbow like pattern on a white ground.*
4947 Garden of Tranquillity : *Two figures, one lying down, some flower heads on rouge ground.*
4948 Carlton China - Black Eye : *Stylistic flower with black eyed centre.*
4958 Carlton China - Papaver or Poppy : *Realistic poppies on yellow.*
4961 Carlton China - New Harebells : *Realistic Harebells.*
4961 Carlton China - Digitalis : *Realistic Foxgloves.*
4963 Carlton China - Dahlia : *Dahlia on cream or white.*
4966 Carlton China - New Garden : *Spires of Daisy like flowers in many colours.*
4977 Carlton China - Papaver or Poppy : *Realistic Poppies on white ground.*
4979 Carlton China - Orange Tree : *Tree with Orange coloured fruit.*

4983 Carlton China - Aster : *Trio of brightly coloured Asters.*
4985 Carlton China - Summer Posy : *Blossom flowers.*
4986 Carlton China - Autumn Trees : *Pendulous trees on a white ground.*
4987 Carlton China - Love-in-a-Mist : *Red and yellow flowers.*
4988 Carlton China - Susan : *Red flowers with five petals named after the flower Black Eyed Susan.*
4989 Carlton China - Flower and Cloud : *Flower flying on small cloud.*
4990 Carlton China - Bright Daisy or Powder Puff : *Colourful daisies on white ground.*
4991 Carlton China - Crooked Tree : *Tree with berries.*
4992 Carlton China - Sweet Pea : *Orange Sweet Peas on white ground.*
4993 Carlton China - Sweet Pea : *Blue Sweet Peas on white ground.*
4994 Carlton China - Sweet Pea : *Orange Sweet Peas on white ground.*
4995 Carlton China - Enamelled Berries or Berry Cluster : *Berries with floral design on white.*
4998 Carlton China - Birds and Trees or Autumn Trees : *Birds and Trees on a white ground.*

Patterns 5000 - 5999

5000 Carlton China - Clematis : *Bold Clematis flowers.*
5001 Carlton China - Moon House : *House with a Moon on a mottled sky.*
5002 Carlton China - Gloaming : *Silhouette version of Bird & Trees (4998).*
5019 Carlton China - Deco Wave : *Deco curves and waves. Orange, Black and Gold.*
5023 Carlton China - Deco Wave : *Deco curves and waves. Turquoise, Black and Gold.*

Patterns with unknown pattern numbers

Gallant : *Lady and Dandy, matt black ground.*
Glade : *Pan like figure with shadow in forest glade with spires of flowers. Matt blue ground.*
Humming Bird : *Elaborately decorated exotic bird and floral decoration. Blue lustre ground.*
Heinz : *Orange running down green ground.*
New Rainbow : *Multicolored Rainbow pattern.*
Rain Forest : *Storks in Forest.*
Hatching : *Hatched pattern above brown.*
Fairy Dell : *Scene with trees, snow and rabbits.*
Honesty : *Stylised Honesty branches. Orange ground.*
Glacielle Ware : *Glacielle Ware comes in about 4 or 5 different animals / bird designs.*
Tree & Swallow : *Swallows flying past slender stemmed tree with wide canopy of pendulous foliage. Matt cream ground.*
Forest Tree : *Exotic birch like trees. Slender tree rising to a wide pendulous canopy of foliage. Matt blue ground with orange and green foliage.*
Tutankhamen : *Gloss Light Blue & Yellow. Egyptian Motifs in colours and gilt.*
Sketching Bird : *Exotic tree with pendant foliage and exotic bird flying by. Bleu Royale.*
Peach Blossom : *Pink blossom sprays on pale blue ground.*

Bird of Paradise : *Bird of Paradise with long plumed tail flying among oriental trees. Pale green ground.*
Sketching Bird : *Exotic tree with pendant foliage and exotic bird flying by. Matt pale green ground.*
Silk Sands : *Contour like lines on pink ground with gilt.*
Chinese Lanterns : *Floral decoration with Chinese Lanterns and a Dragon Fly. Rouge ground.*
Cock & Peony : *Two cockerels standing amongst foliage. Also has a variety of beautifully enamelled flowers including peonies. Armand Lustre backstamp. Mottled orange ground. Armand.*
River Fish : *Beautiful realistic looking fish swimming amongst gilt seaweed. Rouge ground.*
Denim : *Blue denim jeans and shirt.*
Paradise Bird & Tree with Cloud : *Bird of Paradise with long plumed tail flying across clouds and among oriental trees. Mustardy Yellow ground.*
Carlton China - River Fish : *Beautiful realistic looking fish swimming amongst seaweed. Blue ground.*
Rainbow Portal : *Bird sitting on a bough and a cameo with multicoloured stripes. White or pale yellow ground.*
Primula and Leaf : *Primula flowers in bright colours and a butterfly. Pale blue ground.*
Owls : *Realistic Owls with a moon.*
Fairy Carnival : *Beautiful design of Fairies. Extremely rare!*

List of pattern numbers by pattern name

Allium: 4636
Almond Blossom: 1905, 2445, 3033
Anemone: 3694
Animal (Squirrel, Deer or Fox): 4019
Apple Blossom: 3522
Apple and Blossom: 3041
Aquilegia: 4923
Arrowhead: 3416
Aurora: 3412
Autumn Breeze: 3839, 3840
Autumn Daisy: 3802
Autumn Leaf: 3766
Autumn Trees & Ferns: 3517
Awakening: 3450, 3452, 3453, 3456, 3494, 3496, 3497
Azalea: 4140
Babylon: 4125, 4126, 4137, 4158, 4168, 4189
Bamboo: 4676, 4769
Banded: 4128, 4130
Banded and Crosstitch: 3976
Bands: 3720
Barge: 2519
Basket of Flowers: 2124, 2151, 2184, 2185, 2189
Basket of Fruit: 2539, 2556
Bathing Belle: 3681, 3684, 3688, 3796
Beanstalk: 4081
Beech Nut: 4281, 4282
Beehives: 3883, 3884
Bell: 3774, 3785, 3786, 3788, 3792, 3855

Berries and Bands: 2446, 2454, 2460, 2461, 2931
Bird: 421
Bird & Chequered Border: 2218, 2221
Bird & Pine Cone: 3046
Bird & Tree Peony: 595, 2466, 2866
Bird of Paradise: 3191, 4117, 4118, 4234, 4239, 4418
Birds and Blossom: 2089
Birds on Bough: 2794, 3394
Black Crow: 4105
Blossom & Spray: 3968, 4045, 4047
Bluebells: 3294, 3862, 3872, 3874, 3875
Blush Ware: 110, 253, 524, 585, 649, 670, 708, 732, 975, 1075, 1219, 1230, 1246, 1340, 1358, 1414, 1509, 1518, 1572, 1621, 1624, 1664, 1681, 1739, 1747, 1749, 1752, 1786, 1799, 1848, 1863, 1902, 1928, 1935, 1942, 2040, 2339, 2366, 2659
Blush Ware - Arvista: 428, 476, 561, 1031, 1057, 1630, 1652, 1879, 1946, 1990, 2561, 2562
Blush Ware - Azalea: 347
Blush Ware - Camellia: 184, 425, 843, 848, 849, 860, 1153, 2300, 2700
Blush Ware - Carnation: 483, 1038, 1041, 1582, 1693, 1732, 1733, 2486
Blush Ware - Carnation Spray: 621, 1242
Blush Ware - Catalpa: 661
Blush Ware - Cherry Blossom: 2406
Blush Ware - Chrysanthemum: 401, 405, 406, 407, 409, 504, 1089, 1091, 1372, 2407, 2410
Blush Ware - Cistus: 52, 74, 1474, 1769, 1804, 2494, 2798
Blush Ware - Clematis: 821, 826
Blush Ware - Convolvulous: 376, 2662, 2669
Blush Ware - Cornflower: 709

Blush Ware - Cornucopia: 637, 653, 739, 832, 1162, 2083, 2086, 2474
Blush Ware - Daffodil: 641
Blush Ware - Dahlia: 682, 683, 735, 878, 1653, 1741, 1878, 1982, 2458
Blush Ware - Daisies: 2224, 2227
Blush Ware - Daisy: 686
Blush Ware - Diadem: 1650
Blush Ware - Dianthus: 438, 458
Blush Ware - Dog Rose: 1400, 1524
Blush Ware - Floral: 2377
Blush Ware - Gladioli: 1750
Blush Ware - Heather: 418, 1166, 1713, 1742, 2455, 2713, 2718, 2757, 2923
Blush Ware - Hibiscus: 634, 638, 639, 839, 1635, 2021, 2166, 2510, 2687
Blush Ware - Honeysuckle: 1601
Blush Ware - Honfleur: 666, 921, 1002
Blush Ware - Impatiens: 2560
Blush Ware - Iris: 2833
Blush Ware - Marguerite: 1655, 2301
Blush Ware - Mixed Cottage: 1795
Blush Ware - Nasturtium: 2154, 2749
Blush Ware - Nouveau Poppies: 838, 886, 888
Blush Ware - Pansy: 914
Blush Ware - Peony: 186, 194, 538, 945, 949, 1034, 1658, 1661, 1682, 1683, 1685, 1832, 1839, 1853, 1865, 1869, 1996, 2691, 2853
Blush Ware - Petunia: 491, 694, 695, 698, 1451, 1453, 1467, 1810, 1966, 1987, 2007, 2179
Blush Ware - Picotees: 624
Blush Ware - Poppy: 206, 303, 305, 306, 307, 1015, 1770
Blush Ware - Poppy Spray: 1042

Blush Ware - Primula: 2309
Blush Ware - Queen Victoria: 856
Blush Ware - Rose: 2863, 2872
Blush Ware - Rose Bud: 403
Blush Ware - Rose Garland: 348, 438, 1186
Blush Ware - Roses: 439, 913, 1221
Blush Ware - Royal May: 508, 509, 602, 1229
Blush Ware - Sweet Violet: 142
Blush Ware - Tulips: 578, 2872
Blush Ware - Violet: 237, 1283, 1315, 1332
Blush Ware - Wild Rose: 659, 1123, 1125, 1609, 1918, 1919, 1939, 1947, 1974, 1986, 2215
Bookends - Asymmetric Flower: 3535
Bookends - Fan: 3532, 3533
Bookends - Saddleback: 3537
Bookends - Two Tone: 3337
Brodsworth: 2586
Butterfly: 3290, 4122, 4123
Cameo Wren: 3115
Camouflage: 3440
Canadian Views: 4461, 4462
Candy Flowers: 3669
Carlton China - Afternoon Stroll: 4878
Carlton China - Arrow Border: 4294
Carlton China - Aster: 4983
Carlton China - Autumn Trees: 4986
Carlton China - Bird Cartouche: 4421
Carlton China - Birds and Trees or Autumn Trees: 4998
Carlton China - Black Eye: 4948
Carlton China - Blue & Gold: 4577, 4741
Carlton China - Bordered Baubles: 4671
Carlton China - Bouquet: 4879, 4897
Carlton China - Bright Daisy or Powder Puff: 4990

Carlton Ware Patterns and Shapes

Carlton China - Bright Sunshine: 4744
Carlton China - Bud Eye: 4942
Carlton China - Butterflies & Seaweed: 4813
Carlton China - Butterfly: 4683
Carlton China - Canterbury Border or New Bluebells: 4360, 4536, 4805, 4910
Carlton China - Carlton China - Chinese Figures: 4799
Carlton China - Celebration or Technicolour Posies: 4909
Carlton China - Charleston: 4929
Carlton China - Cherries: 4649
Carlton China - Chinese Lanterns: 4906
Carlton China - Chintz Tulip: 4722
Carlton China - Clematis: 5000
Carlton China - Cottage Garden or Hollyhocks: 4904
Carlton China - Crocus or Spring Border: 4526
Carlton China - Crooked Tree: 4991
Carlton China - Dahlia: 4963
Carlton China - Deco Wave: 5019, 5023
Carlton China - Diamond Band: 4762
Carlton China - Digitalis: 4961
Carlton China - Dragons: 4534
Carlton China - Enamelled Berries or Berry Cluster: 4821, 4865, 4870, 4886, 4995
Carlton China - Enchanted Garden: 4605
Carlton China - English Rose: 4614, 4618
Carlton China - Fantail Birds on Branch: 4864, 4900
Carlton China - Festive Border: 4838
Carlton China - Field Scabious: 4664
Carlton China - Floral Band: 4660
Carlton China - Floral Spray: 4812
Carlton China - Floral Trumpet: 4818
Carlton China - Flower and Cloud: 4989
Carlton China - Gallant: 4611

Carlton China - Gilt Festoon: 4727
Carlton China - Gloaming: 5002
Carlton China - Gothic Band: 4576
Carlton China - Gothic Border or Gilt Crosses: 4451, 4514, 4517, 4734, 4735
Carlton China - Greek Keys: 4168
Carlton China - Hanging Baubles: 4928
Carlton China - Hibiscus: 4653
Carlton China - Honeysuckle: 4648
Carlton China - Imari: 4658
Carlton China - Lace: 4723
Carlton China - Love-in-a-Mist: 4668, 4987
Carlton China - Meadow Tree: 4861, 4876
Carlton China - Moon House: 5001
Carlton China - New Delphinium: 4753, 4925
Carlton China - New Garden: 4880, 4881, 4885, 4966
Carlton China - New Harebells: 4961
Carlton China - New Mikado: 4550
Carlton China - New Wisteria: 4639
Carlton China - Nosegay: 4516
Carlton China - Orange Tree: 4979
Carlton China - Orange Tree or Coppice: 4503
Carlton China - Orchard: 4675
Carlton China - Orchard Walk: 4609
Carlton China - Papaver or Poppy: 4958, 4977
Carlton China - Pendant Bubbles: 4574
Carlton China - Peony: 4030
Carlton China - Pimpernel or Lilac Posy: 4777
Carlton China - Playing Cards or Bridge Set: 4608
Carlton China - Posies: 4824
Carlton China - Rainbow: 4940, 4943
Carlton China - Reproduction Swansea: 4419
Carlton China - River Fish: 4801

Carlton Ware Patterns and Shapes

Carlton China - Spider Flower or Cornflower: 4614, 4644, 4645, 4888
Carlton China - Spring Flower: 4908
Carlton China - Spring Medley: 4761
Carlton China - Springtime: 4578, 4754, 4775
Carlton China - Starburst Tree & Birds: 4907, 4913
Carlton China - Strawberry Tree: 4676, 4763, 4769
Carlton China - Summer Border or Cottage Flowers: 4527, 4911
Carlton China - Summer Posy: 4923, 4985
Carlton China - Sunshine: 4693
Carlton China - Susan: 4988
Carlton China - Swags of Flowers: 4758
Carlton China - Sweet Pea: 4992, 4993, 4994
Carlton China - Sylvan Trees: 4903
Carlton China - Target: 4655
Carlton China - Tidal Border: 4482
Carlton China - Trailing Lobelia: 4636, 4637
Carlton China - Trellis Border: 4402
Carlton China - Tulip Garden: 4823
Carlton China - Vine Border: 4515, 4894
Carlton China - Weeping Willow: 4764
Carlton China - Wild Garden: 4927
Carlton China - Zig-Zag Tree: 4889, 4912
Carlton China - no name: 4235, 4461, 4510, 4544, 4581, 4603, 4632, 4650, 4651, 4654, 4657, 4665, 4710, 4794, 4905, 4916
Carnation: 1981
Carnival: 3305
Carre: 3658, 3659
Cartouche of Flowers: 2033, 2216
Chequered Border: 128
Cherry: 3272, 3417

Cherry Blossom: 4002, 4003
Chevrons: 3657, 3671
Chinaland: 2948, 2949, 2950, 3014, 3015, 3895
Chinese Bird: 3196, 3197, 3198, 3296, 3527, 3544
Chinese Bird & Cloud: 3274, 3275, 3275, 3327
Chinese Figures: 3199
Chinese Quail: 522
Chinese Tea Garden: 2936
Chinoiserie: 2752, 2755, 2810, 2972, 3222
Chinoiserie design: 2359
Chintz: 2046, 2047, 2069
Chorisia: 1846
Christmas Tree: 3729
Chrysanthemum: 1775, 2930
Cinquefoil: 4191, 4192
Citrus Fruit: 2961
Clematis: 3525, 3545
Cock & Peony: 2250, 2280, 2281, 2282, 2285, 2287, 2288, 2308, 2398, 2816
Cock & Peony Spray: 2405
Contours: 4291
Cornflower: 2385, 2392
Corolla: 3225, 3226, 3227, 3228
Crab & Lobster Ware: 3908, 3910
Crepes: 4515
Crested Bird and Water Lily: 3529, 3530, 3536
Cretonne: 2913
Crocus and Cloud: 4156
Cubist Butterfly: 3190, 3194, 3195, 3223, 3233, 3469
Dahlia & Butterfly: 3606
Daisies: 4139
Daisy: 3673, 3691, 3693, 3714
Daisy & Stripe: 3341

Carlton Ware Patterns and Shapes

Dancers: 2905
Dancing Deer: 3886
Dancing Figures: 614, 2178, 2284
Daydream: 4246
Deco Fan: 3552
Delphinium: 3273, 3487, 3837
Devils Copse: 3765, 3767, 3769, 3787, 3809, 3817, 3859
Diamond: 3546, 3547, 3549, 3550, 3678
Diaper: 3270
Dragon: 2006, 2053, 2062, 2064, 2066, 2067, 2102, 2103, 2818, 2887, 2903, 2993, 3251, 4717, 4914
Dragon & Traveller: 3594, 3594, 3595, 3597, 3656, 3660
Dragon and Cloud: 3237, 3331, 3332, 3333, 3351
Dragon in Cartouche: 3145, 3146
Drip Ware: 3771, 3772, 3773, 3917
Duck: 4455, 4459, 4490, 4499, 4500, 4501, 4502, 4503, 4605, 4608
Dutch: 3250
Eastern Splendour: 4641, 4642, 4643, 4644, 4645, 4646, 4647
Eclipse: 3551
Eden (Tiger Tree): 3989, 4241, 4242
Eden Canopy: 4248, 4249
Egyptian Fan: 3695, 3696, 3696, 3697, 3698
Eighteenth Tee: 2630, 2633, 2636
Embellished Gilt: 2979, 3063, 3078
Embossed - Buttercup: 3993, 3994
Embossed - Foxglove: 4285, 4286, 4621
Embossed - Grape: 4463, 4464
Embossed - Hazel Nut: 4504, 4505, 4620
Embossed - Hydrangea: 4448, 4449
Embossed - Oak Tree: 3810, 3811
Embossed - Poppy & Daisy: 4388, 4389

Embossed - Primula: 4368, 4369
Embossed - Rock Garden: 3876
Embossed - Water Lily: 4235
Embossed - Wild Rose: 4427, 4428
Enchantment Medallion: 4907, 4908
Engine Turned Ware: 3977, 3978, 3979, 3980, 3981, 3982, 3999
Ensign: 3510
Entangled Droplets: 3555
Explosion: 3447, 3454
Explosion & Butterfly: 3452
Fairy Dell: 3645, 3665
Fairy Shadow: 3564, 3574, 3576
Fairy and Sunflower: 2369
Fan: 3557, 3558
Fantasia: 3388, 3389, 3400, 3406, 3421, 3427
Farrago: 3297, 3362
Feathertailed Bird and Flower: 3354, 3355
Fighting Cocks: 4161, 4186, 4199, 4202, 4380, 4401, 4417, 4422
Fighting Glade: 4184, 4198, 4212, 4377
Figurine - Curtsy: 4262
Figurine - Grandma: 4275, 4276, 4302
Figurine - Jean: 4314
Figurine - Joan: 4273, 4301
Figurine - Monica: 4260, 4261
Figurine - Nan: 4264
Figurine - Nell: 4268, 4269
Figurine - Peggy: 4270, 4271
First Blush of Day: 1220
Fish & Seaweed: 4539
Flies: 2093, 2095, 2099, 2105, 2109, 2112, 2131, 2133, 2134, 2174, 2420, 2456, 2469, 2473, 2939

Carlton Ware Patterns and Shapes

Flies Border: 2642
Floral Comets: 3385, 3387, 3401, 3405, 3422, 3428
Floral Mist: 3913
Floral Scallops: 3234
Floribunda: 3236
Flow Blue: 230, 566, 616, 1225, 1274, 1406, 1619, 1631, 1950, 2319
Flow Blue - Arvista: 561
Flow Blue - Catalpa: 547, 1911
Flow Blue - Chrysanthemum: 1635
Flow Blue - Daffodil: 1646
Flow Blue - Diadem: 777
Flow Blue - Dragons & Unicorn: 2787
Flow Blue - Florida: 220
Flow Blue - Flower Garland: 586
Flow Blue - Honfleur: 1639
Flow Blue - Iris: 1422
Flow Blue - May: 876
Flow Blue - Multi- Flowers: 1941
Flow Blue - Petunia: 534
Flow Blue - Poppy: 751, 752, 1006, 1031, 1041, 1960
Flower & Falling Leaf: 3948, 3949, 3950, 3952
Flower Medley: 3588, 3596
Flower and Fruit: 3249
Flowering Papyrus: 3242
Forest Night: 3997
Forest Tree: 3238, 3239, 3240, 3244, 3244, 3248, 3250, 3253, 3254, 3265, 3283, 3641, 3648, 4426
Freehand Red Sunflower: 3519
Fruit: 2560, 2564, 2565, 2567, 3571
Fruit Bough: 2909
Fruit Branch: 2920

Gallant: 2804, 2839, 2863, 2864, 2867, 2868, 2869, 2872, 2872, 2893, 2953, 2954, 2956
Galleon: 3019, 3020, 3753, 3953, 3957
Garden: 3390, 3396, 3413, 3433, 3438, 3471, 3474, 3475, 3476, 3477, 3478, 3479, 3501, 3581, 3609
Garden Gate: 3863
Garden of Tranquillity: 4947
Gazania: 3592
Gentian: 3358
Geometric Clouds: 2212
Geometrica: 3566
Gilt Scallop: 3795
Grecian Figures: 601, 602, 604
Grecian Figures with no Figures: 602
Green Trees: 3569
Gum Tree: 3768, 3789, 3790, 3794, 3838
Gypsy: 3506
Hammered Pewter: 3902
Harebells: 4014, 4015, 4016, 4136, 4154
Harvest Fruit: 4305
Hazelnut: 3946
Heatwave: 4092
Herbaceous Border: 3801
Heron & Magical Tree: 3965, 4108, 4125, 4150, 4153, 4159, 4160, 4182, 4273, 4293, 4313, 4321, 4325, 4326, 4332
Hiawatha: 3589, 3590
Holly: 3418
Hollyhocks: 3818, 3819, 3820, 3827, 3854, 3972, 3973
Honesty: 3278
Humming Bird: 3462
Humming Bird with Tree: 3884, 4355
Humming Bird without Bird: 3462

Iceland Poppy: 3507, 3646, 4192, 4193, 4194, 4220, 4221, 4228
Incised Diamond: 3901, 3905
Incised Square: 3900
Insects: 850
Intersection: 3690
Iris: 3498
Italian Scenes: 2591
jacobean Figures: 3956, 3956, 3957
Jaggered Bouquet: 3439, 3457, 3489
Jazz: 3352, 3353, 3361
Jazz Poppy: 3503
Jazz Stitch: 3655
Jigsaw: 3431
Kaleidescopic: 3565
Kang Hsi: 596, 599
Kang Hsi Chinoiserie: 2021
Kang Hsi Fish: 597
Kien Lung: 2031, 2053
Kingfisher: 2517, 2530, 2537, 2621, 2858
Kingfisher & Water Lily: 4391, 4491, 4560, 4561, 4562, 4580, 4603, 4606, 4607
Lace Cap Hydrangea: 3639, 3966, 3967, 3969
Lace Frieze: 3173
Landscape Tree: 3141, 3142
Langouste: 4633, 4634
Lazy - Daisy: 3414
Leaf: 3857, 3861, 3873
Leaf & Dots: 4218
Leaf and Catkin: 3918, 3919
Leaves: 4040
Liberty Stripe: 3662
Lightning: 3356, 3357, 3692, 3716

Lilac: 4279, 4310
Lily of the Valley: 4457, 4458, 4488
Long Tailed Bird and Tree Peony: 2634, 2832, 2834
Lovebirds: 2121, 2326, 2328, 2333, 2782
Magical Tree (Rosetta): 3505
Magpies: 2907, 2907, 2908, 2908, 2911, 2912, 2975, 2976
Malvern: 4801, 4901, 4909
Mandarin Tree: 3672, 3701, 3702, 3703, 3719, 3791, 3793
Mandarins Chatting: 3653, 3654, 3672, 3675, 3680
Marguerite Daisy: 4277
Marigold: 3271
Marrakesh: 3289
Mayflower: 3049, 3161, 3165
Meadow: 3077, 3078
Medley: 3587, 3591, 3593, 3599, 3600, 3845
Melange: 3601, 3601
Metropolis: 3420
Mikado: 1883, 1886, 2199, 2240, 2264, 2270, 2314, 2340, 2355, 2356, 2357, 2361, 2363, 2364, 2370, 2399, 2410, 2422, 2442, 2470, 2881, 2910, 2914, 2927, 2978, 3048, 3158, 3201, 3910, 4373, 4422, 4433, 4434, 4678, 4805
Mikado in Cartouche: 2367, 2368, 3178
Mikado without Mikado: 2927
Mirage: 3915
Modern Crocus: 3803
Moderne: 3886, 3887, 3888
Moderne Lady: 2654
Mondrian: 3570
Moonlight: 3075, 3076, 3118, 3127

Moonlight Cameo: 2944, 2944, 2945, 2946, 2947, 2960, 2964, 2969, 2980, 3392
Neapolitan: 3445, 3841, 3842
Needlepoint: 3815, 3816
New Anemone: 4213, 4219, 4231, 4245
New Bird of Paradise: 4794, 4795, 4805
New Chinese Bird: 3304
New Chinese Bird & Cloud: 3320, 3321, 3322
New Delphinium: 3526
New Flies: 2837, 3023, 3024, 3025, 3028
New Laburnam: 3867, 3867
New Mikado: 2091, 2428, 2727, 2728, 2729, 2740, 2788, 2814, 2815, 2825, 2830, 2990, 3137, 3495, 3843, 3860, 4104, 4109, 4320, 4328, 4329, 4346, 4362, 4398, 4416, 4419
New Mikado (Part): 4508
New Mikado with Lady: 2814
New Mikado without Mikado: 2428, 2814
New Prunus Spray: 2463
New Storks: 4280, 4283, 4304, 4339, 4340, 4342, 4343, 4344, 4348, 4367, 4400, 4421, 4440, 4443, 4507
New Violets: 4374, 4376
Nightingale: 3562, 3598
Nightingale Garden: 3568
Norwegian Flowers: 3661
Norwegian Lady: 3665
Norwegian Miss: 3668
Nosegay: 4489, 4514, 4515, 4517, 4518, 4519, 4527, 4528
Old Stone Ware: 3770, 3770, 3775, 3776, 3777, 3778, 3779, 3780, 3781, 3782, 3783, 3784, 3804, 3829, 3830, 3847, 3877, 3878, 3879, 3896, 3904, 3920, 3998
Old Wisteria: 2191, 2238

Orange Blossom: 2721, 2722, 2723, 2724, 2725
Orange Embossed: 3042, 3052
Oranges: 3528
Orchard: 2885, 2886, 3064
Orchid: 3255, 3325
Oriental Water Garden: 2477
Palm Blossom: 4278, 4297, 4298
Paradise Bird & Tree: 3147, 3150, 3151, 3155, 3157, 3159, 3202, 3241, 3350
Paradise Bird & Tree with Cloud: 3143, 3144, 3149, 3154, 3252
Parkland: 3423, 3523, 3524
Parrots: 3016, 3017, 3018, 3037, 3095
Pastoral: 4185
Peach Blossom: 2030, 2371, 2436, 2480
Peach Melba: 3448, 3459
Pearl Insignia: 4733, 4734
Persian: 2882, 2883, 2884, 3065, 3067, 3068, 3069, 3131
Persian Flowers or Turkish: 3050, 3071, 3116
Persian Garden: 3892, 3893, 3894
Persian Rose: 3975
Pheasant: 4805, 4934, 4935
Pheasant Cartouche: 628, 827
Pheasant and Rose: 2857
Pin Stripe: 4609, 4610, 4611
Pink Carnation: 2143
Plain: 601, 852, 2917, 3065, 3843, 3844, 3846, 3849, 3911, 3933, 3965, 4000, 4001, 4009, 4011, 4013, 4021, 4037, 4100, 4108, 4109, 4110, 4141, 4142, 4146, 4149, 4157, 4158, 4166, 4178, 4179, 4181, 4183, 4188, 4258, 4274, 4284, 4341, 4350, 4352, 4353, 4356, 4357, 4397, 4417, 4437, 4460, 4484, 4506, 4599, 4623, 4624, 4625, 4626, 4627, 4628, 4672, 4710, 4841

Carlton Ware Patterns and Shapes

Plain with Floral: 4783
Plain with Leaves: 4157
Pomander Pendant: 2723, 2843, 2845
Pomona: 3324, 3328
Prickly Pansy: 3424, 3449, 3455, 3499
Primula: 3742, 3745, 3746
Primula and Leaf: 4119, 4120, 4121, 4155, 4201
Prunus: 3193
Prunus and Bird: 2412, 2413, 2421, 2431, 2831
Quince: 2412
Rabbits at Dusk: 4243, 4247, 4247, 4249, 4257
Rainbow Fans: 3699, 3700, 3713, 3721
Rainbow Portal: 2497, 2500
Rayure: 3955
Red Devil: 3765, 3767, 3769
Red Rose: 528
Reproduction Swansea China: 624
Ring Posy Bowls: 3909
River Fish: 2437, 2440, 2441, 3360
Rockery & Pheasant: 2041, 2071, 2186, 2244
Rose Bud: 1172
Rose Marie: 3504
Rose Medallion: 2334
Rose Trellis: 2080
Roses: 2286
Rosetta: 3645
Rudolf's Posy: 3408
Russian: 3567
Sagitta: 3415
Scalloped Lace: 2935
Scimitar: 3651, 3652
Scroll: 3411
Seagulls: 3502

Secretary Bird: 4017, 4018, 4106, 4107
Shabunkin: 3970, 3971
Shadow Imprint: 3465
Shagreen: 3033, 3053, 3054, 3056, 3057, 3069
Shamrock: 3235
Silk Sands: 4286, 4287, 4289
Sketching Bird: 3852, 3889, 3890, 3891, 3907, 3951, 3952, 3960, 4211, 4354, 4355, 4376, 4393, 4435
Sketching Bird with no Bird: 3891
Snowdrops: 4375
Spangle Tree or Tiger Tree: 4163
Spider's Web: 4103, 4109, 4242, 4243, 4244, 4252, 4254, 4259, 4327, 4330, 4331, 4347, 4363, 4366, 4399, 4420, 4439, 4509
Spots: 3229, 3231, 3912, 3916, 4011, 4223, 4224, 4225, 4226, 4227, 4232, 4322, 4323, 4324, 4372, 4379, 4404, 4406, 4408, 4418, 4442, 4511
Spray of Flowers: 2779
Spring: 3865, 3885, 3897
Stag: 3359
Starflower: 4215, 4216
Stars: 4475
Stellata or Wild Cherry: 3291, 3326
Stork: 722, 723
Stork and Bamboo: 2822, 2932, 2933, 2934, 3470
Strata: 3553
Summer Flowers: 3925, 3926, 3927, 3958
Summer Medley: 3663
Sunflower: 3982, 3996
Sunflower Geometric: 3313, 3333, 3334, 3339
Sunrise: 2922
Swallow & Cloud: 3073, 3074, 3075, 3134, 3134, 3174, 3243, 3314

Carlton Ware Patterns and Shapes

Swansea Flowers: 2044
Sylvan: 3650, 3715, 3718
Sylvan Glade: 3500
Temple: 2481, 2482, 2552, 2681, 2820, 2880, 2928, 2929, 2941, 2971, 3003, 3026, 3027, 3047, 3048, 3087, 3129, 3130, 3130, 3185, 4108, 4204, 4205, 4208, 4214
Temple without Temple: 2880
Temple Flowers: 3093
Tendrillon: 3858
The Hunt: 2962
Thistle Heads: 4808, 4809
Tiger Lily: 3667
Towering Castle: 3458
Trailing: 2896
Tree & Clouds: 4217, 4292, 4303
Tree & Cottage: 3563
Tree & Swallow: 3279, 3280, 3281, 3282, 3283, 3285, 3384
Triple Band: 3959
Tube Lined Fields and Trees: 4138
Tube Lined Flower: 3945
Tube Lined Marigold: 4012
Tube Lined Poppy & Bell: 3974
Tube Lined Tree: 3943, 3944
Tube Lined Tulip: 4162
Tutankhamen: 2686, 2689, 2706, 2708, 2709, 2710, 2711, 2711, 2780, 3404
Twin Tone: 4520, 4521, 4522, 4523, 4525, 4532, 4551, 4552, 4553, 4559, 4601, 4614, 4615, 4616, 4617, 4618
Tyrolean Bands: 4076
Vertical Stripes: 4077, 4078, 4079, 4080, 4083, 4084
Victorian Garden: 3643
Victorian Lady: 3451, 3491

Vine: 4385, 4387, 4395, 4402, 4405, 4411, 4423, 4441, 4444, 4480, 4481, 4512
Violets: 3043
Vogue: 3868
Wagon Wheels: 3812, 3813, 3814
Water Lily: 4435, 4436, 4492, 4563, 4564, 4565, 4566, 4604
Wild Duck: 3922, 3923, 3924, 3927, 3947, 4042
Will o'wisp: 3929, 3939
Willow: 2041, 2341, 2351, 2352, 2841, 2851, 2851, 2852, 2854, 2858
Wind & Flower: 3508
Windswept: 4581, 4582, 4583, 4622
Wisteria: 3866
Worcester Birds: 2145, 2175, 2195, 2196
Worcester Birds without Birds: 2175
Zig Zag: 3299
Ziggarette: 3554

Carlton Ware Shapes

Carlton Ware produced thousands of different shapes in their portfolio. Each shape was normally given a number and the design would have been recorded. Records of the shape numbers from 1001 onwards, which were placed in large books, still exist and provide a valuable source of information about Carlton Ware.

We are aware that some shapes listed have not surfaced, to our knowledge, and therefore may never have been produced by Carlton Ware. Or, possibly, just one piece was made and is now lost.

Records of shape numbers up to 1000 have not been found; possibly they did not exist in a book form and if they did this might have been destroyed when Carlton Ware finally went to the receivers. We have managed to fill in some of the details by physically finding an item with a particular shape number. In addition we have copies of photographs of some of the Vase shapes produced by Carlton Ware. Most of these shape numbers are below 1000 and were used by Carlton Ware throughout its lifetime. For example, the Ginger Jar with shape number 125.

We have included a Price Guide for the embossed range. For pieces that might have been produced with a variety of different patterns, such as the Ginger Jar, it's not possible to give a price guide as it does depend on the pattern! Some pieces have not been seen and we have therefore not been able to provide a price guide.

Shapes 1 – 499

98 Various Patterns : *Vase*
111 Various Patterns : *Conical Vase*
121 Various Patterns : *Bulbous Temple Jar with lid*
123 Various Patterns : *Flower Vase*
125 Various Patterns : *Ginger Jar, 5 sizes*
128 Various Patterns : *Square Vase with narrow stem*
129 Various Patterns : *Bulbous Temple Jar with lid*
130 Various Patterns : *Temple Jar with Lion*
135 Various Patterns : *Vase*
136 Various Patterns : *Octagonal Vase*
139 Various Patterns : *Bulbous Vase*
140 Various Patterns : *Elongated Ginger Jar*
144 Various Patterns : *Conical Ginger Jar*
147 Various Patterns : *Vase*
148 Various Patterns : *Vase*
149 Various Patterns : *Vase*
150 Various Patterns : *Vase*
152 Various Patterns : *Cylindrical Vase with narrower collar*
153 Various Patterns : *Temple Jar with Lion*
155 Various Patterns : *Pot Pourri*
157 Various Patterns : *Vase*
158 Various Patterns : *Vase*
161 Various Patterns : *Vase*
162 Various Patterns : *Urn*
164 Various Patterns : *Vase*
165 Various Patterns : *Trumpet vase*
166 Various Patterns : *Temple Jar with lid*

Carlton Ware Patterns and Shapes

167 Various Patterns : *Vase*
168 Various Patterns : *Hexagonal Vase with lid*
172 Various Patterns : *Bulbous vase with narrow collar*
173 Various Patterns : *Vase*
174 Various Patterns : *Pregnant Vase*
198 Various Patterns : *Bowl*
213 Various Patterns : *Bowl*
215 Various Patterns : *Pot Pourri*
217 Various Patterns : *Cylindrical Vase*
218 Various Patterns : *Vase*
221 Various Patterns : *Powder Bowl with Lady*
222 Various Patterns : *Bowl*
224 Various Patterns : *Cylindrical vase*
225 Various Patterns : *Curved Cylindrical Vase*
226 Various Patterns : *Vase*
231 Various Patterns : *Pen Holder*
232 Various Patterns : *Ink Holder*
238 Various Patterns : *Pot Pourri*
241 Various Patterns : *Preserve with lid*
244 Various Patterns : *Vase with lid*
245 Fruit Basket : *Small Preserve Pot* : £45 - £65
245 Various Patterns : *Vase with lid*
283 Various Patterns : *Vase*
284 Various Patterns : *Vase*
294 Various Patterns : *Vase*
297 Various Patterns : *Rose Bowl*
298 Various Patterns : *Bowl, 4 sizes*
304 Various Patterns : *Lighter*
311 Various Patterns : *Ginger Jar*
314 Various Patterns : *Vase*
325 Various Patterns : *Vase*
326 Various Patterns : *Vase*
331 Fruit : *Jaffa Preserve and Stand* : £30 - £50

349 Various Patterns : *Gondola*
406 Various Patterns : *Vase*
437 Various Patterns : *Vase*
442 Various Patterns : *Vase*
443 Various Patterns : *Vase*
456 Various Patterns : *Vase*
457 Various Patterns : *Vase*
463 Various Patterns : *Vase*
464 Various Patterns : *Vase*
465 Various Patterns : *Vase*
466 Various Patterns : *Vase*
467 Various Patterns : *Vase*
487 Various Patterns : *Vase*
496 Various Patterns : *Jug*

Shapes 500 – 999

550 Various Patterns : *Cigarette Box*
620 Old Salad : *Preserve and Stand* : £50 - £75
640 Various Patterns : *Vase*
697 Various Patterns : *Vase*
711 Fruit Basket : *Preserve Pot* : £55 - £75
743 Various Patterns : *Vase with Handles*
760 Fruit Basket : *Bowl* : £30 - £45
761 Fruit Basket : *Cruet* : £120 - £170
777 Various Patterns : *Vase*
786 Various Patterns : *Vase*
787 Various Patterns : *Milk Jug*
830 Fruit Basket : *Jug and Stand* : £70 - £90
876 Fruit Basket : *Comport* : £50 - £80
899 Various Patterns : *Square Ashtray* : £20 - £40
925 Anemone : *Preserve Cover* : see 1174
928 Anemone : *Tray* : £75 - £110
932 Anemone : *Plate* : £75 - £110
933 Anemone : *Leaf Tray, one hole for handle* : £80 - £150
935 Anemone : *Plate* : £75 - £110
945 Anemone : *Biscuit Barrel* : £250 - £350
946 Anemone : *Square Salad Bowl & Servers* : £350 - £450
949 Gum Nut : *Round Plate* : £20 - £35
950 Gum Nut : *Long Tray* : £25 - £40
952 Gum Nut : *Preserve Pot* : £40 - £60
970 Anemone : *Small Bowl* : £45 - £70
975 Anemone : *Flower Jug, Pitcher, 3 sizes* : £200 - £400

976 Anemone : *Bowl* : £75 - £110
978 Anemone : *Jug* : £100 - £130
979 Anemone : *Preserve Base* : see 1174
983 Anemone : *Cress Dish and Tray* : £150 - £190
995 Fruit Basket : *Pitcher* : £75 - £95
997 Anemone : *Preserve* : £120 - £175

Shapes 1000 - 1499

1001 Various Patterns : *Toy Teapot, no 3*
1002 Novelty : *Deer Serviette Holder* : £30 - £50
1003 Ornament : *Dick Whittington*
1004 Novelty : *Clergyman Bell* : £30 - £50
1005 Novelty : *Maid Bell* : £30 - £50
1006 Novelty : *Page Bell* : £30 - £50
1007 Novelty : *Dandy Bell* : £30 - £50
1008 Novelty : *Clergyman Cigarette Box or Preserve* : £30 - £50
1009 Gum Nut : *Triangular Tray 9ins* : £25 - £40
1010 Gum Nut : *Triangular Tray 7ins* : £25 - £40
1011 Gum Nut : *Triangular Tray 6ins* : £25 - £40
1012 Novelty : *Crinoline Lady Bell* : £110 - £160
1013 Various Patterns : *Jug*
1014 Anemone : *Round Plate 4ins* : £75 - £110
1015 Anemone : *Round Plate 8ins* : £75 - £110
1016 Ornament : *Santa Claus & Mickey Mouse*
1017 Ornament : *Fairy with Mushroom*
1018 Ornament : *Fairy on Leaf*
1019 Ornament : *Fairy Kneeling*
1020 Fish Band : *Drummer*
1021 Fish Band : *Fife*
1022 Fish Band : *Trumpet*
1023 Fish Band : *Fiddle*
1024 Fish Band : *Drummer*
1025 Fish Band : *Banjo*

1026 Anemone : *Tea Pot* : £300 - £420
1027 Anemone : *Sugar* : £60 - £85
1028 Anemone : *Cream* : £60 - £85
1029 Anemone : *Cup* : £150 - £200 with 1030
1030 Anemone : *Saucer* : see 1029
1031 Anemone : *Puff (Bowl with feet plus lid)* : £160 - £190
1032 Anemone : *Mayonnaise (Puff with spoon)* : £185 - £265
1033 Anemone : *Sugar Sifter* : £90 - £125
1034 Various Patterns : *Bowl with Bulb Feet*
1035 Gum Nut : *Grapefruit* : £30 - £60
1036 Gum Nut : *Toast Rack, 3 bar* : £30 - £50
1037 Gum Nut : *Sauceboat* : £30 - £50 with 1038
1038 Gum Nut : *Sauceboat Stand* : see 1037
1039 Pear : *Salt & Pepper* : £30 - £50
1039 Various Patterns : *Vase*
1040 Gum Nut : *Sauce Container* : £30 - £50
1041 Anemone : *Trinket Tray* : £75 - £100
1042 Anemone : *Bee Box* : £100 - £120
1043 Gum Nut : *Sugar Bowl* : £15 - £30
1044 Gum Nut : *Milk or Creamer* : £15 - £30
1045 Gum Nut : *Cruet Set* : £35 - £60
1046 Ornament : *Old Woman in Shoe*
1047 Ornament : *Red Riding Hood*
1048 Acorn : *Salt & Pepper* : £15 - £30
1049 Ornament : *Mickey Mouse with Sled*
1050 Ornament : *Mickey Mouse*
1051 Ornament : *Mickey Mouse on Plane*
1052 Ornament : *Mickey Mouse*
1053 No details :
1054 No details :
1055 No details :

Carlton Ware Patterns and Shapes

1056 Ornament : *Pip Squeak & Wilfred Band*
1057 No details :
1058 No details :
1059 No details :
1060 No details :
1061 Ornament : *Pip Squeak & Wilfred Band*
1062 Various Patterns : *Bowl - Velox, similar to Cone Ashtray*
1063 Gum Nut : *Salad Spoon* : see 1066
1064 Gum Nut : *Salad Fork* : see 1066
1065 Jaffa : *Sugar* : £30 - £50
1066 Gum Nut : *Salad Bowl* : £50 - £70 with 1063 & 1064
1067 Anemone : *Vase* : £100 - £120
1068 Anemone : *Covered Mug* : £190 - £250
1069 Anemone : *Flower Pot* : £70 - £100
1070 Stone Ware : *Vase - Rings* : £15 - £30
1071 Stone Ware : *Ribbed Vase* : £15 - £30
1072 Stone Ware : *Vase* : £15 - £30
1073 Stone Ware : *Round Ash Tray, 3 rests* : £5 - £10
1074 Stone Ware : *Jug* : £15 - £30
1075 Stone Ware : *Vase, 2 handles each side offset* : £15 - £30
1076 Stone Ware : *Bowl with 2 handles* : £15 - £30
1077 Stone Ware : *Vase* : £15 - £30
1078 Stone Ware : *Beaker* : £10 - £20
1079 Stone Ware : *Puff Box* : £15 - £30
1080 Stone Ware : *Candle Stick* : £10 - £20
1081 Stone Ware : *Bowl on Foot* : £15 - £30
1082 Gum Nut : *Toast Rack, 5 bar* : £40 - £60
1083 Ornament : *Hand Mirror with Face*
1084 Gum Nut : *Triangular Tray 8ins* : £25 - £40
1085 Ornament : *Thermometer Frame*
1086 Gum Nut : *Rectangular Tray* : £25 - £40

1087 Crinoline : *Mustard, Salt & Pepper* : £75 - £100
1088 Jaffa : *Lemon Squeezer, Large Size* : £30 - £50
1089 Gum Nut : *Leaf Butter* : £25 - £45
1090 Ornament : *Squirrel Tooth Brush Holder*
1091 Ornament : *Guardsman Tooth Brush Holder*
1092 Ornament : *Sailor Tooth Brush Holder*
1093 Ornament : *Soldier Tooth Brush Holder*
1094 Oven Ware : *Preserve or Jam Jar Container*
1095 Cancelled :
1096 Anemone : *Butter, small* : £45 - £70
1097 Anemone : *Morning Tray* : £100 - £125 with 1029
1098 Oak Tree : *Jug or Pitcher* : £120 - £160
1099 Bluebell : *Jug* : £200 - £300
1100 Gum Nut : *Sauceboat, Large Size* : £30 - £50 with 1101
1101 Gum Nut : *Sauceboat Stand, Large Size* : see 1100
1102 Ornament : *21st Key, Large Size*
1103 Stone Ware : *Dog* : £150 - £200
1104 Stone Ware : *Vase* : £15 - £30
1105 Stone Ware : *Vase* : £15 - £30
1106 Stone Ware : *Ribbed Vase* : £15 - £30
1107 Stone Ware : *Bowl* : £15 - £30
1108 Stone Ware : *Vase* : £15 - £30
1109 Stone Ware : *Vase* : £15 - £30
1110 Stone Ware : *Bowl* : £15 - £30
1111 Stone Ware : *Mug* : £10 - £20
1112 Stone Ware : *Jug* : £10 - £20
1113 Stone Ware : *Bowl on Foot* : £10 - £20
1114 Stone Ware : *Owl Cruet* : £20 - £35
1115 Stone Ware : *Pot* : £10 - £20
1116 Stone Ware : *Dessert Plate* : £10 - £20
1117 Stone Ware : *Bulb Bowl* : £10 - £20
1118 Stone Ware : *Bulb Bowl* : £10 - £20

Carlton Ware Patterns and Shapes

1119 Stone Ware : *Tobacco Jar* : £20 - £40
1120 Stone Ware : *Vase No 5* : £15 - £30
1121 Stone Ware : *Vase No 4* : £15 - £30
1122 Stone Ware : *Vase /4* : £15 - £30
1123 Stone Ware : *Jug, 1 handle* : £15 - £30
1124 Stone Ware : *Jug, 2 handles* : £15 - £30
1125 Various Patterns : *Jug, Flat Sided*
1126 Gum Nut : *Mayonnaise Bowl , Unhandled* : £35 - £55
1127 Advertising Ware : *Dimple Jug, Large Size* : £10 - £20
1128 Advertising Ware : *Dimple Ash Tray* : £10 - £20
1129 Various Patterns : *Tall Round Ash Tray, 2 rests* : £20 - £40
1130 Ornament : *Yale Key*
1131 Various Patterns : *Square Ash Bowl, 4 rests*
1132 Cat : *Toy Tea Ware*
1133 Dimple : *Jug, Small Size*
1134 Dimple : *Jug*
1135 Various Patterns : *Round Ash Bowl*
1136 Various Patterns : *Round Ash Tray, Solid*
1137 Rabbit : *Toy Tea Ware*
1138 Novelty : *Crinoline Lady Napkin Holder* : £60 - £90
1139 Various Patterns : *Posie Bowl, 4 sizes*
1140 Stone Ware : *Jug, No 1 & 2* : £15 - £30
1141 Various Patterns : *Oblong Ash Bowl*
1142 Various Patterns : *Triangular Ash Bowl*
1143 Oak Tree : *Ashtray* : £40 - £60
1144 Oak Tree : *Charger* : £100 - £150
1145 Oak Tree : *Candlestick, single* : £50 - £60
1146 Oak Tree : *Jug, 8ins* : £100 - £130
1147 Oak Tree : *Cigarette Box* : £40 - £70
1148 Oak Tree : *Bowl, handled* : £60 - £90

1149 Oak Tree : *Toast Rack, 3 bar* : £40 - £50
1150 Various Patterns : *Octagonal Shaving Brush Handle*
1151 Various Patterns : *Vase on Foot*
1152 Various Patterns : *Vase, Size 5, 6*
1153 Various Patterns : *Vase, Size 5, 6*
1154 Various Patterns : *Vase, Size 5, 6*
1155 Oak Tree : *Match Holder* : £45 - £60
1156 Various Patterns : *Vase, Square Top*
1157 Various Patterns : *Vase, Footed Cone*
1158 Cat : *Mug*
1159 Cat : *Fruit Plate*
1160 Cat : *Muffin*
1161 Stone Ware : *Lamp, as vase 1071* : £20 - £30
1162 Oak Tree : *Vase* : £50 - £70
1163 Oak Tree : *Vase, two handled* : £80 - £110
1164 Oak Tree : *Book Ends* : £140 - £170
1165 Oak Tree : *Oval Bowl* : £30 - £45
1166 Oak Tree : *Toast Rack, 5 bar* : £50 - £60
1167 Oak Tree : *Cheese Dish and Cover* : £80 - £100
1168 Oak Tree : *Butter, covered, square* : £60 - £80
1169 Oak Tree : *Leaf Butter* : £25 - £35
1170 Lemon : *Segmented Dish* : £40 - £60
1171 Stone Ware : *Vase, as 1071* : £15 - £30
1172 Stone Ware : *Vase, as 1072* : £15 - £30
1173 Various Patterns : *Oval shaped Bowl, two handled*
1174 Anemone : *Preserve Pot* : £120 - £175 with 925 & 979
1175 Oak Tree : *Preserve with Base* : £60 - £80
1176 Various Patterns : *Vase 16ins (/00) 14ins (/0)*
1177 Stone Ware : *Square Box* : £20 - £35
1178 Stone Ware : *Crinoline Lady* : £40 - £70
1179 Stone Ware : *Rat* : £150 - £200
1180 Stone Ware : *Goose* : £250 - £300

Carlton Ware Patterns and Shapes

1181 Stone Ware : *Penguin* : £150 - £200
1182 Stone Ware : *Rabbit* : £150 - £200
1183 Oak Tree : *Cruet Set* : £130 - £160
1184 Anemone : *Tea Cup as 1029* : see 1029
1185 Oak Tree : *Cream* : £35 - £50
1186 Oak Tree : *Sugar* : £35 - £50
1187 Oak Tree : *Leaf Tray (s, m, l)* : £25 - £60
1188 Oak Tree : *Biscuit* : £70 - £100
1189 Oak Tree : *Sauceboat and Stand* : £40 - £60
1190 Oak Tree : *Sugar Sifter* : £70 - £90
1191 Oak Tree : *Jug, 6ins, 1 pint* : £120 - £150
1192 Oak Tree : *Double Candlestick* : £60 - £70
1193 Oak Tree : *Cigarette Holder and Ashtray* : £45 - £70
1194 Oak Tree : *Triple Tray* : £50 - £70
1195 Various Patterns : *Jug, as 1125 but shrunk*
1196 Various Patterns : *Jug*
1197 Novelty : *Pelican Cruet* : £30 - £60
1198 Various Patterns : *Pot Pourri (Base 1157 with new cover)*
1199 Various Patterns : *Powder Puff (897 with Wicker Knob)*
1200 Various Patterns : *Small Grecian Jug*
1201 Various Patterns : *Jug, Barrel Shape*
1202 Ornament : *Scot Toothbrush Holder*
1203 Ornament : *Irish Toothbrush Holder*
1204 Ornament : *Welsh Toothbrush Holder*
1205 Stone Ware : *Triangular Ash Tray* : £5 - £10
1206 Cat : *Ash Tray* : £10 - £15
1207 Various Patterns : *Triangular Jug*
1208 Oak Tree : *Bon-bon dish* : £30 - £50
1209 Various Patterns : *Lamp, converted from 1105/4*
1210 Various Patterns : *Modern Cigarette or Card Holder*
1211 Stone Ware : *Book End* : £20 - £40

1212 Stone Ware : *Book End* : £20 - £40
1213 Mugs & Jugs, Musical : *Humpty Dumpty* : £100 - £200
1214 Oak Tree : *Bowl, 3ins* : £40 - £70
1215 Various Patterns : *Round Ash Tray*
1216 Various Patterns : *Vase converted to Jug (1181)*
1217 Gazelle : *Candle Stick*
1218 Various Patterns : *Large Round Ash Tray as 1215*
1219 Various Patterns : *Medium Ash Tray*
1220 Various Patterns : *Drip Ash Tray, large size*
1221 Various Patterns : *Drip Ash Tray, small size*
1222 Various Patterns : *Posy Bowl, small size, Ring*
1223 Gazelle : *Pot*
1224 Various Patterns : *Posy Bowl, (1217 covered Vase)*
1225 Various Patterns : *Footed Vase*
1226 Fruit : *Grapefruit slices* : £10 - £20
1227 Various Patterns : *Offside Handled Vase*
1228 Various Patterns : *Bowl*
1229 Various Patterns : *Cigarette Holder, Ring*
1230 Various Patterns : *Ashtray, single cigarette rest on each side* : £15 - £20
1231 Various Patterns : *Vase*
1232 Various Patterns : *Vase, two offset handles each side, 2 sizes*
1233 Various Patterns : *Two Handled Vase, 2 sizes*
1234 Various Patterns : *Two Handled Vase, handles offset, 2 sizes*
1235 Various Patterns : *Three Handled Vase*
1236 Various Patterns : *Oval Dish*
1237 Rock Garden : *Tray, Elliptical* : £30 - £50
1238 Rock Garden : *Flower Jug, Tall* : £110 - £150
1239 Rock Garden : *Vase, two offset handles each side* : £40 - £60

Carlton Ware Patterns and Shapes

1240 Rock Garden : *Posy Bowl* : £45 - £55
1241 Rock Garden : *Leaf Butter, small handle, large size* : £20 - £35
1242 Various Patterns : *Ring 2 handled Vase*
1243 Rock Garden : *Cigarette Vase, unholed handles* : 330 - £40
1244 Rock Garden : *Vase, offset handle each side* : £50 - £80
1245 Moderne : *Tea Set* : £300 - £400
1246 Moderne : *Coffee Set* : £300 - £400
1247 Rock Garden : *Soup Bowl, unholed handles* : £35 - £50
1248 Rock Garden : *Ashtray* : £20 - £40
1249 Rock Garden : *Flower Trough* : £30 - £45
1250 Rock Garden : *Jug or Pitcher, two handles on one side* : £40 - £55
1251 Rock Garden : *Candlestick* : £35 - £50
1252 Rock Garden : *Ashtray and Match or Cigarette Holder* : £45 - £60
1253 Rock Garden : *Vase, Bulbous, handles on one side* : £40 - £60
1254 Rock Garden : *Vase, offset handles each side* : £40 - £60
1255 Guinness : *Round Ash Tray* : £20 - £40
1256 Various Patterns : *Vase converted to Lamp (1104/4 as Lamp)*
1257 Advertising Ware : *Abbotts Choice Jug* : £15 - £20
1258 Advertising Ware : *Abbotts Choice Ash Tray* : £15 - £20
1259 Various Patterns : *Vase with handle from 1140*
1260 Mugs & Jugs, Musical : *Hunting Scene Jug* : £40 - £80
1261 Ornament : *Santa*

Dr Czes & Yvonne Kosniowski

1262 Rock Garden : *Cruet Set* : £80 - £100
1263 Dovecote Range : *Oblong Jug* : £20 - £30
1264 Rock Garden : *Leaf Butter, small handle, small size* : £20 - £35
1265 Rock Garden : *Preserve with Lid* : £70 - £90
1266 Blackberry/Raspberry : *Preserve* : £80 - £120
1267 Lobster : *Oval Salad* : £100 - £160 with 1273
1268 No details :
1269 Lobster : *Round Salad* : £100 - £160 with 1273
1270 Crab : *Butter* : £20 - £40
1271 Haig : *Cigar Ash Bowl* : £10 - £20
1272 Lobster : *Oblong Dish* : £30 - £50
1273 Lobster : *Servers* : see 1267, 1269
1274 Dolls Head : *Open Top, 4ins*
1275 Various Patterns : *Ash Tray*
1276 Dolls Head : *Paramount 400*
1277 Lobster : *Preserve* : £40 - £70
1278 Lobster : *Round Plate, 4 sizes* : £20 - £50
1279 Dolls Head : *Open Top, 6.5ins*
1280 Crab & Lobster : *Triangular Dish* : £20 - £40
1281 Advertising Ware : *Craven A Square Ash Tray* : £5 - £10
1282 Guinness : *Ash Tray with several rests* : £20 - £40
1283 Various Patterns : *Ash Tray*
1284 Mugs & Jugs, Musical : *Hangsman* : £150 - £250
1285 Mugs & Jugs, Musical : *Hangsman* : £80 - £150
1286 Various Patterns : *Diamond Dish, 2 sizes*
1287 Rock Garden : *Sauceboat and Stand* : £55 - £85
1288 Dolls Head : *Paramount 350*
1289 Mugs & Jugs, Musical : *Hunting Scene Mug* : £40 - £80
1290 Incised : *Ash Tray*
1291 Incised : *Jug as 496*

Carlton Ware Patterns and Shapes

1292 Incised : *Vase with incised Diamond*
1293 Incised : *Plaque, 12ins*
1294 Incised : *Oval Dish as 1237*
1295 Incised : *Jug as 786*
1296 Incised : *Vase as 443/6ins*
1297 Incised : *Vase as 1176/4ins*
1298 Incised : *Biscuit Jar as 998*
1299 Incised : *Cigarette Box as 923*
1300 Incised : *Vase as 466*
1301 Incised : *Bowl as 1062*
1302 Incised : *Preserve & Stand as 800*
1303 Incised : *Ash Tray as 1136*
1304 Incised : *Vase as 442*
1305 Incised : *Triangle Book Ends*
1306 Incised : *Vase as 443/10ins*
1307 Incised : *Ash Tray as 794*
1308 Incised : *Vase as 741*
1309 Incised : *Jug as 788*
1310 Incised : *Posy Bowl*
1311 Various Patterns : *Flower Ring Plain Candlestick*
1312 Dolls Head : *Paramount 300*
1313 Novelty : *Punch Egg Timer*
1314 Novelty : *Pope Egg Timer*
1315 Novelty : *Policeman Egg Timer*
1316 Novelty : *Golliwog Egg Timer*
1317 Various Patterns : *Store Jar, as 905, 6ins x 4 ins*
1318 Various Patterns : *Jug, as 814 shrunk handle*
1319 Various Patterns : *Hexagonal Shaving Brush Handle*
1320 Incised : *Posy Bowl, small size*
1321 Incised : *Cigarette Holder, as 1210*
1322 Incised : *Vase, as 1232 large size*
1323 Incised : *Posy Bowl, medium size*
1324 Incised : *Diamond Shape Tray as 1286*

1325 Incised : *Vase as 1227*
1326 Incised : *Double Posy Bowl*
1327 Various Patterns : *Flower Ring, 4 sizes*
1328 Royalty : *King Henry VIII Bowl* : £750 - £1,000
1329 Advertising Ware : *Milk Jug (White & Mackey)* : £15 - £30
1330 Mugs & Jugs, Musical : *Huntsman Mug Plain* : £40 - £80
1331 Dolls Head : *Paramount 500*
1332 Royalty : *Confederation Jug* : £500 - £750
1333 Various Patterns : *Barrel Jug*
1334 Crab & Lobster : *Sauce Boat* : £20 - £40
1335 Crab & Lobster : *Sauce Stand, small size* : £10 - £20
1336 Rock Garden : *Lamp* : £200 - £250
1337 Rock Garden : *Charger or Plaque* : £150 - £200
1338 Crab & Lobster : *Sauce Container* : £15 - £30
1339 Crab & Lobster : *5 bar Toast Rack* : £50 - £80
1340 Various Patterns : *Modern Triangular Tray, 9ins*
1341 Various Patterns : *Modern Oblong Dish, 3 sizes*
1342 Various Patterns : *Modern Butter, with handle*
1343 Various Patterns : *Modern Round Salad*
1344 Dolls Head : *Paramount 600, size 7*
1345 Various Patterns : *Brush Book*
1346 Various Patterns : *Modern Preserve, 2 sizes*
1347 Various Patterns : *Modern Jug, 3 sizes*
1348 Crab & Lobster : *Low Round Salad* : £30 - £60
1349 Dolls Head : *Paramount, size 8*
1350 Crab & Lobster : *Shallow Oblong Dish* : £30 - £60
1351 Various Patterns : *Artists Palette, numbered sample 1*
1352 Various Patterns : *Artists Palette, numbered sample 13*
1353 Rock Garden : *Lamp, unhandled* : £200 - £250

Carlton Ware Patterns and Shapes

1354 Crab & Lobster : *Cheese* : £30 - £60
1355 Novelty : *Legs of Man*
1356 Rings : *Jug, as 1112*
1357 Rings : *Vase, 8ins, as 1121*
1358 Rings : *Vase, 8ins, as 1122*
1359 Rings : *Vase , 8ins, as 1109*
1360 Rings : *Vase 2 handles, as 1075*
1361 Rings : *Vase Handled, as 1105*
1362 Various Patterns : *Posy Hoop*
1363 Various Patterns : *VAT 69 Jug*
1364 Crab & Lobster : *3 Bar Toast Rack* : £40 - £70
1365 Various Patterns : *Oblong Shallow Tray*
1366 Various Patterns : *Modern Cruet*
1367 Curled Lettuce : *Diamond Dish* : £10 - £20
1368 Dolls Head : *Paramount Open Top*
1369 Various Patterns : *Posy Bar*
1370 Fish : *Candle Holder*
1371 Various Patterns : *Modern Beaker & Cover*
1372 Curled Lettuce : *Sauce Boat and Tray* : £30 - £40
1373 Various Patterns : *Flower Bowl, Plate with stem holder*
1374 Curled Lettuce : *Butter* : £10 - £20
1375 Curled Lettuce : *Oblong Tray* : £10 - £20
1376 Various Patterns : *Toy Tea Set*
1377 Various Patterns : *Round Ash Tray*
1378 Various Patterns : *Oblong Ash Tray with rests*
1379 Various Patterns : *Oblong Ash Tray*
1380 Curled Lettuce : *Knife* : £10 - £20
1381 Various Patterns : *Oval Ash Tray, 2 rests*
1382 Curled Lettuce : *Crescent Dish* : £10 - £20
1383 Curled Lettuce : *Salad Bowl* : £30 - £40
1384 No details :
1385 Curled Lettuce : *Square Plate, 4 sizes* : £10 - £20

1386 Curled Lettuce : *Triple Tray* : £15 - £25
1387 Various Patterns : *Circular Butter, 2 ears* : £10 - £20
1388 Various Patterns : *Vase, 2 sizes*
1389 Curled Lettuce : *Sauce Boat and Tray* : £30 - £40
1390 Curled Lettuce : *Diamond Tray, less elongated than 1367* : £10 - £20
1391 Curled Lettuce : *Salad Servers* : £15 - £30
1392 Curled Lettuce : *Mayonnaise Bowl & Stand* : £30 - £40
1393 Various Patterns : *Ash Tray with 3 rests*
1394 Various Patterns : *Modern Cheese*
1395 Buttercup : *Butter* : £40 - £70 with 1402
1396 Strawberry : *Jam*
1397 Various Patterns : *Bon Bon, as Puff Base 897 to verge*
1398 Various Patterns : *Oblong Cigarette Box, no feet*
1399 Various Patterns : *Card Table Ash Tray*
1400 Various Patterns : *Modern Knife*
1401 Various Patterns : *Modern Spoon*
1402 Buttercup : *Butter Knife* : see 1402
1403 Tulip : *Spoon, also for Strawberry* : £15 - £25
1404 Tulip : *Jam or Butter, 2 sizes* : £25 - £40
1405 Various Patterns : *Shaving Brush Handle, small size*
1406 Haig : *Jug, modernised* : £20 - £45
1407 Various Patterns : *Wall Pocket Vase*
1408 Various Patterns : *Ash Bowl*
1409 Various Patterns : *Coronation Mug*
1410 Various Patterns : *Footed Bowl*
1411 Various Patterns : *Jug, introduced October 1936*
1412 Curled Lettuce : *Cress Drainer & Tray* : £30 - £50
1413 Various Patterns : *Candle Stick*
1414 Royalty : *King Edward VIII* : £500 - £750
1415 Various Patterns : *Cake Plate & Knife*

Carlton Ware Patterns and Shapes

1416 Tulip : *Jug, 6 sizes* : £40 - £90
1417 Tulip : *Oval Dish* : £30 - £40
1418 Tulip : *Preserve* : £45 - £75
1419 Tulip : *Plate, 3 sizes* : £25 - £55
1420 Tulip : *Square Jug, 2 sizes* : £50 - £70
1421 Tulip : *Handled Crescent Plate, 3 sizes* : £40 - £80
1422 Tulip : *Sugar Sifter* : £60 - £95
1423 Animals : *Lion Cubs sitting* : £400 - £450
1424 Animals : *Sea Lion* : £300 - £400
1425 Animals : *Polar Bear* : £300 - £400
1426 Animals : *Lioness* : £450 - £500
1427 Animals : *Lion Cubs lying down* : £400 - £450
1428 Various Patterns : *Lemonade Jug*
1429 Various Patterns : *Lemonade Beaker*
1430 Animals : *Lion* : £450 - £500
1431 Various Patterns : *Large Spill*
1432 Royalty : *Sphere* : see 1434
1433 Various Patterns : *Vase, 9ins*
1434 Royalty : *King George VI* : £400 - £600 with 1432
1435 Royalty : *Queen Elizabeth* : £400 - £600
1436 Various Patterns : *Vase, 2 offset handles*
1437 Animals : *Lizard Vase with Neck* : £300 - £400
1438 Animals : *Lizard Vase without neck* : £300 - £400
1439 Tulip : *Morning Tea Set (Tea for Two)* : £200 - £300
1440 Animals : *Scotch Terrier Standing* : £100 - £150
1441 Animals : *Scotch Terrier Sitting* : £100 - £150
1442 Animals : *Fox Terrier* : £100 - £150
1443 Various Patterns : *Round Ash Tray, 6 rests*
1444 Various Patterns : *Round Ash Tray, 7 rests*
1445 Animals : *Spaniel Dog* : £100 - £150
1446 Animals : *Lamb* : £100 - £150
1447 Animals : *Stag* : £100 - £150
1448 Animals : *Fox* : £100 - £150

1449 Animals : *Mouse on Log* : £100 - £150
1450 Animals : *Mouse on Nest* : £100 - £150
1451 Animals : *Sea Gulls* : £300 - £400
1452 Various Patterns : *Trinket Tray*
1453 Tulip : *Salad* : £45 - £75
1454 Various Patterns : *Trinket Box*
1455 Various Patterns : *Puff Box, as 1454*
1456 Various Patterns : *Sphere Lamp*
1457 Tulip : *Servers* : £30 - £50
1458 Various Patterns : *Round Flat Bowl, 14ins*
1459 Tulip : *Cruet* : £60 - £95
1460 Various Patterns : *Lamp, Jug 1411 converted*
1461 Tulip : *Biscuit* : £60 - £95
1462 Advertising Ware : *Bovril Cup* : £20 - £45
1463 Advertising Ware : *Bovril Cup* : £20 - £45
1464 Guinness : *Ash Tray, as 1282* : £20 - £40
1465 Various Patterns : *Shaving Brush Handle*
1466 Animals : *Lizard on Rock* : £300 - £400
1467 Animals : *Blue Tits* : £300 - £400
1468 Animals : *Fish on Stand* : £100 - £150
1469 Animals : *Alsatian Dogs* : £450 - £500
1470 Animals : *Group of Sheep* : £300 - £400
1471 Animals : *Heron in Flight* : £300 - £400
1472 Daisy : *Jam or Butter* : £20 - £40
1473 Blackberry/Raspberry : *Jam or Butter* : £30 - £45
1474 Pear : *Butter* : £15 - £25
1475 Animals : *Greyhounds* : £450 - £500
1476 Daisy : *Knife* : £15 - £25
1477 Blackberry/Raspberry : *Spoon* : £20 - £40
1478 Buttercup : *Salad Bowl* : £90 - £150 with 1479
1479 Buttercup : *Salad Bowl Servers* : see 1478
1480 Animals : *Crab* : £100 - £150
1481 Animals : *Snake Charmer* : £100 - £150

Carlton Ware Patterns and Shapes

1482 Buttercup : *Plate, 6ins, 7ins, 8ins, 9ins* : £30 - £75
1483 Buttercup : *Bowl, Oval, 3 sizes* : £30 - £75
1484 Various Patterns : *Shaving Brush Handle*
1485 Guinness : *Oblong Ash Tray* : £20 - £40
1486 Buttercup : *Preserve & Stand* : £90 - £155
1487 Engine Turned : *Plate, 4 sizes* : £30 - £50
1488 Engine Turned : *Vase* : £40 - £80
1489 Engine Turned : *Vase, 4 sizes* : £40 - £80
1490 Engine Turned : *Vase* : £40 - £80
1491 Engine Turned : *Bowl, 7ins* : £30 - £50
1492 Engine Turned : *Vase, 4 sizes* : £40 - £80
1493 Engine Turned : *Biscuit Barrel* : £50 - £75
1494 Engine Turned : *Puff Bowl with lid, as 1495 with no hole in lid* : £30 - £50
1495 Engine Turned : *Sugar* : £30 - £40
1496 Engine Turned : *Trinket Box with lid, 2 sizes* : £30 - £50
1497 Engine Turned : *Vase, 3 sizes* : £40 - £80
1498 Engine Turned : *Vase, 3 sizes* : £40 - £80
1499 Engine Turned : *Beaker* : £30 - £40

Dr Czes & Yvonne Kosniowski

Shapes 1500 - 1999

1500 Engine Turned : *Cruet* : £80 - £80
1501 Buttercup : *Cruet (on a Tomato Cruet Frame)* : £120 - £180
1502 Engine Turned : *Cylinder Vase* : £40 - £80
1503 Various Patterns : *Pewter Teapot*
1504 Various Patterns : *Pewter Cream*
1505 Various Patterns : *Pewter Sugar*
1506 Animals : *Giraffe* : £200 - £300
1507 Animals : *Kangaroo* : £200 - £300
1508 Animals : *Borzois Dog* : £200 - £300
1509 Animals : *Leopard* : £200 - £300
1510 Buttercup : *Triple Tray* : £100 - £150
1511 Buttercup : *Bon-Bon Dish* : £35 - £70
1512 Buttercup : *Cress Dish and Tray* : £70 - £110
1513 Buttercup : *Sauce Boat and Tray* : £50 - £70
1514 Buttercup : *Comport* : £50 - £80
1515 Blackberry/Raspberry : *Crescent Tray* : £40 - £60
1516 Blackberry/Raspberry : *Plate* : £30 - £45
1517 Ornament : *Vase*
1518 Ornament : *Mandarin*
1519 Ornament : *Plain Finger Bowl*
1520 Ornament : *Water Carrier*
1521 Ornament : *Coolie*
1522 Buttercup : *Morning Tea Set (Tea for two)* : £400 - £600
1523 Buttercup : *Footed Bowl* : £50 - £80
1524 Buttercup : *Jug, 2 sizes* : £70 - £110
1525 Buttercup : *Reamer* : £100 - £150
1526 Buttercup : *Toast Rack, Combination* : £120 - £170

Carlton Ware Patterns and Shapes

1527 Bee : *Butter Bee Box*
1528 Buttercup : *Sauce Container* : £50 - £80
1529 Buttercup : *Crescent Plate, 2 sizes* : £40 - £70
1530 Buttercup : *Covered Butter or Cheese* : £200 - £400
1531 Buttercup : *Cheese Tray* : £60 - £100
1532 Buttercup : *Toast Rack, 5 Bar* : £80 - £120
1533 Buttercup : *Toast Rack, 3 Bar* : £70 - £100
1534 Buttercup : *Round Butter* : £30 - £50
1535 Ornament : *Mans Head*
1536 Ornament : *Indian Group*
1537 Leaf : *Nut Leaf Knife* : £10 - £20
1538 Leaf : *Ivy Leaf Butter* : £20 - £30
1539 Leaf : *Vine Leaf Jam or Butter* : £20 - £30
1540 Old Water Lily : *Butter* : £35 - £65 with 1541
1541 Old Water Lily : *Knife* : see 1540
1542 Curled Lettuce : *Cheese Plate* : £20 - £40
1543 Mugs & Jugs, Musical : *Flower Mug* : £80 - £150
1544 Flower : *Cruet*
1545 Blackberry/Raspberry : *Sandwich Tray* : £40 - £60
1546 Blackberry/Raspberry : *Diamond Tray* : £40 - £60
1547 Blackberry/Raspberry : *Oblong Tray* : £40 - £60
1548 Blackberry/Raspberry : *Covered Cheese* : £180 - £225
1549 Mugs & Jugs, Musical : *Ghoules* : £100 - £200
1550 Fruit : *Apple Jam* : £10 - £20
1551 Wild Rose : *Butter* : £20 - £40 with 1554 or 1555
1552 Crocus : *Butter* : £30 - £70
1553 Crocus : *Knife* : £10 - £20
1554 Wild Rose : *Knife* : see 1551
1555 Wild Rose : *Spoon* : see 1551
1556 Fruit : *Apple Spoon* : £10 - £20
1557 Plain : *Knife Handle*
1558 Buttercup : *Cheese Knife* : £20 - £30

1559 Blackberry/Raspberry : *Oval Tray* : £30 - £50
1560 Blackberry/Raspberry : *Round Salad* : £30 - £50
1561 Engine Turned : *Lamp, 12ins, no handle* : £50 - £75
1562 Engine Turned : *Lamp, 11ins, handled* : £50 - £75
1563 Various Patterns : *Modern Tea Set*
1564 Blackberry/Raspberry : *Salad Servers* : £40 - £60
1565 Blackberry/Raspberry : *Biscuit Barrel* : £175 - £225
1566 Various Patterns : *Coffee Set*
1567 Stone Ware : *Lamp, 1108/2 converted* : £15 - £30
1568 Various Patterns : *Lamp, 226/10 converted*
1569 Various Patterns : *Lamp, 456/8 converted*
1570 Blackberry/Raspberry : *Morning Tea Set (Tea for two)* : £330 - £450
1571 Various Patterns : *Triangular Tray*
1572 Various Patterns : *Oval Bowl*
1573 Engine Turned : *Lamp, 1502 converted* : £50 - £75
1574 Buttercup : *Juicer and Jug* : £60 - £90
1575 Various Patterns : *Toy Tea Set*
1576 Thistle : *Butter or Jam* : £30 - £50
1577 Thistle : *Butter Knife* : £15 - £25
1578 Thistle : *Jam Spoon* : £15 - £25
1579 Thistle : *Ashtray* : £25 - £50
1580 Blackberry/Raspberry : *Bon-bon dish* : £30 - £50
1581 Blackberry/Raspberry : *Fruit* : £20 - £45
1582 Various Patterns : *Rita Coffee Set*
1583 Buttercup : *Sugar Shaker* : £100 - £150
1584 Blackberry/Raspberry : *Sauceboat and Stand* : £70 - £90
1585 Buttercup : *Covered Mug* : £150 - £200
1586 Blackberry/Raspberry : *Jug* : £60 - £90
1587 Buttercup : *Open Jam, also called Grapefruit* : £90 - £120

Carlton Ware Patterns and Shapes

1588 Water Lily : *Open Jam, also called Grapefruit* : £100 - £120
1589 Various Patterns : *Shaving Brush Handle*
1590 Engine Turned : *Ash Tray, 1 rest* : £30 - £40
1591 Various Patterns : *Lamp, 443/10 converted*
1592 Various Patterns : *Scotch Cruet*
1593 Blackberry/Raspberry : *Sauce Container* : £25 - £45
1594 Various Patterns : *Modern Jug, handle at side*
1595 Buttercup : *Egg Cruet* : £190 - £260
1596 Various Patterns : *Modern Salad Servers*
1597 Buttercup : *Butter Pat* : £30 - £50
1598 Blackberry/Raspberry : *Cruet* : £100 - £150
1599 Blackberry/Raspberry : *Butter Pat* : £20 - £35
1600 Various Patterns : *Triangular Salad, as 1571 with foot*
1601 Various Patterns : *Triangular Dessert Plate*
1602 Blackberry/Raspberry : *Jug with Lemon Squeezer* : £60 - £85
1603 Red Currant : *Butter or Jam* : £20 - £30
1604 Various Patterns : *Modern Butter Pat*
1605 Red Currant : *Butter Knife* : £10 - £20
1606 Red Currant : *Jam Spoon* : £10 - £20
1607 Red Currant : *Preserve* : £50 - £80
1608 Various Patterns : *Oval Scalloped Dish*
1609 Various Patterns : *Oval Scalloped Comport*
1610 Various Patterns : *Bon Bon Dish, as 1397 with rim at outside edges*
1611 Various Patterns : *Bowl, as 1062 Velox with rim*
1612 Various Patterns : *Ash Tray, as 797 with rim*
1613 Buttercup : *Bulb Bowl, 10ins* : £50 - £80
1614 Apple Blossom : *Leaf Tray* : £30 - £50
1615 Various Patterns : *Parisienne Tea Set*
1616 Rope : *Vase* : £30 - £50

Dr Czes & Yvonne Kosniowski

1617 Apple Blossom : *Triangular Tray 4ins, 6ins, 9ins* : £30 - £50
1618 Apple Blossom : *Preserve* : £65 - £95
1619 Various Patterns : *Modern Shallow Dish*
1620 Various Patterns : *Glasgow Exhibition Ash Tray*
1621 Apple Blossom : *Butter* : £30 - £50
1622 Various Patterns : *Octagonal Bon Bon with Foot*
1623 Various Patterns : *Octagonal Bon Bon without Foot*
1624 Novelty : *Bird on Horseshoe*
1625 Novelty : *Bird on Ring*
1626 Various Patterns : *Footed Bon Bon Dish*
1627 Various Patterns : *Bon Bon Dish without Foot*
1628 Various Patterns : *Footed Bon Bon Dish*
1629 Various Patterns : *Bon Bon Dish without Foot*
1630 Various Patterns : *Rita Tea Set*
1631 Various Patterns : *Oblong Bon Bon Dish Footed*
1632 Various Patterns : *Oblong Bon Bon Dish without Foot*
1633 Various Patterns : *Bon Bon Dish Footed*
1634 Various Patterns : *Bon Bon Dish Footed without Foot*
1635 Various Patterns : *Diamond Bon Bon Dish Footed*
1636 Various Patterns : *Diamond Bon Bon Dish without Foot*
1637 Red Currant : *Leaf Tray* : £30 - £50
1638 Apple Blossom : *Vase, 3 sizes* : £70 - £100
1639 Cone : *Sugar Sifter*
1640 Rope : *Vase, rope top & bottom, 3 sizes* : £30 - £50
1641 Rope : *Vase, rope top & bottom, 3 sizes* : £30 - £50
1642 Rope : *Vase, rope top & bottom, 3 sizes* : £30 - £50
1643 Rope : *Vase, rope top & bottom, 3 sizes* : £30 - £50
1644 Rope : *Vase, rope top & bottom, 2 sizes* : £30 - £50

1645 Rope : *Vase, rope bottom only, as 1641, 2 sizes* : £30 - £50
1646 Rope : *Vase, rope bottom only, as 1642, 2 sizes* : £30 - £50
1647 Rope : *Vase, rope bottom only, as 1643, small size* : £30 - £50
1648 Apple Blossom : *Vase, Bulbous, 3 sizes* : £70 - £100
1649 Apple Blossom : *Vase, 3 sizes* : £70 - £100
1650 Apple Blossom : *Cheese Plate* : £35 - £55
1651 Apple Blossom : *Cheese Knife* : £20 - £30
1652 Apple Blossom : *Sauceboat and Stand* : £55 - £80
1653 Apple Blossom : *Cruet Set* : £80 - £100
1654 Apple Blossom : *Spoon* : £20 - £30
1655 Apple Blossom : *Butter Knife* : £20 - £30
1656 Red Currant : *Leaf Jam* : £20 - £30
1657 Red Currant : *Preserve, with leaves on side* : £40 - £60
1658 Red Currant : *Cheese Tray* : £30 - £60 with 1659
1659 Red Currant : *Cheese Tray Knife* : see 1658
1660 Red Currant : *Sauceboat and Stand* : £30 - £50
1661 Buttercup : *Butter Pat Knife* : £20 - £30
1662 Blackberry/Raspberry : *Butter Pat Knife* : £20 - £40
1663 Apple Blossom : *Salad Servers* : £50 - £70
1664 Apple Blossom : *Bon-bon dish* : £35 - £50
1665 Apple Blossom : *Oval Bowl, 3 sizes* : £40 - £70
1666 Various Patterns : *Triple Candlestick*
1667 Various Patterns : *Double Candlestick*
1668 Apple Blossom : *Cress Dish* : £55 - £80
1669 Apple Blossom : *Footed Bowl* : £45 - £70
1670 Apple Blossom : *Morning Tea Set (Tea for two)* : £250 - £400
1671 Apple Blossom : *Salad* : £75 - £100
1672 Various Patterns : *Ash Tray & Cigarette Holder*

1673 Various Patterns : *Cracker Toast Rack*
1674 Various Patterns : *Conical Vase*
1675 Various Patterns : *Conical Vase*
1676 Various Patterns : *Modern Oval Jug*
1677 Various Patterns : *Modern Round Jug*
1678 Various Patterns : *Ash Bowl*
1679 Red Currant : *Double Butter* : £30 - £50
1680 Apple Blossom : *Double Butter* : £40 - £60
1681 Guinness : *Menu Stand* : £20 - £40
1682 Various Patterns : *Cigarette Box*
1683 Various Patterns : *Ash Tray*
1684 Various Patterns : *Pen Tray*
1685 Mugs & Jugs, Musical : *Grandfather Clock* : £150 - £250
1686 Apple Blossom : *Jug, 2 sizes* : £70 - £100
1687 Apple Blossom : *Beaker and Cover* : £95 - £135
1688 Apple Blossom : *Triple Tray* : £35 - £60
1689 Apple Blossom : *Mayonnaise Bowl, Stand and Ladle* : £85 - £120
1690 Various Patterns : *Vase*
1691 Various Patterns : *Vase with Wavy Sides*
1692 Various Patterns : *Vase with small handles, two each side, 4 sizes*
1693 Various Patterns : *Vase with small handles, three each side, 4 sizes*
1694 Various Patterns : *Vase with small handles, two each side, 4 sizes*
1695 Various Patterns : *Vase with small handles, two each side, 4 sizes*
1696 Apple Blossom : *Toast Rack* : £80 - £110
1697 Apple Blossom : *Jug, Tall* : £250 - £320
1698 Novelty : *Judge Serviette Holder* : £45 - £80
1699 Novelty : *Scotchman Serviette Holder* : £45 - £80

Carlton Ware Patterns and Shapes

1700 Apple Blossom : *Jug, double handle, 3 sizes* : £175 - £250

1701 Apple Blossom : *Egg Frame and 4 Egg Cups* : £110 - £140

1702 Novelty : *Judge Bottle Stopper* : £40 - £70

1703 Novelty : *Scotchman Bottle Stopper* : £40 - £70

1704 Apple Blossom : *Covered Cheese* : £175 - £225

1705 Crinoline Lady : *Cruet Set* : £120 - £180

1706 Various Patterns : *Ribbed Toy Tea Set*

1707 Apple Blossom : *Serviette Holder* : £40 - £70

1708 Red Currant : *Napkin Ring* : £40 - £80

1709 Buttercup : *Napkin Ring* : £100 - £160

1710 Apple Blossom : *Vase* : £70 - £90

1711 Novelty : *Double Horse Shoe & Doves*

1712 Various Patterns : *Bowl, Conical, 12ins*

1713 Various Patterns : *Candlestick*

1714 Apple Blossom : *Toy Teaware* : £250 - £500

1715 Bell : *Posy Holder* : £30 - £40

1716 Novelty : *Humpty Dumpty Lamp*

1717 Wedding Cake : *Fence Cake Decoration*

1718 Water Lily : *Posy Holder* : £40 - £60

1719 Various Patterns : *Ash Tray, as 1683 without rests*

1720 Apple Blossom : *Morning Set on Tray* : £250 - £500

1721 Various Patterns : *Vase, as 1675 handled*

1722 Various Patterns : *Vase, two double handles*

1723 Apple Blossom : *Sugar - Toy Set size* : £30 - £50

1724 Wild Rose : *Wall Pocket* : £70 - £100

1725 Cottage : *Small House*

1726 Ornament : *Gnome, 1.125ins*

1727 Various Patterns : *Fluted Wall Pocket*

1728 Apple Blossom : *Mayonnaise Bowl, unhandled* : £40 - £60

1729 Apple Blossom : *Pickle Dish* : £20 - £30

1730 Red Currant : *Jam Pot Holder* : £40 - £60
1731 Ornament : *Gnome*
1732 Daffodil : *Posy Holder* : £50 - £70
1733 Various Patterns : *Hexagonal Bowl*
1734 Various Patterns : *Double Candle Stick, modelled May 1939*
1735 Various Patterns : *Ribbed Round Bowl*
1736 Tulip : *Posy Holder* : £35 - £55
1737 Various Patterns : *Storage Jar, 9ins*
1738 Water Lily : *Cruet Set* : £100 - £160
1739 Fruit : *Lemon Preserve* : £20 - £35
1740 Arum Lily : *Posy Holder* : £40 - £65
1741 Water Lily : *Twin Lobed Plate* : £50 - £70
1742 Wedding Cake : *Fence, large, as 1717 altered for Robin*
1743 Wedding Cake : *Fence, small, from Hunting series*
1744 Gladioli : *Bracket* : £200 - £300
1745 Cottage : *Windmill*
1746 Poppy : *Bracket* : £140 - £170
1747 Crocus : *Serving Dish, 2 sizes* : £30 - £70
1748 Tomato : *Oval Tray* : £30 - £50
1749 Various Patterns : *Mug, 2 sizes*
1750 Water Lily : *Serving Bowl, Oval Bowl* : £50 - £70
1751 Pyrethrum : *Jam* : £45 - £80 with 1757
1752 Wallflower : *Butter or Jam* : £45 - £60 with 1763 or 1758
1753 Anemone : *Butter* : £25 - £35
1754 Clover/Shamrock : *Clover Tray* : £20 - £40
1755 Various Patterns : *Modern Ashtray, 2 rests on one side* : £15 - £20
1756 Apple Blossom : *Cream, Tall* : £35 - £55
1757 Pyrethrum : *Spoon* : see 1751
1758 Wallflower : *Butter Knife* : see 1752

Carlton Ware Patterns and Shapes

1759 Crocus : *Comport* : £45 - £70
1760 Crocus : *Bon Bon Dish* : £50 - £80
1761 Anemone : *Spoon* : £25 - £35
1762 Anemone : *Knife* : £25 - £35
1763 Wallflower : *Jam Spoon* : see 1752
1764 Basket : *Fruit Basket* : £40 - £60
1765 Crocus : *Flower Jug, Pitcher, 2 sizes* : £200 - £250
1766 Crocus : *Bulb Bowl* : £60 - £100
1767 Narcissus : *Jug* : £70 - £120
1768 Begonia : *Butter & Knife, Jam & Spoon* : £45 - £60 each set
1769 Forget-me-not : *Butter & Knife, Jam & Spoon* : £45 - £60 each set
1770 Novelty : *Lady Serviette Holder* : £60 - £90
1771 Campion : *Butter & Knife, Jam & Spoon* : £45 - £60 each set
1772 Leaf : *Candle Stick* : £10 - £20
1773 Water Lily : *Cheese Tray & Knife* : £60 - £90
1774 Water Lily : *Cress Dish and Tray* : £70 - £100
1775 Basket : *Handled Flower Basket* : £80 - £120
1776 Water Lily : *Sauce Boat and Tray* : £50 - £80
1777 Water Lily : *Handled Basket* : £90 - £120
1778 Water Lily : *Salad Bowl* : £80 - £120 with 1782
1779 Water Lily : *Candlestick* : £30 - £50
1780 Daffodil : *Candle Holder* : £45 - £60
1781 Water Lily : *3 Lobed Tray* : £60 - £90
1782 Water Lily : *Salad Bowl Servers* : see 1778
1783 Water Lily : *Plate, 9ins, 6ins* : £30 - £50
1784 Water Lily : *Butter or Jam, Knife, Spoon* : £35 - £65
1785 Wedding Cake : *Slipper*
1786 Water Lily : *Morning Tea Set (Tea for two)* : £350 - £500
1787 Water Lily : *Covered Beaker* : £90 - £150

1788 Water Lily : *Jug, 3 sizes* : £60 - £80
1789 Water Lily : *Bon Bon* : £40 - £70
1790 Wedding Cake : *Pillar, 4.5ins*
1791 Wedding Cake : *Slipper, evening style*
1792 Various Patterns : *Ribbed Toy Tea Set*
1793 Wedding Cake : *Boot*
1794 Wedding Cake : *Double Slipper*
1795 Wedding Cake : *Basket*
1796 Wedding Cake : *Slipper & Dove*
1797 Wedding Cake : *Bell*
1798 Water Lily : *3 Way Tray* : £80 - £100
1799 Apple Blossom : *Toyware* : £250 - £500
1800 Wedding Cake : *Corinthian Pillar. 4ins*
1801 Water Lily : *Toast Rack, 5 bar* : £60 - £100
1802 Ornament : *Polar Bear & Santa Claus*
1803 Basket : *Handled Vase/ Basket, 2 sizes* : £50 - £80
1804 Water Lily : *Preserve Pot* : £50 - £90
1805 Water Lily : *Biscuit Barrel* : £150 - £220
1806 Water Lily : *Jug, Juicer & Tray* : £50 - £80
1807 Various Patterns : *Butter, .25lbs, with curved lid*
1808 Crocus : *Mug with Cover* : £140 - £190
1809 Crocus : *Preserve Jar with Lid* : £80 - £120
1810 Basket : *Handled Vase, 2 sizes* : £50 - £80
1811 Tulip : *Candle Holder* : £25 - £40
1812 Ornament : *War Ship*
1813 Ornament : *Nurse*
1814 Ornament : *Militia Man*
1815 Ornament : *Sailor with Kit Bag*
1816 Ornament : *Balloon Barge*
1817 Ornament : *Bridal Pair*
1818 Ornament : *Doll*
1819 Ornament : *Polar Bear*
1820 Water Lily : *Covered Cheese* : £150 - £200

Carlton Ware Patterns and Shapes

1821 Ornament : *Tiny Robin*
1822 Ornament : *Military Bridal Pair*
1823 Ornament : *Santa on Sleigh*
1824 Ornament : *Medium Robin*
1825 Ornament : *Airman*
1826 Ornament : *Anti Aircraft Gun*
1827 Ornament : *Snow Baby Falling*
1828 Ornament : *Snow Baby Sitting*
1829 Ornament : *Snow Baby Lying & Standing*
1830 Ornament : *Cupid Sitting*
1831 Ornament : *Sailor, movable arms*
1832 Crocus : *Posy Holder, movable arms* : £60 - £80
1833 Ornament : *Policeman, movable arms*
1834 Ornament : *Nurse, movable arms*
1835 Ornament : *Soldier, movable arms*
1836 Ornament : *Bridegroom, movable arms*
1837 Ornament : *Old Bill*
1838 Ornament : *Dancing Figure*
1839 Ornament : *Figure*
1840 Ornament : *Figure with Cape*
1841 Ornament : *Airman, movable arms*
1842 Ornament : *Skater*
1843 Ornament : *Santa*
1844 Ornament : *Slipper, as 1796 without Dove*
1845 Ornament : *Hitler, movable head*
1846 Ornament : *Footballer, movable head*
1847 Ornament : *Golfer, movable head*
1848 Cottage : *Church for Windmill series*
1849 Ornament : *Girl with bag*
1850 Ornament : *Dutch Boy & Girl*
1851 Ornament : *Babies on Bear*
1852 Ornament : *Eskimo & Hut*
1853 Incised : *Cigarette Box, incised wood grain*

1854 Ornament : *Bride, movable arms*
1855 Arum Lily : *Candle Holder* : £35 - £55
1856 Incised : *Tray, as 1608 incised*
1857 Ornament : *Old Bill, movable head*
1858 Ornament : *W A A T, movable head*
1859 Ornament : *Fence from Hunting series 757*
1860 Ornament : *Large Horse Shoe*
1861 Ornament : *Small Horse Shoe*
1862 Ornament : *Large Dove*
1863 Ornament : *Small Dove*
1864 Ornament : *21 on key, medium*
1865 Ornament : *Mushroom Bowl*
1866 Dogshead : *Ashtray with Foxhound* : £5 - £10
1867 Margarite : *Flower Vase* : £40 - £60
1868 Lily : *Flower Vase* : £25 - £40
1869 Clover/Shamrock : *Butter* : £20 - £40
1870 Foxglove : *Leaf Tray* : £25 - £35
1871 Incised : *Bowl, Wood incised*
1872 Poppy : *Flower Vase* : £25 - £40
1873 Campion : *Flower Vase* : £40 - £60
1874 Clover/Shamrock : *Shamrock Cress Dish & Stand* : £30 - £50
1875 Foxglove : *Butter Dish* : £25 - £35
1876 Basket : *Salad Bowl* : £80 - £120 with 1944
1877 Various Patterns : *Flower Vase*
1878 Various Patterns : *Barley Bowl*
1879 Foxglove : *Salad Bowl & Servers* : £90 - £150
1880 Various Patterns : *Coffee Cup*
1881 Foxglove : *Preserve Pot and Cover* : £60 - £80
1882 Foxglove : *Flower Jug, Pitcher* : £130 - £180
1883 Foxglove : *Morning Tea Set (Tea for two)* : £300 - £400
1884 Foxglove : *Handled Basket* : £75 - £120

Carlton Ware Patterns and Shapes

1885 Foxglove : *Jug, 3 sizes* : £45 - £95
1886 Foxglove : *Beaker and Cover* : £90 - 120
1887 Foxglove : *Cheese Plate and Knife* : £45 - £75
1888 Foxglove : *Bon-bon dish* : £40 - £60
1889 Incised : *Tray, as 236*
1890 Incised : *Vase, as 1693*
1891 Incised : *Mug, as 1749*
1892 Incised : *Candle Stick, as 1667*
1893 Incised : *Jug, as 1676*
1894 Incised : *Bon Bon, cancelled*
1895 Foxglove : *Toast Rack* : £70 - £90
1896 Foxglove : *Cruet Set* : £70 - £100
1897 Foxglove : *Sauceboat and Stand* : £50 - £80
1898 Foxglove : *Butter & Knife, Jam & Spoon* : £40 - £60 each set
1899 Ornament Stand : *No 1, reserved for Hovells*
1900 Ornament Stand : *No 2, reserved for Hovells*
1901 Ornament Stand : *No 3, reserved for Hovells*
1902 Ornament Stand : *No 4, reserved for Hovells*
1903 Foxglove : *Oval Bowl, 3 sizes* : £20 - £50
1904 Foxglove : *Plate* : £20 - £40
1905 Wedding Cake : *Base*
1906 Wedding Cake : *Base*
1907 Basket : *Covered Beaker* : £100 - £170
1908 Basket : *Single Handled Sandwich Tray* : £40 - £60
1909 Basket : *Bon Bon* : £30 - £50
1910 Basket : *Lemon Squeezer* : £80 - £100
1911 Basket : *Handled Basket* : £100 - £150
1912 Basket : *Preserve Pot and Cover* : £90 - £120
1913 Basket : *Cress Dish & Stand* : £50 - £100
1914 Dogshead : *Ashtray with Alsatian* : £5 - £10
1915 Dogshead : *Ashtray with Spaniel* : £5 - £10
1916 Dogshead : *Ashtray with Terrier* : £5 - £10

1917 Dogshead : *Ashtray with Setter* : £5 - £10
1918 Dogshead : *Ashtray with Bull Dog* : £5 - £10
1919 Various Patterns : *Covered Butter*
1920 Various Patterns : *Covered Butter for South America*
1921 Various Patterns : *Cup & Saucer*
1922 Basket : *Serving Open Bowl* : £40 - £70
1923 Incised : *Vase,, 1694/4 incised*
1924 Incised : *Bon Bon with two handles, as 1623*
1925 Incised : *Vase with three handles each side, as 1695E*
1926 Incised : *Oval Tray, as 1572*
1927 Incised : *Vase, as 1694E*
1928 Incised : *Vase, as 1694C*
1929 Incised : *Comport, as 1609*
1930 Incised : *Bon Bon, as 1633*
1931 Incised : *Bon Bon, as 1629*
1932 Incised : *Vase, as 1692D*
1933 Incised : *Butter, as 1387*
1934 Incised : *Candle Stick, as 1713*
1935 Incised : *Preserve and Stand with Modern Sugar*
1936 Incised : *Ash Tray, as 1683*
1937 Incised : *Square Ash Tray, as 899*
1938 Incised : *Vase, as 1695C*
1939 Incised : *Bon Bon, as 1626*
1940 Incised : *Vase, as 1692H*
1941 Incised : *Vase, as 1693G*
1942 Incised : *Vase, as 1695J*
1943 Cancelled :
1944 Basket : *Salad Bowl Servers* : see 1876
1945 Various Patterns : *Shaving Brush Handle*
1946 Chestnut : *Leaf Tray*
1947 Daisy : *Dish, 9ins* : £40 - £70
1948 Wedding Cake : *Base, as 1906 with holes*

Carlton Ware Patterns and Shapes

1949 Wedding Cake : *Base, as 1948 with holes lower position*
1950 Various Patterns : *Ash Tray*
1951 Daisy : *Bowl, 6ins* : £40 - £70
1952 Water Lily : *Ash Tray* : £20 - £40
1953 Clematis : *Leaf Plate* : £30 - £50
1954 Chestnut : *Supper Tray*
1955 Chestnut : *Preserve*
1956 Chestnut : *Salad & Servers*
1957 Clematis : *Beaker & Cover* : £90 - £120
1958 Clematis : *Oval Bowl, 3 sizes* : £35 - £65
1959 Clematis : *Sauceboat and Stand* : £65 - £90
1960 Clematis : *Tall Cream* : £30 - £50
1961 Clematis : *Supper Tray* : £30 - £50
1962 Clematis : *Cress Dish and Stand* : £70 - £95
1963 Clematis : *Plate, 2 sizes* : £30 - £50
1964 Clematis : *Butter* : £25 - £40
1965 Various Patterns : *Unhandled Beaker, War Office*
1966 Various Patterns : *Worcester Cup & Saucer*
1967 Various Patterns : *Jug, 2 sizes*
1968 Various Patterns : *Opal Cup*
1969 Various Patterns : *Teapot*
1970 Various Patterns : *Unhandled Cup*
1971 Various Patterns : *Opal Cup altered*
1972 Mugs & Jugs, Musical : *Hangsman, Plain Handle* : £40 - £80
1973 Shell : *Bowl* : £30 - £50
1974 Swirl : *Coffee Set*
1975 Primula : *Leaf Tray* : £20 - £40
1976 Shell : *Bon Bon* : £20 - £40
1977 Various Patterns : *Dish, two handled with a Swirl*
1978 Shell : *Flower Vase, No 1, 6ins* : £30 - £50
1979 Shell : *Vase, No 2, 6ins* : £30 - £50

Dr Czes & Yvonne Kosniowski

1980 Shell : *Oval Vase* : £30 - £50
1981 Shell : *Oval Dish* : £30 - £50
1982 Primula : *Butter or Jam* : £30 - £50 with 2052 each set
1983 Various Patterns : *Bowl on 3 feet*
1984 Various Patterns : *Vase*
1985 Various Patterns : *Round Ash Tray, 2 protruding rests in centre*
1986 Various Patterns : *Square Ash Tray, 2 protruding rests in centre*
1987 Various Patterns : *Round Flattened Dish, 6 handles*
1988 Various Patterns : *Diamond Dish, 2 handles*
1989 Various Patterns : *Tobacco Jar*
1990 Various Patterns : *Round Box (Powder)*
1991 Cherry : *Preserve* : £30 - £50
1992 Shell : *Oval Bowl* : £40 - £60
1993 Embossed Flower : *Vase, cancelled*
1994 Shell : *Butter* : £30 - £50
1995 Wallflower : *Vase*
1996 Shell : *Jug, 10ins* : £40 - £70
1997 Shell : *Double Vase* : £40 - £70
1998 Shell : *Sugar* : £30 - £50
1999 Shell : *Cream Jug* : £30 - £50

Carlton Ware Patterns and Shapes

Shapes 2000 - 2499

2000 Delphinium : *Vase*
2001 Various Patterns : *Bon Bon, as 1626*
2002 Various Patterns : *Bon Bon, as 1627*
2003 Various Patterns : *Oval Tray, 3 sizes*
2004 Various Patterns : *Narrow Vase with Folds*
2005 Primula : *Salad Bowl, Fork and Spoon* : £100 - £150
2006 Various Patterns : *Jug*
2007 Various Patterns : *Bowl*
2008 Apple Blossom : *Lamp* : £180 - £250
2009 Various Patterns : *Jug*
2010 Poppy and Daisy : *Round Bowl* : £60 - £90
2011 Various Patterns : *Oval Bon Bon*
2012 Primula : *Cruet* : £100 - £150
2013 Delphinium : *Shallow Bowl*
2014 Delphinium : *Deeper Bowl*
2015 Delphinium : *Conical Bowl*
2016 Delphinium : *Dish*
2017 Delphinium : *Vase*
2018 Delphinium : *Vase*
2019 Delphinium : *Flower Vase, 3 sizes*
2020 Wallflower : *Sugar*
2021 Wallflower : *Cream*
2022 Wallflower : *Preserve*
2023 Wallflower : *Cruet*
2024 Embossed Flower : *Cup & Saucer*
2025 Wallflower : *Butter*

2026 Wallflower : *Large Oblong Tray*
2027 Wallflower : *Small Oblong Tray*
2028 Wallflower : *Salad Set*
2029 Wallflower : *Triple Tray*
2030 Late Buttercup or Buttercup Garland : *Powder Bowl, Covered Bowl* : £40 - £60
2031 Embossed Birds : *Tray, 2 handles*
2032 Wallflower : *Egg Cup*
2033 Poppy and Daisy : *Oval Tray* : £50 - £80
2034 Poppy and Daisy : *Vase, 3 sizes* : £80 - £180
2035 Embossed Flowers : *Vase, 3 feet*
2036 Primula : *Butter, Triangular* : £20 - £35
2037 Various Patterns : *Round Bowl*
2038 Primula : *Morning Tea Set (Tea for two)* : £250 - £400
2039 Primula : *Dish, 4 sizes* : £20 - £40
2040 Primula : *Long Dish* : £25 - £50
2041 Primula : *Preserve and Lid* : £50 - £80
2042 Poppy and Daisy : *Bowl, 3 dips, 3 sizes* : £50 - £140
2043 New Daisy : *Vase, 2 sizes* : £60 - £90
2044 New Daisy : *Oval Tray* : £60 - £90
2045 New Daisy : *Sugar and Cream* : £50 - £70 each
2046 Late Buttercup or Buttercup Garland : *Oval Tray* : £30 - £40
2047 Late Buttercup or Buttercup Garland : *Morning Tea Set (Tea Pot, Sugar, etc)* : £175 - £250
2048 Primula : *Bon-bon dish* : £30 - £50
2049 Primula : *Sauceboat and Stand* : £40 - £60
2050 Various Patterns : *Cocktail Cup, metal foot*
2051 Poppy and Daisy : *Bowl/Plate, 2 sizes* : £50 - £80
2052 Primula : *Jam Spoon & Butter Knife* : £20 - £40, also see 1982
2053 Poppy and Daisy : *Bon-bon dish* : £40 - £70

Carlton Ware Patterns and Shapes

2054 Poppy and Daisy : *Large Footed Bowl, Fluted* : £70 - £100
2055 Late Buttercup or Buttercup Garland : *Tray* : £30 - £50
2056 New Daisy : *Preserve* : £60 - £90
2057 Poppy and Daisy : *Round Vase, 3 sizes* : £60 - £160
2058 Rope : *Lamp Base* : £70 - £100
2059 Various Patterns : *Comport, as 2011 Bon Bon*
2060 Guinness : *Round Ash Tray, 3 rests* : £20 - £40
2061 Late Buttercup or Buttercup Garland : *Jug, 2 sizes* : £40 - £60
2062 Late Buttercup or Buttercup Garland : *Bon-bon dish* : £20 - £30
2063 Late Buttercup or Buttercup Garland : *Comport* : £40 - £60
2064 Late Buttercup or Buttercup Garland : *Salad Bowl* : £40 - £60
2065 Late Buttercup or Buttercup Garland : *Bread & Butter Plate* : £20 - £30
2066 Late Buttercup or Buttercup Garland : *Sauceboat and Stand* : £40 - £60
2067 Various Patterns : *Cocktail Cup with foot*
2068 Late Buttercup or Buttercup Garland : *Bowl* : £40 - £60
2069 Late Buttercup or Buttercup Garland : *Butter and Knife* : £30 - £45
2070 Various Patterns : *Round Ash Tray, 3 rests*
2071 Various Patterns : *Square Ash Tray, 4 rests*
2072 Various Patterns : *Bowl, 3 feet*
2073 Various Patterns : *Vase, 2 handles*
2074 Late Buttercup or Buttercup Garland : *Cruet Set* : £60 - £90
2075 Various Patterns : *Bowl*

2076 Various Patterns : *Bowl, as 2072 with no feet*
2077 Various Patterns : *Salt & Pepper, Modern style modified*
2078 Various Patterns : *Tray, 3 sizes*
2079 Poppy and Daisy : *Lamp Base* : £90 - £120
2080 Various Patterns : *Fluted Lamp*
2081 Various Patterns : *Plain Lamp*
2082 Ornament : *Small Dogs Head from 12ins Vase 130, 1.625ins tall*
2083 Ornament : *Large Dogs Head from vase, 2.25ins tall*
2084 Various Patterns : *Musical Bottle*
2085 Various Patterns : *Comport from Tray 2037 with tall and low foot*
2086 Hydrangea : *Vase* : £70 - £90
2087 Shell : *Tray* : £30 - £50
2088 Various Patterns : *Oval Bowl*
2089 Various Patterns : *Vase with Ringed feet, 4 sizes*
2090 Various Patterns : *Bon Bon*
2091 Various Patterns : *Dessert Plate from 2085 Comport*
2092 Salad Ware : *Butter* : £10 - £20
2093 Salad Ware : *Triangular Plate, 3 sizes* : £20 - £40
2094 Salad Ware : *Salad Bowl & Servers* : £50 - £70
2095 Salad Ware : *Tray, 3 sizes* : £10 - £30
2096 Salad Ware : *Sauceboat and Stand* : £20 - £40
2097 Rope Pattern : *Round Vase*
2098 Various Patterns : *Mug, 4 sizes*
2099 Salad Ware : *Cucumber Tray* : £30 - £40
2100 Rope Pattern : *Tray*
2101 Rope Pattern : *Butter*
2102 Rope Pattern : *Triangular Ash Tray, 3 rests*
2103 Rope Pattern : *Triangular Vase*
2104 Rope Pattern : *Bon Bon*
2105 Rope Pattern : *Cigarette Box Lid*

Carlton Ware Patterns and Shapes

2106 Rope Pattern : *Oval Bowl, 3 sizes*
2107 Rope Pattern : *Tall Oval Bowl*
2108 Wild Rose : *Oval Dish 4ins, 6ins, 8ins, 9ins* : £30 - £60
2109 Cherry : *Oval Plate, 3 sizes* : £20 - £40
2110 Rope Pattern : *Comport*
2111 Rope Pattern : *Round Vase*
2112 Rope Pattern : *Post Bowl*
2113 Various Patterns : *Ash Bowl, 3 rests*
2114 Wild Rose : *Butter & Knife, Jam & Spoon* : £20 - £40 each set
2115 Wild Rose : *Morning Tea Set (Tea Pot, Sugar, etc)* : £250 - £450
2116 Wild Rose : *Oval Bowl, 3 sizes* : £40 - £60
2117 Wild Rose : *Cruet Set* : £70 - £100
2118 Wild Rose : *Toast Rack* : £60 - £90
2119 Wild Rose : *Supper Tray (Long Tray)* : £20 - £50
2120 Wild Rose : *Preserve with cover* : £50 - £80
2121 Wild Rose : *Sauceboat and Stand* : £50 - £80
2122 Wild Rose : *Bon Bon* : £45 - £70
2123 Wild Rose : *Salad Bowl and Servers* : £70 - £90
2124 Wild Rose : *Jug, 2 sizes* : £60 - £100
2125 Lobster : *Plate* : £20 - £30
2126 Cherry : *Oval Bowl, 3 sizes* : £30 - £50
2127 Cherry : *Preserve Jar, Lid & Ladle* : £50 - £80
2128 Cherry : *Tall Cream* : £30 - £60
2129 Cherry : *Sugar* : £30 - £60
2130 Cherry : *Cream* : £30 - £60
2131 Salad Ware : *Cruet* : £40 - £60
2132 Wild Rose : *Mayonnaise Bowl & Ladle* : £70 - £100
2133 Cherry : *Plate, 3 sizes* : £20 - £40
2134 Cherry : *Butter & Knife, Jam & Spoon* : £40 - £70 each

2135 Cherry : *Cruet Set* : £70 - £100
2136 Cherry : *Salad Bowl & Servers* : £80 - £120
2137 Cherry : *Bon Bon* : £30 - £50
2138 Various Patterns : *Combined Ash Tray & Cigarette Holder*
2139 Various Patterns : *Combined Ash Tray & Cigarette Box, Lid without rests*
2140 Various Patterns : *Rectangular Ash Tray, 2 rests*
2141 Various Patterns : *Cigarette Box and double Ash Tray*
2142 Various Patterns : *Triangular Ash Tray, 3 rests*
2143 Various Patterns : *Hexagonal Ash Tray, 3 rests*
2144 Various Patterns : *Cigarette Box, Tray with Lid*
2145 Shell : *Powder Bowl* : £40 - £80
2146 Card Series : *Bridge Butter Pat or Ashtray Set* : £40 - £80
2147 Various Patterns : *Triangular Ash Tray, hollow, 3 rests*
2148 Various Patterns : *Tray* : £40 - £65
2149 Various Patterns : *Square Bowl, 2 sizes*
2150 Various Patterns : *Jug, 3 sizes*
2151 Various Patterns : *Rectangular Ash Tray, 1 rest*
2152 Various Patterns : *Globular Lamp*
2153 Cherry : *Mug* : £30 - £60
2154 Hydrangea : *Vase, Tall, 3 sizes* : £100 - £160
2155 Cherry : *Jug, 2 sizes* : £50 - £80
2156 Leaf : *Tray* : £30 - £40
2157 Various Patterns : *Coffee Set*
2158 Cherry : *Toast Rack* : £30 - £60
2159 Various Patterns : *Round Bowl, 3 sizes* : £20 - £30
2160 Various Patterns : *Bowl as 1387 Butter, 2 sizes*
2161 Hydrangea : *Tray, 3 sizes* : £60 - £120
2162 Various Patterns : *Oval Bowl, 3 sizes*

Carlton Ware Patterns and Shapes

2163 Various Patterns : *Round Bowl, 2 sizes*
2164 Various Patterns : *Bon Bon with Knobs*
2165 Hydrangea : *Flat Bowl, 2 sizes* : £70 - £110
2166 Advertising Ware : *Dewars Jug* : £20 - £40
2167 Hydrangea : *Vase* : £70 - £90
2168 Various Patterns : *Bowl with 2 handles*
2169 Hydrangea : *Bon-bon dish* : £50 - £80
2170 Hydrangea : *Round Bowl* : £110 - £170
2171 Hydrangea : *Wall Vase* : £70 - £110
2172 Hydrangea : *Preserve with Cover* : £80 - £120
2173 Hydrangea : *Sugar & Cream* : £60 - £80 each
2174 Hydrangea : *Oval Bowl, 2 sizes* : £80 - £130
2175 Bell Handle : *Butter*
2176 Hydrangea : *Footed Bowl* : £100 - £140
2177 Bell Handle : *Tray, 3 sizes*
2178 Bell Handle : *Ash Tray, 1 rest*
2179 Bell Handle : *Vase, 2 Bell handles*
2180 Bell Handle : *Cigarette Box*
2181 Bell Handle : *Oval Bowl*
2182 Bell Handle : *Comport*
2183 Bell Handle : *Sugar & Cream*
2184 Various Patterns : *Butter*
2185 Lobster : *Tray, 1 lobster, 3 sizes* : £20 - £30
2186 Lobster : *Salt & Pepper* : £20 - £40
2187 Various Patterns : *Triangular Butter*
2188 Various Patterns : *Butter & Knife*
2189 Various Patterns : *Lamp*
2190 Various Patterns : *Lamp*
2191 Various Patterns : *Vase*
2192 Various Patterns : *Ash Tray, 18 rests*
2193 Fluted : *Vase*
2194 Embossed Flower : *Oval Dish, Flower centre*
2195 Grape : *Round Dish* : £50 - £70

2196 Shell : *Dish* : £20 - £40
2197 Grape : *Round Dish* : £50 - £70
2198 Various Patterns : *Bowl, as 2003 Tray*
2199 Various Patterns : *Double Candle Stick*
2200 Various Patterns : *Plain Biscuit Barrel*
2201 Various Patterns : *Ash Tray, green glaze*
2202 Various Patterns : *Cigarette Box with Ash Tray Lid, green glaze*
2203 Grape : *Two Way Tray* : £50 - £98
2204 Various Patterns : *Vinegar Jar, 4ins*
2205 Various Patterns : *Gondola*
2206 Fluted : *Oval Tray*
2207 Fluted : *Sugar & Cream*
2208 Grape : *Preserve and Stand* : £60 - £90
2209 Hydrangea : *Two way Tray* : £90 - £110
2210 Hydrangea : *Five way Tray* : £120 - £170
2211 Grape : *Jug, 2 sizes* : £50 - £90
2212 Various Patterns : *Vinegar Jar, 3ins*
2213 Various Patterns : *Vinegar Jar, 3.25ins*
2214 Grape : *Three Way Tray, handled* : £70 - £110
2215 Card Series : *Ashbowl, Cube, with Dice indents* : £25 - £40
2216 Various Patterns : *Soup & Stand*
2217 Grape : *Cruet Set* : £120 - £160
2218 Lobster : *Serving Tray, 2 lobsters, 2 sizes* : £30 - £60
2219 Hydrangea : *Three way Tray* : £100 - £130
2220 Grape : *Five Way Tray, handled* : £90 - £130
2221 Grape : *Planter, Oblong Dish, 2 sizes* : £60 - £80
2222 Guinness : *Bridge Ash Tray* : £20 - £40
2223 Various Patterns : *Bon Bon*
2224 Grape : *Cigarette Box, Covered Box* : £60 - £90
2225 Grape : *Mug or Beaker* : £40 - £60
2226 Grape : *Sugar & Cream* : £40 - £60 each

Carlton Ware Patterns and Shapes

2227 Grape : *Toast Rack* : £70 - £100
2228 Grape : *Candlestick* : £40 - £60
2229 Various Patterns : *Swirl Candle Holder*
2230 Lobster : *3 Way Round Tray* : £40 - £70
2231 Lobster : *Egg Tray* : £60 - £80
2232 Lobster : *5 Way Round Tray* : £50 - £80
2233 Various Patterns : *Heart Ash Tray, 3 rests*
2234 Various Patterns : *Heart Ash Tray, 3 rests*
2235 Spiral : *Cigarette Box Cover, use 1398 for base*
2236 Spiral : *Vase, as 125/5*
2237 Spiral : *Round Ash Tray*
2238 Spiral : *Round Bowl, 3 sizes*
2239 Spiral : *Oval Ash Tray*
2240 Spiral : *Bon Bon*
2241 Various Patterns : *Open handle Tray, as 2184 Butter, 3 sizes*
2242 Lobster : *5 Way Round Tray, Low Relief* : £40 - £70
2243 Lobster : *3 Way Round Tray, Low Relief* : £40 - £70
2244 Ribbed : *Cigarette Box*
2245 Ribbed : *Ash Tray*
2246 Various Patterns : *Cigarette Box, as large 2139*
2247 Various Patterns : *Comport, as 2223 Bon Bon*
2248 Various Patterns : *Oval Ash Tray*
2249 Various Patterns : *Rectangular Cigarette Box*
2250 Various Patterns : *Ash Tray*
2251 Various Patterns : *Combined Ash Tray & Cigarette Box*
2252 Various Patterns : *Combined Ash Tray & Cigarette Box*
2253 Grape : *Five Way Tray, unhandled* : £80 - £120
2254 Grape : *Three Way Tray, unhandled* : £60 - £80
2255 Ornament : *Horse Shoe, 1.5ins*
2256 Card Series : *Ashbowl, Cube* : £25 - £40

2257 Poppy : *Plate, 3 sizes* : £40 - £70
2258 Scroll : *Tray, 3 sizes*
2259 Various Patterns : *Lamp base*
2260 Various Patterns : *Oval Vase, 6ins*
2261 Hydrangea : *Wall Vase, Flat Back, 2 sizes* : £80 - £120
2262 Various Patterns : *Five Way Tray*
2263 Poppy : *Jug* : £60 - £90
2264 Hydrangea : *Flat Back Lamp Base* : £90 - £130
2265 Ribbed : *Round Bowl*
2266 Card Series : *Oblong Butter* : £10 - £20
2267 Various Patterns : *Covered vase, Buddha knob*
2268 Grape : *Round Dish, 13ins* : £50 - £70
2269 Grape : *Oval Tray* : £50 - £70
2270 Various Patterns : *Ash Tray*
2271 Various Patterns : *Cigarette Box*
2272 Grape : *Dessert Plate, 5ins* : £30 - £40
2273 Fluted : *Covered vase, Buddha knob*
2274 Various Patterns : *Ashtray*
2275 Clematis : *Basket Tray, one hole* : £35 - £50
2276 Poppy : *3 Way Tray* : £60 - £90
2277 Hazel Nut : *Tray/Dish* : £20 - £40
2278 Poppy : *5 Way Tray* : £100 - £150
2279 Spiral : *Vase, 3 sizes*
2280 Spiral : *Oblong Ash Tray*
2281 Poppy : *Oval Bowl, double poppy, 3 sizes* : £50 - £80
2282 Spiral : *Single Candle Stick*
2283 Spiral : *Double Candle Stick*
2284 Poppy : *Butter & Knife, Jam & Spoon* : £50 - £80 each set
2285 Poppy : *Preserve with lid & spoon* : £70 - £110
2286 Spiral : *Comport, tall & low*
2287 Poppy : *Bon Bon* : £40 - £60

Carlton Ware Patterns and Shapes

2288 Poppy : *Sugar and Cream* : £40 - £70 each
2289 Poppy : *Salad Bowl* : £90 - £130 with 2291
2290 Poppy : *Toast Rack, combination* : £80 - £120
2291 Poppy : *Servers* : see 2289
2292 Poppy : *Tea Pot* : £140 - £200
2293 Poppy : *Cruet* : £100 - £150
2294 Poppy : *Sauceboat & Stand* : £60 - £80
2295 Grape : *Cigarette Box, different to 2224* : £60 - £90
2296 Grape : *Oval Bowl* : £50 - £70
2297 Grape : *Ashtray* : £30 - £50
2298 Guinness : *Glass & Toucan* : £250 - £350
2299 Grape : *Bon Bon* : £40 - £60
2300 Various Patterns : *Lamp, Brookes booked 26 May 1955*
2301 Grape : *Comport* : £50 - £70
2302 Various Patterns : *Lamp, Elliot & Snears booked 20 August 1955*
2303 Grape : *Turned over Bowl, 16 July 1955* : £50 - £70
2304 Grape : *Candlestick* : £40 - £60
2305 Coral : *Vase, 28 July 1955*
2306 Hazel Nut : *Butter or Jam* : £20 - £40 with 2327 each set
2307 Hazel Nut : *Sauce Boat and Stand* : £20 - £40
2308 Guinness : *Kangaroo* : £100 - £150
2309 Hazel Nut : *Salt & Pepper, large* : £15 - £35
2310 Hazel Nut : *Oval Serving Dish, 2 sizes* : £30 - £50
2311 Hazel Nut : *Jug, 3 sizes* : £40 - £80
2312 Fluted : *Bowl*
2313 Hazel Nut : *Salad Bowl* : £50 - £80 with 2321
2314 Various Patterns : *Ash Tray*
2315 Advertising Ware : *Schweppes Ash Tray* : £5 - £10
2316 Hazel Nut : *Oval Bowl, 3 sizes* : £25 - £50
2317 Guinness : *Ostrich* : £100 - £150

Dr Czes & Yvonne Kosniowski

2318 Hazel Nut : *Boomerang Tray, 2 sizes* : £30 - £60
2319 Guinness : *Tortoise* : £100 - £150
2320 Guinness : *Seal* : £100 - £150
2321 Hazel Nut : *Servers* : see 2313
2322 Guinness : *Small Glass & Toucan* : £100 - £150
2323 Advertising Ware : *Kensitas Ash Tray* : £5 - £10
2324 Hazel Nut : *Tea Pot* : £35 - £60
2325 Guinness : *Toucan Lamp, with shade* : £300 - £400
2326 Hazel Nut : *Bon-bon Dish* : £20 - £40
2327 Hazel Nut : *Knife & Spoon* : see 2306
2328 Various Patterns : *Vase*
2329 Various Patterns : *Bowl, 3 conical legs*
2330 Hazel Nut : *Cruet* : £25 - £50
2331 Guinness : *Zoo Keeper* : £100 - £150
2332 Various Patterns : *Vase*
2333 Various Patterns : *Bowl, 3 conical legs*
2334 Various Patterns : *Vase*
2335 Various Patterns : *Vase*
2336 Leaf : *Salad Set with Servers, 2 sizes* : £40 - £70
2337 Coral : *Vase, 27 April 1956*
2338 Various Patterns : *Tray, 3 sizes*
2339 Coral : *Vase*
2340 Various Patterns : *Oval Bowl with flat end, 2 sizes*
2341 Various Patterns : *Vase*
2342 Coral : *Tray, 3 sizes*
2343 Various Patterns : *Footed Bowl*
2344 Coral : *Ash Tray*
2345 Various Patterns : *Oval Tray, panelled edge, 3 sizes*
2346 Leaf : *Sauce Boat & Stand* : £15 - £30
2347 Advertising Ware : *Brandyman* : £60 - £80
2348 Various Patterns : *Triangular Tray*
2349 Various Patterns : *Vase*
2350 Various Patterns : *Pin Tray*

Carlton Ware Patterns and Shapes

2351 Various Patterns : *Vase*
2352 Advertising Ware : *Gilbey Ash Tray, Round, 9 rests* : £5 - £10
2353 Various Patterns : *Ash Tray, 2 sizes*
2354 Various Patterns : *Jug with handle*
2355 Various Patterns : *Bowl, 2 sizes*
2356 Advertising Ware : *Tio Pepe, loose hat*
2357 Hazel Nut : *Television Set (Cup & Tray)* : £40 - £50
2358 Hazel Nut : *Morning Tea Set (Tea for two)* : £120 - £200
2359 Leaf : *Sauce Boat* : £10 - £20
2360 Guinness : *Toucan in flight on Charger* : £100 - £150
2361 Leaf : *Butter & Knife, Jam & Spoon* : £25 - £40 each set
2362 Various Patterns : *Crinkled Bowl*
2363 Leaf : *Long Tray* : £20 - £40
2364 Various Patterns : *Lamp*
2365 Guinness : *Ash Tray, 13 October 1956* : £20 - £40
2366 Leaf : *Turned-over Leaf Bowl, 2 sizes* : £20 - £40
2367 Leaf : *Tray, 4 sizes* : £10 - £30
2368 Leaf : *Two way Tray* : £20 - £40
2369 Leaf : *Cruet Set (Pepper, Salt, Mustard and Frame)* : £30 - £50
2370 Leaf : *Egg Set* : £40 - £60
2371 Leaf : *Covered Cheese* : £40 - £60
2372 Leaf : *Preserve Jar and Saucer* : £30 - £50
2373 Leaf : *Posy Holder* : £20 - £30
2374 Leaf : *Toast Rack* : £25 - £45
2375 Guinness : *Menu Holder, 4 November 1956* : £20 - £40
2376 Leaf : *Handled Basket, 2 sizes* : £15 - £35
2377 Leaf : *Three way Tray* : £25 - £45
2378 Guinness : *Blue Ash Bowl* : £20 - £40

2379 Various Patterns : *Service Plate*
2380 Various Patterns : *Lamp Base*
2381 Leaf : *Morning Tea Set (Tea Pot, Sugar, etc)* : £80 - £150
2382 Leaf : *Salt & Pepper, large* : £10 - £25
2383 Leaf : *Television Set (Tray with cup)* : £15- £25
2384 Various Patterns : *Plain Tray*
2385 Leaf : *Tea Pot, 2 sizes* : £25 - £50
2386 Leaf : *Candlestick* : £10 - £20
2387 Leaf : *Bon Bon* : £10 - £20
2388 Leaf : *Oval Bowl, 3 sizes* : £10 - £40
2389 Leaf : *Pin or Trinket Box* : £10 - £20
2390 Leaf : *Handled Basket* : £15 - £35
2391 Various Patterns : *Wall Lamp*
2392 Various Patterns : *Ash Bowl*
2393 Various Patterns : *Lamp, as 2335*
2394 Windswept : *Tray* : £10 - £20
2395 Windswept : *Jug* : £10 - £20
2396 Windswept : *Preserve and Stand* : £20 - £30
2397 Various Patterns : *Perforated Lamp Base, as 2152*
2398 Guinness : *Drayman (man pulling horse in cart)* : £250 - £350
2399 Guinness : *3 Flying Toucans* : £300 - £400
2400 Novelty : *Pheasant Cruet* : £40 - £70
2401 Guinness : *Drayman Plaque* : £100 - £150
2402 New Daisy : *Lamp, 2043 upside down* : £60 - £90
2403 Windswept : *Cream, Sugar, Cup and Saucer* : £10 - £20 each
2404 Windswept : *5ins Plate* : £10 - £20
2405 Windswept : *Tea Pot, 2 sizes* : £20 - £45
2406 Windswept : *Sauceboat and Stand* : £20 - £35
2407 Windswept : *Toast Rack* : £20 - £30

Carlton Ware Patterns and Shapes

2408 Windswept : *Butter & Knife, Jam & Spoon* : £15 - £25 each set
2409 Windswept : *Ashtray* : £10 - £20
2410 Advertising Ware : *Dunhill Table Lighter*
2411 Windswept : *Two way Tray* : £15 - £25
2412 Advertising Ware : *Gordons Ash Tray, Triangular, 3 rests, open back* : £5 - £10
2413 Advertising Ware : *Gordons Ash Tray, Triangular, 3 rests, open face* : £5 - £10
2414 Windswept : *Cruet Set (Pepper, Salt, Mustard and Frame)* : £20 - £40
2415 Windswept : *Cheese Dish and Stand* : £15 - £30
2416 Windswept : *Cress Dish and Stand* : £25 - £40
2417 Leaf : *Mayonnaise Bowl, Ladle & Stand* : £40 - £60
2418 Novelty : *Cat Ash Tray* : £5 - £10
2419 Pinstripe : *Tall Jug* : £15 - £25
2420 Advertising Ware : *Noilly Prat Wine Pourer*
2421 Guinness : *Toucan Jug* : £100 - £150
2422 Windswept : *Coffee Set (inc 6 C&S)* : £100 - £150
2423 Windswept : *Egg Tray* : £15 - £30
2424 Windswept : *Salad Bowl and Servers* : £25 - £50
2425 Windswept : *Barbecue Set (4 cups on stand) & Crescent Plate (Side Tray)* : £25 - £40 & £15 - £25
2426 Windswept : *Plate, large size* : £10 - £20
2427 Various Patterns : *Hors d'oeuvre Dish*
2428 Pinstripe : *Butter & Knife, Jam & Spoon* : £20 - £40 each set
2429 Pinstripe : *Plate 5ins* : £10 - £20
2430 Pinstripe : *Long Tray* : £20 - £40
2431 Fruit : *Cruet Set (Fruit)* : £30 - £50
2432 Various Patterns : *Bowl*
2433 Haig : *Ash Tray, as 1381, no rests, oval inside* : £5 - £10

Dr Czes & Yvonne Kosniowski

2434 Haig : *Ash Tray, as 1381, 2 rests, oval inside* : £5 - £10
2435 Pinstripe : *Cruet Set (Pepper, Salt, Mustard and Frame)* : £30 - £50
2436 Various Patterns : *Handled Round Jug*
2437 Haig : *Oval Jug* : £10 - £15
2438 Windswept : *Soup Jug or Hot Water Jug* : £20 - £40
2439 Pinstripe : *Tray, 2 sizes* : £15 - £30
2440 Novelty : *Modern Cruet* : £25 - £45
2441 Novelty : *Mushroom Cruet* : £50 - £75 (£75 - £100 with spots)
2442 Linen & Other : *Vase* : £20 - £30
2443 Linen & Other : *Coffee Pot, Cup & Saucer, Sugar & Cream* : £30 - £50, £20 - £40, £30 - £50
2444 Linen & Other : *Butter* : £10 - £20
2445 Linen & Other : *Triangular Plate, 3 sizes* : £20 - £60
2446 Linen & Other : *Bowl, 2 sizes* : £20 - £40
2447 Linen & Other : *Tall Narrow Vase* : £20 - £40
2448 Linen & Other : *Wall Vase* : £20 - £40
2449 Linen & Other : *Jug* : £30 - £50
2450 Linen & Other : *Candle Holders* : £25 - £35
2451 Pinstripe : *Morning Tea Set (Tea for two)* : £80 - £150
2452 Pinstripe : *Preserve and Stand* : £30 - £50
2453 Pinstripe : *Two way Tray* : £20 - £35
2454 Pinstripe : *Three way Tray* : £25 - £45
2455 Pinstripe : *Sauceboat and Stand* : £20 - £30
2456 Pinstripe : *Tall Cup with Saucer* : £15 - £25
2457 Pinstripe : *Pin Tray* : £10 - £20
2458 Pinstripe : *Television Set (Tray with cup)* : £20 - £30
2459 Advertising Ware : *Babycham* : £50 - £100
2460 Advertising Ware : *Boothe Ash Tray, 6 rests* : £5 - £10

Carlton Ware Patterns and Shapes

2461 Pinstripe : *Cheese Dish and Stand* : £40 - £60
2462 Pinstripe : *Toast Rack* : £30 - £50
2463 Guinness : *Miniature Glass* : £40 - £60
2464 Pinstripe : *Tea Pot* : £25 - £50
2465 Pinstripe : *Egg Set* : £40 - £60
2466 Pinstripe : *Salad Set - Bowl with Servers* : £40 - £60
2467 Pinstripe : *Salt & Pepper, large* : £10 - £25
2468 Wood : *Tray*
2469 Wood : *Jug*
2470 Langouste : *Serving Dish, 2 lobsters, 2 sizes* : £30 - £60
2471 Langouste : *5 Way Round Tray* : £50 - £80
2472 Advertising Ware : *Babycham, no grass* : £50 - £100
2473 Langouste : *Butter, no lobster* : £10 - £20
2474 Langouste : *Tray, 1 lobster, 3 sizes* : £20 - £50
2475 Langouste : *3 Way Round Tray* : £40 - £70
2476 Langouste : *Mayonnaise Set with stand & ladle* : £30 - £60
2477 Advertising Ware : *Bullman Morris* : £100 - £200
2478 Advertising Ware : *Babycham, for Ash Tray* : £50 - £80
2479 Novelty : *Childs Drawing Butter*
2480 Convolvulus : *Tray, 3 sizes* : £25 - £35
2481 Langouste : *Salad Set with servers* : £60 - £80
2482 Wood : *Carved Wood Tray*
2483 Tulip : *Tray* : £30 - £40
2484 Novelty : *Childs Drawing Tray*
2485 Convolvulus : *Jug* : £30 - £50
2486 Novelty : *Childs Drawing Cruet Set (houses from drawing)*
2487 Wood : *Tea Pot*
2488 Convolvulus : *Preserve Pot and Tray* : £30 - £50

2489 Convolvulus : *Morning Tea Set (Tea for two)* : £90 - £150
2490 Convolvulus : *Salt & Pepper* : £25 - £40
2491 Convolvulus : *Butter & Knife, Jam & Spoon* : £25 - £40
2492 Langouste : *Plate* : £20 - £30
2493 Langouste : *Salt & Pepper* : £20 - £40
2494 Convolvulus : *Two way Tray* : £25 - £35
2495 Convolvulus : *Cruet* : £30 - £50
2496 Convolvulus : *Tray, short width, 2 sizes* : £20 - £30
2497 Convolvulus : *Vinegar and Oil Pots (with stoppers)* : £25 - £40
2498 Convolvulus : *Three way Tray* : £25 - £35
2499 Convolvulus : *Salad Bowl and Servers* : £50 - £80

Shapes 2500 - 2999

2500 Convolvulus : *Covered Cheese* : £40 - £60
2501 Convolvulus : *Bowl, 2 sizes* : £30 - £40
2502 Various Patterns : *Preserve & Stand*
2503 Novelty : *Squirrel Cruet* : £40 - £70
2504 Convolvulus : *Tea Pot, 2 sizes* : £30 - £60
2505 Haig : *Round Ash Tray with triangular top* : £5 - £10
2506 Haig : *Square Ash Tray* : £5 - £10
2507 Convolvulus : *Tray, long width* : £30 - £40
2508 Convolvulus : *Sauceboat and Tray* : £25 - £40
2509 Convolvulus : *Lamp Base* : £35 - £50
2510 Convolvulus : *Soup Cup* : £10 - £20
2511 Convolvulus : *Coffee Pot* : £40 - £70
2512 Convolvulus : *Mayonnaise, Ladle and Tray* : £40 - £70
2513 Convolvulus : *Toast Rack* : £25 - £45
2514 Fruit : *Apple Preserve and Stand* : £20 - £35
2515 Magnolia : *Preserve Pot and Tray* : £30 - £50
2516 Various Patterns : *Button*
2517 Embossed Flower : *Button*
2518 Convolvulus : *Vase, medium* : £20 - £30
2519 Convolvulus : *Vase, tall* : £25 - £35
2520 Convolvulus : *Vase, squat* : £20 - £30
2521 Convolvulus : *Bowl* : £20 - £30
2522 Various Patterns : *Lighter Holder*
2523 Convolvulus : *Vase, tall* : £25 - £35
2524 Convolvulus : *Double Vase, crescent* : £25 - £40
2525 Aladdins Lamp : *Lighter Holder* : £20 - £50
2526 Fruit : *Pear Butter* : £10 - £20
2527 Fruit : *Apple Butter* : £10 - £20

2528 Fruit : *Lemon Butter* : £10 - £20
2529 Fruit : *Pineapple Butter* : £10 - £20
2530 Fruit : *Knife or Spoon for Butter Set* : £15 - £25 each
2531 Magnolia : *Oval Plate, 2 sizes* : £20 - £30
2532 Various Patterns : *Plate, 5ins*
2533 Orchid : *Tray, large size* : £30 - £50
2534 Novelty : *Sampan Cruet* : £40 - £70
2535 Novelty : *Mug, Embossed Figure & Thistle*
2536 Novelty : *Sir Walter Raleigh Lighter Holder*
2537 Convolvulus : *Hot Water Pot* : £35 - £60
2538 Shelf : *Preserve & Stand*
2539 Ornament : *Zulu*
2540 Ornament : *Dutchman*
2541 Ornament : *Cossack*
2542 Ornament : *Spaniard*
2543 Ornament : *Scotsman*
2544 Shelf : *Cruet Set* : £30 - £50
2545 Shelf : *Oval Tray*
2546 Langouste : *Butter, with lobster* : £15 - £25
2547 Various Patterns : *Tray*
2548 Various Patterns : *Round Trinket Box, 2 sizes*
2549 Various Patterns : *Rectangular Cigarette Box*
2550 Advertising Ware : *Martell Ash Bowl* : £5 - £10
2551 Various Patterns : *Pin Tray*
2552 Various Patterns : *Candle Stick*
2553 Various Patterns : *Specimen Vase, 2 sizes*
2554 Various Patterns : *Specimen Vase, 3 sizes*
2555 Various Patterns : *Specimen Vase, 3 sizes*
2556 Guinness : *Salt & Pepper* : £50 - £80
2557 Advertising Ware : *Colibri Lighter Holder*
2558 Magnolia : *Butter & Knife, Jam & Spoon* : £25 - £40 each set
2559 Magnolia : *Double Candlestick* : £15 - £30

Carlton Ware Patterns and Shapes

2560 Magnolia : *Jug, 1 pint* : £15 - £30
2561 Magnolia : *Pin Box, Covered* : £20 - £30
2562 Magnolia : *Covered Bon Bon, Trinket Box* : £20 - £30
2563 Magnolia : *Single Candlestick* : £10 - £25
2564 Magnolia : *Long Tray* : £25 - £35
2565 Various Patterns : *Single Candlestick*
2566 Guinness : *Toucan Wall Plaque* : £100 - £150
2567 Various Patterns : *Double Candlestick*
2568 Various Patterns : *Triple Candlestick*
2569 Novelty : *Motor Boat Lighter Holder*
2570 Advertising Ware : *Carreras Ash Tray* : £5 - £10
2571 Magnolia : *Covered Cheese* : £50 - £80
2572 Novelty : *Shell Cruet* : £30 - £50
2573 Various Patterns : *Octagonal Ash Tray*
2574 Orchid : *Flower Jug* : £65 - £90
2575 Orchid : *Cigarette Box* : £45 - £70
2576 Orchid : *Trinket Box with legs, including lid* : £45 - £70
2577 Orchid : *Ashtray* : £25 - £40
2578 Orchid : *Bud Vase (no handle)* : £50 - £80
2579 Orchid : *Oval Bowl* : £25 - £40
2580 Orchid : *Vase, Squat* : £50 - £80
2581 Various Patterns : *Octagonal Ash Tray, open top*
2582 Orchid : *Tray, 2 sizes* : £25 - £40
2583 Advertising Ware : *Flowers Brewmaster Model* : £50 - £75
2584 Guinness : *Mug, half pint* : £50 - £80
2585 Orchid : *Bon Bon Dish* : £40 - £60
2586 Orchid : *Low Vase* : £40 - £60
2587 Advertising Ware : *Flowers Shakespeare Ash Bowl, figure fluxed on* : £20 - £30
2588 Trinket Set : *Tall Jug*
2589 Trinket Set : *Long Tray*

2590 Trinket Set : *Bowl, 2 sizes*
2591 Fruit : *Pear Preserve with Apple Preserve Stand* : £20 - £35
2592 Magnolia : *Cup & Saucer, Sugar, Cream* : £20 - £30 each
2593 Magnolia : *Two way Tray* : £25 - £35
2594 Magnolia : *Double Butter* : £20 - £30
2595 Magnolia : *Salad Bowl and Servers* : £60 - £80
2596 Magnolia : *Salt & Pepper* : £25 - £40
2597 Magnolia : *Sugar Shaker* : £25 - £40
2598 Magnolia : *Dessert Bowl* : £20 - £30
2599 Magnolia : *Tea Pot, 2 sizes* : £90 - £120
2600 Advertising Ware : *Williams & Humbert Sherry Girl*
2601 Magnolia : *Three way Tray* : £25 - £40
2602 Guinness : *Waterford Tankard* : £30 - £50
2603 Trinket Set : *Lamp Base*
2604 Magnolia : *Coffee Pot, Cup & Saucer* : £80 - £100, £20 - £30
2605 Magnolia : *Tray, 3 sizes* : £20 - £30
2606 Advertising Ware : *Berhard & Mayes Lighter Holder*
2607 Magnolia : *Bowl, 2 sizes* : £15 - £30
2608 Various Patterns : *Preserve*
2609 Convolvulus : *Bud Vase, from large Salt* : £20 - £30
2610 Magnolia : *Hot Milk Jug* : £80 - £100
2611 Magnolia : *Sauceboat and Tray* : £30 - £60
2612 Magnolia : *Soup Jug* : £80 - £100
2613 Magnolia : *Egg Set* : £40 - £60
2614 Advertising Ware : *Flowers Shakespeare Figure, 10ins* : £50 - £75
2615 Magnolia : *Handled Soup Cup* : £15 - £30
2616 Magnolia : *Cruet* : £40 - £55
2617 Magnolia : *Oil and Vinegar* : £30 - £50
2618 Magnolia : *Mayonnaise, Ladle and Tray* : £30 - £60

Carlton Ware Patterns and Shapes

2619 Guinness : *Lamp Base, as 1640* : £30 - £50
2620 Magnolia : *Toast Rack* : £45 - £65
2621 Magnolia : *Vase, Tall* : £40 - £60
2622 Magnolia : *Vase, Squat* : £30 - £50
2623 Magnolia : *Vase, Bud* : £30 - £50
2624 Magnolia : *Vase, Open Top* : £30 - £50
2625 Magnolia : *Covered Butter, rectangular* : £40 - £60
2626 Magnolia : *Large Stand for Oil etc* : £20 - £30
2627 Guinness : *Salt, Pepper, Mustard & Spoon* : £60 - £90
2628 Honeysuckle : *Long Tray, 13.75 ins*
2629 Honeysuckle : *Jug*
2630 Fruit : *Vegetable Cruet Set* : £30 - £50
2631 Various Patterns : *Square Ash Bowl*
2632 Guinness : *Candlestick* : £40 - £60
2633 Honeysuckle : *Preserve & Stand*
2634 Honeysuckle : *Butter*
2635 Fruit : *Tomato Cruet Set* : £30 - £50
2636 Novelty : *Cottage Light Holder*
2637 Guinness : *Penguin Lamp, with shade* : £300 - £500
2638 Various Patterns : *Round Ash Bowl, 7ins*
2639 Floral Spray : *Preserve & Stand* : £20 - £30
2639 Orbit : *Preserve & Stand* : £30 - £50
2640 Various Patterns : *Ash Tray, 3 rests*
2641 Floral Spray : *Butter & Knife, Jam & Spoon* : £20 - £30 each
2641 Orbit : *Butter & Knife, Jam & Spoon* : £30 - £40 each
2642 Floral Spray : *Plate, 3 sizes* : £10 - £30
2642 Orbit : *Plate, 3 sizes* : £20 - £50
2643 Guinness : *Bowl* : £30 - £50
2644 Floral Spray : *Coffee Pot, Cup & Saucer* : £50 - £90
2644 Orbit : *Coffee Pot, Cup & Saucer* : £95 - £170
2645 Carlton Village : *Inn* : £40 - £60

2646 Carlton Village : *Smithy* : £40 - £60
2647 Carlton Village : *Water Mill* : £40 - £60
2648 Carlton Village : *Wind Mill* : £150 - £300
2649 Carlton Village : *Church* : £40 - £60
2650 Carlton Village : *Cottage* : £40 - £60
2651 Carlton Village : *Butter Market* : £100 - £170
2652 Carlton Village : *Shop* : £40 - £60
2653 Carlton Village : *Hall* : £40 - £60
2654 Floral Spray : *Cruet Set (Frame is Magnolia)* : £30 - £50
2654 Orbit : *Cruet Set (Frame is Magnolia)* : £50 - £80
2655 Floral Spray : *Sauce Boat (Stand is 2629)* : £20 - £30
2655 Orbit : *Sauce Boat (Stand is 2629)* : £30 - £50
2656 Floral Spray : *Mayonnaise Bowl & Ladle (Stand is 2629)* : £30 - £40
2656 Orbit : *Mayonnaise Bowl & Ladle (Stand is 2629)* : £40 - £60
2657 Floral Spray : *Egg Frame (Cups are Magnolia)* : £30 - £40
2657 Orbit : *Egg Frame (Cups are Magnolia)* : £40 - £60
2658 Floral Spray : *Salad Bowl & Servers* : £30 - £40
2658 Orbit : *Salad Bowl & Servers* : £40 - £60
2659 Floral Spray : *Tray, Triangular, 3 sizes* : £15 - £30
2659 Orbit : *Tray, Triangular, 3 sizes* : £25 - £55
2660 Haig : *Triangular Ash Tray, 1 rest* : £5 - £10
2661 Fruit : *Apple Salt and Pepper* : £20 - £30
2662 Fruit : *Pear Salt and Pepper* : £20 - £30
2663 Guinness : *Sea Lion Lamp Base & Revolving Shade* : £400 - £600
2664 Floral Spray : *Cheese Dish & Stand* : £25 - £45
2664 Orbit : *Cheese Dish & Stand* : £45 - £65
2665 Floral Spray : *Long Tray, Elongated* : £20 - £30
2665 Orbit : *Long Tray, Elongated* : £30 - £40

Carlton Ware Patterns and Shapes

2666 Floral Spray : *Sugar, Cream, Tea Cup & Saucer* : £10 - £20 each
2666 Orbit : *Sugar, Cream, Tea Cup & Saucer* : £25 - £35 each
2667 Floral Spray : *Oil & Vinegar* : £20 - £30
2667 Orbit : *Oil & Vinegar* : £30 - £50
2668 Floral Spray : *Two way Tray* : £20 - £35
2668 Orbit : *Two way Tray* : £30 - £50
2669 Floral Spray : *Three way Tray* : £20 - £35
2669 Orbit : *Three way Tray* : £30 - £50
2670 Floral Spray : *Soup Jug* : £30 - £50
2670 Orbit : *Soup Jug* : £50 - £70
2671 Floral Spray : *Double Butter* : £10 - £20
2671 Orbit : *Double Butter* : £20 - £30
2672 Floral Spray : *Salt & Pepper, large* : £20 - £30
2672 Orbit : *Salt & Pepper, large* : £35 - £60
2673 Advertising Ware : *Petlick Ash Tray* : £5 - £10
2674 Floral Spray : *Individual Fruit* : £10 - £20
2674 Orbit : *Individual Fruit* : £20 - £30
2675 Floral Spray : *Sugar Shaker* : £20 - £30
2675 Orbit : *Sugar Shaker* : £40 - £60
2676 Floral Spray : *Jug, 2 sizes* : £20 - £40
2676 Orbit : *Jug, 2 sizes* : £40 - £60
2677 Floral Spray : *Bowl, 2 sizes* : £10 - £25
2677 Orbit : *Bowl, 2 sizes* : £20 - £35
2678 Floral Spray : *Soup Cup & Barbecue Tray* : £20 - £30
2678 Orbit : *Soup Cup & Barbecue Tray* : £30 - £45
2679 Floral Spray : *Tea Pot, 2 sizes* : £40 - £70
2679 Orbit : *Tea Pot, 2 sizes* : £50 - £80
2680 Floral Spray : *Hot Water Jug or Small Coffee Pot* : £30 - £50
2680 Orbit : *Hot Water Jug or Small Coffee Pot* : £50 - £70

2681 Floral Spray : *Covered Butter* : £20 - £30
2681 Orbit : *Covered Butter* : £40 - £65
2682 Floral Spray : *Five way Tray* : £20 - £35
2682 Orbit : *Five way Tray* : £30 - £50
2683 Floral Spray : *Vegetable Dish* : £20 - £35
2683 Orbit : *Vegetable Dish* : £30 - £45
2684 Floral Spray : *Powder Bowl* : £20 - £35
2684 Orbit : *Powder Bowl* : £30 - £50
2685 Floral Spray : *Salt, Pepper & Stand, small* : £20 - £30
2685 Orbit : *Salt, Pepper & Stand, small* : £35 - £60
2686 Floral Spray : *Candlestick* : £15 - £30
2686 Orbit : *Candlestick* : £25 - £45
2687 Floral Spray : *Divided Bowl* : £15 - £30
2687 Orbit : *Divided Bowl* : £25 - £35
2688 Floral Spray : *Toast Rack* : £20 - £35
2688 Orbit : *Toast Rack* : £30 - £50
2689 Guinness : *Flower Pot* : £30 - £50
2690 Guinness : *Cheese Containers, 2 sizes* : £45 - £80
2691 Various Patterns : *Vase, large & small*
2692 Various Patterns : *Bowl*
2693 Advertising Ware : *Craven A Ash Bowl* : £5 - £10
2694 Various Patterns : *Vase*
2695 Various Patterns : *Lamp Base, as 2691*
2696 Various Patterns : *Bon Bon*
2697 Various Patterns : *Bud vase, 8ins*
2698 Various Patterns : *Round Cigarette Box*
2699 Various Patterns : *Ash Tray*
2700 Tapestry & Daisy Chain : *Tray* : £10 - £20
2701 Various Patterns : *Covered Vase*
2702 Advertising Ware : *Mackeson Ash Tray* : £5 - £10
2703 Guinness : *Pickle Jar* : £30 - £50
2704 Guinness : *Store Jar* : £30 - £50
2705 Guinness : *Miniature Penguin* : £100 - £150

Carlton Ware Patterns and Shapes

2706 Advertising Ware : *Flowers Ash Bowl* : £5 - £10
2707 Tapestry & Daisy Chain : *Preserve, Cover & Stand* : £20 - £30
2708 Various Patterns : *Gold Border Lighter Holder*
2709 Guinness : *Vase* : £30 - £50
2710 Tapestry & Daisy Chain : *Coffee Pot, Cup & Saucer* : £20 - £30, £10 - £20
2711 Tapestry & Daisy Chain : *Sugar Shaker* : £20 - £30
2712 Tapestry & Daisy Chain : *Cruet* : £25 - £40
2713 Tapestry & Daisy Chain : *Long Tray* : £10 - £20
2714 Tapestry & Daisy Chain : *Round Plate, 3 sizes* : £10 - £30
2715 Tapestry & Daisy Chain : *Two way Tray* : £10 - £20
2716 Tapestry & Daisy Chain : *Three way Tray* : £15 - £25
2717 Tapestry & Daisy Chain : *Double Butter* : £10 - £20
2718 Tapestry & Daisy Chain : *Cheese & Stand* : £20 - £30
2719 Tapestry & Daisy Chain : *Vegetable Dish* : £10 - £20
2720 Guinness : *Hors d'oeuvres, set of 4* : £30 - £50
2721 Tapestry & Daisy Chain : *Five way Tray* : £15 - £25
2722 Guinness : *Crowson Cheese Jar* : £30 - £50
2723 Advertising Ware : *Square Vase* : £5 - £10
2724 Tapestry & Daisy Chain : *Butter & Knife, Jam & Spoon* : £20 - £30 each set
2725 Tapestry & Daisy Chain : *Mayonnaise Bowl, Stand & Ladle* : £20 - £30
2726 Tapestry & Daisy Chain : *Oil & Vinegar* : £20 - £30
2727 Advertising Ware : *Ash Tray* : £5 - £10
2728 Guinness : *Ash Tray* : £20 - £40
2729 Tapestry & Daisy Chain : *Platters, 3 sizes* : £10 - £20
2730 Tapestry & Daisy Chain : *Salad Bowl & Servers* : £20 - £30

2731 Tapestry & Daisy Chain : *Tea Pot, 2 sizes, Cup & Saucer, Sugar, Cream* : £20 - £40 TP, £10 - £20 others each
2732 Tapestry & Daisy Chain : *Salt & Pepper, large* : £20 - £30
2733 Tapestry & Daisy Chain : *Oval Bowl, 2 sizes* : £10 - £25
2734 Tapestry & Daisy Chain : *Individual Fruit* : £10 - £20
2735 Advertising Ware : *Schweppes Cricketers*
2736 Advertising Ware : *Schweppes Golfer*
2737 Tapestry & Daisy Chain : *Soup Cup* : £10 - £20
2738 Tapestry & Daisy Chain : *Covered Bon Bon* : £15 - £25
2739 Advertising Ware : *Schweppes Ascot*
2740 Advertising Ware : *Schweppes Sculptor*
2741 Advertising Ware : *Schweppes Skier*
2742 Tapestry & Daisy Chain : *Sauce Boat & Stand* : £15 - £25
2743 Tapestry & Daisy Chain : *Hot Milk Jug* : £20 - £30
2744 Tapestry & Daisy Chain : *Jug* : £20 - £30
2745 Tapestry & Daisy Chain : *Salt, Pepper & Stand* : £15 - £25
2746 Tapestry & Daisy Chain : *Egg Frame* : £20 - £30
2747 Tapestry & Daisy Chain : *Divided Bowl* : £10 - £20
2748 Tapestry & Daisy Chain : *Covered Butter* : £15 - £25
2749 Tapestry & Daisy Chain : *Toast Rack* : £20 - £30
2750 Guinness : *Keg Harp Ash Bowl* : £20 - £40
2751 Guinness : *Square Ash Tray* : £20 - £40
2752 Guinness : *Miniature Toucan* : £50 - £80
2753 Various Patterns : *Vase*
2754 Tapestry & Daisy Chain : *Sugar, small size* : £10 - £20

Carlton Ware Patterns and Shapes

2755 Advertising Ware : *Johnson Mathey Ash Tray* : £5 - £10
2756 Guinness : *Dish* : £20 - £40
2757 Guinness : *Inn Sign Vase* : £45 - £80
2758 Guinness : *Inn Sign Vase* : £45 - £80
2759 Guinness : *Horse Drawn Bus Ash Tray* : £50 - £80
2760 Guinness : *Continental Ash Bowl* : £30 - £50
2761 Novelty : *Candles & Snuffer Cruet*
2762 Novelty : *Chessman Cruet*
2763 Novelty : *Onion Preserve Pot with Face* : £10 - £20
2764 Novelty : *Lantern Cruet*
2765 Guinness : *Cube Cruet* : £30 - £50
2766 Novelty : *Owl & Pussycat Cruet* : £15 - £25
2767 Guinness : *Pudding Bowl* : £30 - £50
2768 Guinness : *Antique Plate* : £30 - £50
2769 Fruit : *Banana Split Tray* : £10 - £20
2770 Guinness : *Antique Bottle* : £30 - £50
2771 Fruit : *Apple Individual Preserve* : £15 - £25
2772 Fruit : *Lemon Individual Fruit Dish* : £10 - £20
2773 Fruit : *Apple Salad Bowl and Servers* : £30 - £50
2774 Fruit : *Banana Long Tray* : £15 - £25
2775 Fruit : *Pear Egg Frame and Apple Egg Frame* : £40 - £60
2776 Fruit : *Range Centre Piece* : £35 - £55
2777 Fruit : *Knob for covered Butter* : £20 - £35
2778 Fruit : *Apple and Pear Three Way Tray* : £25 - £40
2779 Fruit : *Banana Salt and Pepper Stand* : £20 - £30
2780 Fruit : *Banana Two Way Tray* : £15 - £25
2781 Fruit : *Lemon Cream or Sauceboat* : £15 - £25
2782 Fruit : *Combination Toast Rack, Pear* : £60 - £80
2783 Fruit : *Lemon Individual Preserve* : £15 - £25
2784 Fruit : *Individual Apple and Lemon Preserve Stand* : £10 - £20

2785 Various Patterns : *Jiggered Dishes, 3 sizes*
2786 Various Patterns : *Oval Dish, 4.75ins*
2787 Various Patterns : *Tray*
2788 Various Patterns : *Jiggered Fluted Round Dish*
2789 Novelty : *Mouse covered Cheese Dish*
2790 Novelty : *Cow covered Butter*
2791 Various Patterns : *Gold Scroll Cigarette Box, round*
2792 Novelty : *Squirrel Acorn Preserve* : £40 - £70
2793 Guinness : *Double Tray* : £30 - £50
2794 Athena : *Salt, Pepper* : £15 - £25 with 2796
2795 Athena : *Egg Set* : £20 - £30
2796 Athena : *Salt & Pepper Stand* : see 2794
2797 Various Patterns : *Cup*
2798 Bamboo : *Coffee Pot*
2799 Bamboo : *Two way Tray*
2800 Athena : *Covered Butter* : £15 - £25
2801 Athena : *Long Tray* : £10 - £20
2802 Athena : *Butter* : £10 - £20
2803 Athena : *Vinegar Jug* : £15 - £25
2804 Skye : *Coffee Pot, Coffee Mug* : £20 - £30, £10 - £15
2805 Athena : *Preserve & Stand* : £15 - £25
2806 Athena : *Coffee Mug* : £10 - £20
2807 Athena : *Cheese* : £15 - £25
2808 Athena : *Coffee Pot, Cup & Saucer, Cream, Sugar* : £15 - £25 CP, £10 - £20 others each
2809 Athena : *Hot Milk Jug* : £15 - £25
2810 Athena : *Bowl, 2 sizes* : £10 - £20
2811 Athena : *Tray, 2 sizes* : £10 - £20
2812 Athena : *Toast Rack* : £15 - £25
2813 Skye : *Long Rectangular Tray* : £10 - £15
2814 Skye : *Circular Dish* : £10 - £15
2815 Persian : *Coffee Pot*
2816 Persian : *Coffee Cup & Saucer*

Carlton Ware Patterns and Shapes

2817 Persian : *Tea Pot*
2818 Persian : *Preserve*
2819 Persian : *Hot Water Jug*
2820 Persian : *Cream & Sauce Boat*
2821 Persian : *Plate, 5ins*
2822 Military Figures : *Royal Hussar* : £90 - £140
2823 Persian : *Sugar*
2824 Military Figures : *Royal Horse Guard* : £90 - £140
2825 Persian : *Long Tray*
2826 Persian : *Tray*
2827 Persian : *Cruet Set (Salt, Pepper, Mustard, Frame)*
2828 Persian : *Covered Butter*
2829 Persian : *Salt & Pepper Stand*
2830 Military Figures : *12th Royal Lancers* : £90 - £140
2831 Persian : *Egg Cup Frame*
2832 Persian : *Individual Butter*
2833 Persian : *Large Plate*
2834 Persian : *Oil/Vinegar Bottle*
2835 Military Figures : *Coldstream Guard* : £90 - £140
2836 Athena : *Tea Pot* : £15 - £25
2837 Athena : *Plate, 5ins* : £10 - £20
2838 Various Patterns : *Coffee Percolator*
2839 Various Patterns : *Cube Lighter Base*
2840 Various Patterns : *Low Square Cigarette Box*
2841 Various Patterns : *Tall Square Cigarette Box*
2842 Various Patterns : *Small Square Ash Tray, 4 rests*
2843 Various Patterns : *Large Square Ash Tray, 4 rests*
2844 Various Patterns : *Tea Pot Percolator*
2845 Novelty : *Monk Cruet Set*
2846 Skye : *Square Tray, small* : £10 - £15
2847 Skye : *Three way Tray, oblong* : £10 - £15
2848 Novelty : *Elephant Cruet set*
2849 Skye : *Five way Tray, round* : £10 - £15

2850 Skye : *Television Set (with cup)* : £15 - £20
2851 Bird : *Sweet Tray*
2852 Skye : *Two way Tray, oblong* : £10 - £15
2853 Skye : *Triangular Tray* : £10 - £15
2854 Skye : *Coffee Jug* : £20 - £30
2855 Bird : *Sweet Tray*
2856 Skye : *Butter* : £5 - £10
2857 Skye : *Salt & Pepper* : £10 - £15
2858 Novelty : *Elephant Salt & Pepper Stand*
2859 Bird : *Egg Set (Salt, Pepper, Egg Cup, Frame)*
2860 Bird : *Pepper, Salt & Stand*
2861 Military Figures : *Beefeater Yeoman* : £50 - £80
2862 Advertising Ware : *Ash Bowl, Large Size, Mackesons* : £5 - £10
2863 Novelty : *Monk Salt & Pepper Stand*
2864 Various Patterns : *Beaker*
2865 Bird : *Tray*
2866 Bird : *Tray*
2867 Warwick : *Urn, large*
2868 Various Patterns : *Coffee Percolator*
2869 Advertising Ware : *Booths Ash Tray* : £5 - £10
2870 Advertising Ware : *Colibri Lighter Base*
2871 Various Patterns : *Coffee Percolator*
2872 Vine or Canterbury : *Coffee Pot, Cup & Saucer, Cream, Sugar* : £25 - £40 CP, £10 - £15 others each
2873 Warwick : *Jardiniere*
2874 Warwick : *Rose Bowl*
2875 Warwick : *Urn, medium*
2876 Warwick : *Urn, small*
2877 Warwick : *Jardiniere, small*
2878 Vine or Canterbury : *Tea Cup* : £15 - £20
2879 Haig : *Ice Jug* : £10 - £15
2880 Oslo : *Coffee Set* : £75 - £100

Carlton Ware Patterns and Shapes

2881 Vine or Canterbury : *Cruet* : £20 - £30
2882 Vine or Canterbury : *Egg Set* : £10 - £15
2883 Oslo : *Tea Cup* : £15 - £20
2884 Vine or Canterbury : *Plate, 5ins* : £10 - £15
2885 Vine or Canterbury : *Three way Tray* : £10 - £15
2886 Haig : *Ash Bowl* : £5 - £10
2887 Vine or Canterbury : *Long Tray* : £10 - £15
2888 Skye : *Cream* : £10 - £15
2889 Skye : *Covered Sugar* : £10 - £15
2890 Oslo : *Beaker* : £10 - £15
2891 Vine or Canterbury : *Butter* : £10 - £15
2892 Oslo : *Oil/Vinegar Jug* : £10 - £15
2893 Oslo : *Preserve, as 2902 without embossment* : £15 - £20
2894 Vine or Canterbury : *Salt & Pepper Stand, large, also for Oslo* : £10 - £15
2895 Oslo : *Cheese Cover & Stand, as 2910* : £20 - £30
2896 Oslo : *Long Tray, as 2887* : £15 - £20
2897 Oslo : *Three way Tray, as 2885* : £15 - £20
2898 Oslo : *Plate, 5ins, as 2884* : £15 - £20
2899 Vine or Canterbury : *TV Tray* : £10 - £15
2900 Advertising Ware : *Heinekin Salt & Pepper* : £10 - £15
2901 Vine or Canterbury : *Vinegar Jug* : £10 - £15
2902 Vine or Canterbury : *Preserve, with cover* : £15 - £20
2903 Oslo : *Sauce Boat, as 2920* : £15 - £20
2904 Vine or Canterbury : *Sauce Boat Stand, also for Oslo* : see 2920
2905 Oslo : *Tea Pot, 2 cup, as 2917* : £25 - £40
2906 Advertising Ware : *Heinekin Clog Ash Tray* : £10 - £15
2907 Vine or Canterbury : *Covered Butter* : £20 - £25

2908 Advertising Ware : *Heinekin Salt & Pepper, large* : £10 - £15
2909 Vine or Canterbury : *Beaker* : £10 - £15
2910 Vine or Canterbury : *Covered Cheese* : £20 - £30
2911 Oslo : *Cruet, as 2881* : £20 - £30
2912 Oslo : *Egg Cup, as 2882* : £15 - £20
2913 Various Patterns : *Tahiti Tall Lighter Base*
2914 Various Patterns : *Tahiti Low Lighter Base*
2915 Various Patterns : *Tahiti Round Ash Tray, 3 sizes*
2916 Various Patterns : *Tall Cigarette Box*
2917 Vine or Canterbury : *Tea Pot* : £25 - £40
2918 Various Patterns : *Small Bowl*
2919 Oslo : *TV Tray, as 2899* : £15 - £20
2920 Vine or Canterbury : *Sauce Boat* : £15 - £20 with 2904
2921 Oslo : *Covered Butter, as 2907* : £20 - £25
2922 Money Box - Flat Back : *Owl* : £35 - £50
2923 Money Box - Flat Back : *Horse* : £35 - £50
2924 Haig : *Ash Bowl, centre rests* : £5 - £10
2925 Advertising Ware : *Mustard, Heinekin* : £10 - £15
2926 Various Patterns : *Oblong Pencil Box*
2927 Various Patterns : *Covered Vase, large*
2928 Various Patterns : *Vase, 2 covers, small*
2929 Various Patterns : *Box/Ash Tray, large*
2930 Various Patterns : *Box, small, hole in top*
2931 Various Patterns : *Box, small, 4 holes in top*
2932 Various Patterns : *Coffee Pot*
2933 Haig : *Ice Jug* : £10 - £15
2934 Various Patterns : *Pin Box*
2935 Various Patterns : *Candle Stick*
2936 Various Patterns : *Cancelled*
2937 Various Patterns : *Bud Vase, 3 sizes*
2938 Various Patterns : *Covered Jar*

Carlton Ware Patterns and Shapes

2939 Bathroom : *Squat Ginger Jar, 2 sizes*
2940 Bathroom : *Pin Box*
2941 Bathroom : *Bud Vase, 2 sizes*
2942 Bathroom : *Powder Bowl*
2943 Bathroom : *Candle Stick*
2944 Money Box - Flat Back : *Cat* : £35 - £50
2945 Bathroom : *Oval Tray*
2946 Money Box - Flat Back : *Ark* : £35 - £50
2947 Bathroom : *Beaker*
2948 Bathroom : *Pedestal Soap Dish*
2949 Bathroom : *Low Soap Dish*
2950 Money Box - Flat Back : *Engine* : £35 - £50
2951 Embossed Fruit : *Pepper & Salt, large* : £20 - £45
2952 Various Patterns : *Ash Tray*
2953 Various Patterns : *Pepper & Salt*
2954 Wellington : *Pepper & Salt* : £15 - £25
2954 Sunflower : *Pepper & Salt* : £5 - £10
2955 Various Patterns : *Cruet Set*
2956 Various Patterns : *Bowl*
2957 Various Patterns : *Cruet Set*
2958 Various Patterns : *Sugar*
2959 Various Patterns : *Cup for TV Tray 2962*
2960 Various Patterns : *Vase, small*
2961 Various Patterns : *Cancelled*
2962 Various Patterns : *TV Tray for Cup 2959*
2963 Various Patterns : *Urn*
2964 Various Patterns : *Pin Tray, 6ins*
2965 Various Patterns : *Cream*
2966 Various Patterns : *Coffee Jug*
2967 Various Patterns : *Cancelled*
2968 Various Patterns : *Three Way Tray*
2969 Various Patterns : *Vase, narrow neck*
2970 Various Patterns : *Pin Box, oval*

2971 Various Patterns : *Covered 4 sided Vase*
2972 Various Patterns : *Fluted Bowl with tall or low foot and handles*
2973 Wellington : *Vase, 3 sizes* : £20 - £30
2973 Sunflower : *Vase, 3 sizes* : £10 - £20
2974 Wellington : *Lighter Holder* : £10 - £20
2974 Sunflower : *Lighter Holder* : £5 - £10
2975 Wellington : *Tray* : £10 - £20
2975 Sunflower : *Tray* : £5 - £10
2976 Wellington : *Footed Mug* : £15 - £20
2976 Sunflower : *Footed Mug* : £5 - £10
2977 Wellington : *Cup & Saucer* : £10 - £20
2977 Sunflower : *Cup & Saucer* : £5 - £10
2978 Wellington : *Ashtray* : £10 - £20
2978 Sunflower : *Ashtray* : £5 - £10
2979 Wellington : *Lighter Holder, tall* : £10 - £20
2979 Sunflower : *Lighter Holder, tall* : £5 - £10
2980 Wellington : *Cigarette Box* : £20 - £30
2980 Sunflower : *Cigarette Box* : £10 - £15
2981 Wellington : *Candle Stick (5 flanges)* : £10 - £15
2981 Sunflower : *Candle Stick (5 flanges)* : £5 - £10
2982 Wellington : *Candle Stick (3 flanges)* : £10 - £15
2982 Sunflower : *Candle Stick (3 flanges)* : £5 - £10
2983 Wellington : *Coffee Pot, Cream, Sugar* : £40 - £60
2983 Sunflower : *Coffee Pot, Cream, Sugar* : £20 - £40
2984 Wellington : *Ashtray, large* : £10 - £20
2984 Sunflower : *Ashtray, large* : £5 - £10
2985 Various Patterns : *Fluted Urn*
2986 Wellington : *Preserve* : £10 - £15
2986 Sunflower : *Preserve* : £5 - £10
2987 Various Patterns : *Plain Percolator*
2988 Wellington : *Spice Jar* : £10 - £15
2988 Sunflower : *Spice Jar* : £5 - £10

Carlton Ware Patterns and Shapes

2989 Various Patterns : *House of Lords Ash Tray*
2990 Wellington : *Oil & Vinegar* : £15 - £25
2990 Sunflower : *Oil & Vinegar* : £10 - £15
2991 Wellington : *Soup Cup* : £10 - £20
2991 Sunflower : *Soup Cup* : £5 - £10
2992 Wellington : *Tea Cup* : £10 - £20
2992 Sunflower : *Tea Cup* : £5 - £10
2993 Various Patterns : *Ball Cruet*
2994 Wellington : *Cruet* : £20 - £30
2994 Sunflower : *Cruet* : £10 - £15
2995 Wellington : *Butter Tray* : £10 - £20
2995 Sunflower : *Butter Tray* : £5 - £10
2996 Various Patterns : *Long Tray*
2997 Wellington : *Covered Cheese* : £20 - £30
2997 Sunflower : *Covered Cheese* : £10 - £15
2998 Wellington : *Covered Butter* : £20 - £30
2998 Sunflower : *Covered Butter* : £10 - £15
2999 Various Patterns : *Roman covered Vase*

Shapes 3000 - 3499

3000 Wellington : *Two way Tray* : £10 - £20
3000 Sunflower : *Two way Tray* : £5 - £10
3001 Various Patterns : *Childs Plate, Vintage Ash Tray*
3002 Novelty : *Penguin Salt & Pepper* : £20 - £45
3003 Various Patterns : *Cancelled*
3004 Various Patterns : *Cancelled*
3005 Various Patterns : *Double Pepper & Salt*
3006 Novelty : *Owl Pepper & Salt* : £20 - £45
3007 Novelty : *Elephant Pepper & Salt* : £20 - £45
3008 Novelty : *Poodle Pepper & Salt* : £20 - £45
3009 New Buttercup and Somerset : *Butter* : £10 - £20
3010 Various Patterns : *Vase Lamp*
3011 Various Patterns : *Vase Lamp (Fishtail)*
3012 Various Patterns : *Jug (Inverhouse)*
3013 Various Patterns : *Ash Tray (Inverhouse)*
3014 Novelty : *Bird Pepper & Salt* : £20 - £45
3015 Various Patterns : *Ash Tray*
3016 New Buttercup and Somerset : *Sauce Boat* : £20 - £40
3017 Various Patterns : *Jug*
3018 Novelty : *Tortoise Pepper & Salt* : £20 - £45
3019 Various Patterns : *Bowl or Ash Tray*
3020 Various Patterns : *Cancelled*
3021 New Buttercup and Somerset : *Five way Tray* : £35 - £55
3022 Various Patterns : *Goblet*

Carlton Ware Patterns and Shapes

3023 Various Patterns : *Mug with Face*
3024 New Buttercup and Somerset : *Preserve* : £20 - £30
3025 New Buttercup and Somerset : *Two way Tray* : £30 - £50
3026 New Buttercup and Somerset : *Butter* : £10 - £20
3027 New Buttercup and Somerset : *Coffee Set (Coffee for two)* : £90 - £150
3028 New Buttercup and Somerset : *Salt & Pepper* : £10 - £20
3029 New Buttercup and Somerset : *Covered Butter* : £20 - £40
3030 New Buttercup and Somerset : *Jug* : £20 - £40
3031 New Buttercup and Somerset : *Sauceboat and Stand* : £25 - £45
3032 New Buttercup and Somerset : *Plate, 5ins* : £15 - £30
3033 New Buttercup and Somerset : *Tea Pot* : £40 - £60
3034 Various Patterns : *Cancelled*
3035 New Buttercup and Somerset : *Tray or Oval Dish, large* : £20 - £25
3036 New Buttercup and Somerset : *Tray or Oval Dish, small* : £15 - £20
3037 New Buttercup and Somerset : *Beaker* : £15 - £30
3038 New Buttercup and Somerset : *Cheese & Cover with Stand* : £30 - £50
3039 Perth : *Pepper & Salt*
3040 Advertising Ware : *Carlsburg Ash Bowl* : £5 - £10
3041 Perth : *Coffee Pot*
3042 Various Patterns : *Cancelled*
3043 Advertising Ware : *Tanqueray Ice Jug* : £30 - £50
3044 Various Patterns : *ICTC Artichoke Dish*
3045 Various Patterns : *ICTC Corn on the Cob Tray*
3046 Various Patterns : *ICTC Avocado Dish*

3047 Advertising Ware : *Ballantyne Ice Jug* : £30 - £50
3048 Perth : *Sugar with Lid*
3049 Various Patterns : *Focus Lighter Base*
3050 Various Patterns : *ICTC Egg Cup*
3051 Perth : *Cream Jug*
3052 Perth : *Saucer*
3053 Perth : *Covered Dish, large size*
3054 Perth : *Covered Dish, small size*
3055 Various Patterns : *ICTC Cake Stand*
3056 Money Box : *Cube* : £20 - £30
3057 Tangier : *Ash Tray*
3058 Various Patterns : *Cancelled*
3059 Tangier : *Candle Stick*
3060 Tangier : *Pepper & Salt*
3061 Toby Jug : *Dormouse*
3062 Tangier : *Low Vase*
3063 Fruit : *Strawberry Preserve* : £20 - £40
3064 Fruit : *Pineapple Preserve* : £20 - £40
3065 Fruit : *Blackberry Preserve* : £20 - £40
3066 Fruit : *Raspberry Preserve* : £20 - £40
3067 Fruit : *Peach or Plum Preserve* : £20 - £40
3068 Tangier : *Cigar Jar*
3069 Various Patterns : *ICTC 5 bar Toast Rack*
3070 Tangier : *Bud vase*
3071 Tangier : *Tray*
3072 Tangier : *Pomanda*
3073 Various Patterns : *Rio Ash Tray*
3074 Various Patterns : *Picture Frame Posy Holder, large*
3075 Various Patterns : *Picture Frame Posy Holder, small*
3076 Tangier : *Powder Bowl*
3077 Tangier : *Lighter base*
3078 Tangier : *Cigarette Box, as 3068 but shorter*
3079 Tangier : *Tall vase*

Carlton Ware Patterns and Shapes

3080 Money Box - Flat Back : *Face* : £35 - £50
3081 Various Patterns : *Fish Platter, small*
3082 Various Patterns : *Fish Platter, large*
3083 Various Patterns : *ICTC Salad Plate*
3084 Various Patterns : *ICTC Grapefruit Dish*
3085 Various Patterns : *Lighter Holder*
3086 Money Box - Flat Back : *Pig* : £35 - £50
3087 Novelty : *Honey Pot, with Bee* : £25 - £45
3088 Novelty : *Parsley Sauce Boat, with Fish Head* : £10 - £20
3089 Novelty : *Bread Sauce Jar* : £10 - £20
3090 Novelty : *Horse Radish Preserve Pot, with Face* : £10 - £20
3091 Various Patterns : *String Holder*
3092 Novelty : *Red Cabbage Preserve Pot, with Face* : £10 - £20
3093 Novelty : *Beetroot Preserve Pot, with Face* : £10 - £20
3094 Lampbase : *Cat* : £75 - £100
3095 Lampbase : *Ark* : £75 - £100
3096 Lampbase : *Owl* : £75 - £100
3097 Lampbase : *Engine* : £75 - £100
3098 Lampbase : *Horse* : £75 - £100
3099 Novelty : *Annabelle*
3100 Various Patterns : *Percolator*
3101 Various Patterns : *Goblet*
3102 Various Patterns : *Cancelled*
3103 Spectrum : *Water Jug*
3104 Money Box - Flat Back : *Soldier* : £35 - £50
3105 Spectrum : *Cruet*
3106 Novelty : *Annabelle*
3107 Various Patterns : *Small Vase*
3108 Spectrum : *Beaker*

3109 Spectrum : *Coaster*
3110 Various Patterns : *Egg Cup*
3111 Various Patterns : *Beaker*
3112 Various Patterns : *Goblet*
3113 Spectrum : *Salt & Pepper*
3114 Embossed : *Posy Vase*
3115 Novelty : *Annabelle & Cat*
3116 Various Patterns : *Goblet with base*
3117 Various Patterns : *Wine Decanter*
3118 Various Patterns : *Cover for Ginger Jar*
3119 Embossed : *Soup Bowl*
3120 Embossed : *Soup Tureen*
3121 Face : *Salt & Pepper* : £20 - £45
3122 Novelty : *Alphabet Bowl*
3123 Novelty : *Annabelle with Flowers*
3124 Novelty : *Annabelle with Doll*
3125 Novelty : *Annabelle with Birds*
3126 Novelty : *Annabelle with Teddy*
3127 Various Patterns : *Cancelled*
3128 Money Box - Bug Eyes : *Owl* : £35 - £55
3129 Money Box - Bug Eyes : *Snail* : £35 - £55
3130 Money Box - Bug Eyes : *Bird* : £35 - £55
3131 Money Box - Bug Eyes : *Frog* : £35 - £55
3132 Ornament : *MG Car* : £100 - £200
3133 Various Patterns : *Elgin Coffee Set*
3134 Advertising Ware : *Gordons Gin Ash Tray* : £5 - £10
3135 Various Patterns : *Bottle*
3136 Various Patterns : *Salt*
3137 Various Patterns : *Salt*
3138 Various Patterns : *Salt*
3139 Various Patterns : *Salt*
3140 Various Patterns : *Pepper*
3141 Money Box - Flat Back : *Boot* : £35 - £50

Carlton Ware Patterns and Shapes

3142 Money Box - Flat Back : *Peacock* : £35 - £50
3143 Walking Ware First Range : *Cup* : £30 - £50
3143 Walking Ware First Range : *Egg Cup* : £25 - £40
3143 Walking Ware First Range : *Milk* : £30 - £50
3143 Walking Ware First Range : *Sugar with lid (standing),* : £45 - £65
3143 Walking Ware First Range : *Tea Pot (small)* : £80 - £120
3143 Walking Ware First Range : *Tea Pot (miniature)* : £150 - £200
3144 Novelty : *Curling Stone* : £10 - £20
3145 Novelty : *1st Kiwi Figure*
3146 Advertising Ware : *Gordons Gin Ash Tray* : £5 - £10
3147 Novelty : *Toby Jug, 3 sizes*
3148 Novelty : *Daisy Bowl, 2 sizes*
3149 Money Box : *Tram Car* : £40 - £70
3150 Money Box : *Carousel* : £30 - £40
3151 Novelty : *2nd Kiwi Figure*
3152 Novelty : *Pepper, Female eyes*
3153 Novelty : *Salt, Male Eyes*
3154 Novelty : *Goblin Tea Pot*
3155 Novelty : *Coffee Cup Set*
3156 Novelty : *Lady Powder Bowl, low oval*
3157 Novelty : *Lady Powder Bowl, round*
3158 Novelty : *Lady Powder Bowl, tall*
3159 Money Box : *Rocking Horse* : £35 - £50
3160 Gourmet : *Grapefruit*
3161 Gourmet : *Pear Dish, 3 parts*
3162 Gourmet : *Corn on the Cob*
3163 Gourmet : *Single Egg Cup*
3164 Gourmet : *Double Egg Cup*
3165 Gourmet : *Artichoke*
3166 Novelty : *Golf Ball*

3167 Gourmet : *Escargot*
3168 Gourmet : *Toast Rack*
3169 Gourmet : *Salad Plate*
3170 Novelty : *Curling Stone* : £10 - £20
3171 Novelty : *Hen Egg Dish*
3172 Novelty : *Hen Pepper & Salt* : £20 - £45
3173 Novelty : *Celery Tray*
3174 Money Box : *Pig* : £30 - £50
3175 Apple Blossom - AW : *Sauceboat and Stand* : £40 - £60
3176 Apple Blossom - AW : *Individual Butter* : £20 - £30
3177 Flow Blue - AW : *Toothbrush Jar* : £10 - £20
3178 Apple Blossom - AW : *Long Tray* : £30 - £50
3179 Apple Blossom - AW : *Covered Butter* : £50 - £75
3180 Apple Blossom - AW : *Jug - 1 pint* : £40 - £70
3181 Flow Blue - AW : *Candlestick* : £15 - £25
3182 Apple Blossom - AW : *Pepper and Salt* : £25 - £40
3183 Apple Blossom - AW : *Preserve* : £50 - £80
3184 Flow Blue - AW : *Heart Box* : £10 - £20
3185 Apple Blossom - AW : *Cheese and Stand* : £75 - £125
3186 Apple Blossom - AW : *Crescent Tray* : £25 - £40
3187 Flow Blue - AW : *Footed Box* : £10 - £20
3188 Apple Blossom - AW : *Salad Bowl* : £30 - £50
3189 Apple Blossom - AW : *Leaf Tray* : £25 - £35
3190 Flow Blue - AW : *Tray* : £5 - £10
3191 Flow Blue - AW : *Soap Dish* : £5 - £10
3192 Apple Blossom - AW : *Toast Rack* : £40 - £70
3193 Flow Blue - AW : *Chamber Pot, 2 sizes* : £5 - £15
3194 Walking Ware First Range : *Salt & Pepper* : £50 - £80
3195 Walking Ware First Range : *Tea Pot, large* : £100 - £150

Carlton Ware Patterns and Shapes

3196 Walking Ware First Range : *Coffee or Water Jug* : £70 - £130
3197 Walking Ware First Range : *Sugar with lid, sitting cross legged* : £55 - £85
3198 Walking Ware First Range : *Plate* : £60 - £90
3199 Walking Ware First Range : *Soup Bowl with lid* : £55 - £85
3200 Flow Blue - AW : *Clog* : £5 - £10
3201 Various Patterns : *Plant Pot Holder*
3202 Flow Blue - AW : *Apothecary Jar* : £10 - £20
3203 Flow Blue - AW : *Tankard* : £5 - £10
3204 Flow Blue - AW : *Basin and Ewer* : £25 - £35
3205 Flow Blue - AW : *Kettle* : £10 - £20
3206 Flow Blue - AW : *Trinket Box* : £5 - £10
3207 Gourmet : *Sugar Shaker*
3208 Gourmet : *Salt & Pepper*
3209 Gourmet : *Boat Stand*
3210 Gourmet : *Preserve*
3211 Gourmet : *Cheese & Stand*
3212 Gourmet : *Covered Butter*
3213 Gourmet : *Coffee Jug*
3214 Gourmet : *Coffee Cup*
3215 Gourmet : *Coffee Filter*
3216 Flow Blue - AW : *Iron* : £5 - £10
3217 Novelty : *Books*
3218 Embossed Salad : *Vinegar Jar*
3219 Walking Ware Other Items : *Cow in Bath Butter* : £40 - £60
3220 Novelty : *Pint Tankard with Figure*
3221 Embossed Salad : *Tureen*
3222 Various Patterns : *Ginger Jar, medium*
3223 Various Patterns : *Ginger Jar, small*
3224 Flow Blue - AW : *Caravan Cigarette Box* : £10 - £20

3225 Novelty : *Half Pint Mug with Figure*
3226 Novelty : *Kaning Pepper & Salt*
3227 Walking Ware Other Items : *Kneeling Jubilee Mug* : £60 - £90
3228 Walking Ware First Range : *Tea Pot, miniature* : £150 - £200
3229 Walking Ware First Range : *Biscuit Barrel* : £70 - £130
3230 Toby Jug : *Huntsman*
3231 Toby Jug : *Bandit*
3232 Salad Range : *Soup Bowl* : £10 - £20
3233 Flow Blue - AW : *Tumbler or Goblet* : £5 - £10
3234 Novelty : *Penguin Pepper & Salt, with plinth* : £20 - £45
3235 Novelty : *Covered Dish with Figure Knob*
3236 Novelty : *Fox Covered Dish & Ladle*
3237 Novelty : *Roman Tea Cup*
3238 Novelty : *Boss Egg Cup*
3239 Novelty : *Duck Spout Tea Pot* : £20 - £40
3240 Walking Ware Other Items : *Cow Milk* : £30 - £50
3241 Novelty : *Valentine Mug*
3242 Novelty : *Goose Bowl*
3243 Denim : *Preserve Jar* : £10 - £20
3244 Denim : *Covered Sugar* : £10 - £20
3245 Denim : *Coffee Mug* : £10 - £20
3246 Denim : *Tea Pot & Coffee Pot, large* : £20 - £40
3247 Denim : *Biscuit Barrel, small* : £15 - £30
3248 Denim : *Cream* : £10 - £20
3249 Denim : *Ash Tray* : £10 - £20
3250 Denim : *Biscuit Barrel, large* : £15 - £30
3251 Novelty : *Tuba Egg Cup*
3252 Novelty : *Elephant Tea Pot* : £20 - £40
3253 Haig : *Round Water Jug* : £10 - £20

Carlton Ware Patterns and Shapes

3254 Haig : *Antique Water Jug* : £10 - £20
3255 Green Apple Range : *Tea Pot, Cheese, etc*
3256 Novelty : *Bow Tie Pepper, Salt & Mustard* : £10 - £20
3257 Novelty : *Cosy Egg Cup, stacking*
3258 Novelty : *Disney Tea Cup*
3259 Novelty : *Disney Egg Cup*
3260 Novelty : *Duck Egg Cup*
3261 Novelty : *Camel Tea Pot* : £20 - £40
3262 Dovecote Range : *Coffee Pot* : £40 - £60
3262 Dovecote Range : *Cream* : £20 - £30
3262 Dovecote Range : *Sugar* : £30 - £50
3262 Dovecote Range : *Cup & Saucer* : £20 - £30
3263 Novelty : *Tuba Mug*
3264 Novelty : *Double Bags Pepper & Salt*
3265 Novelty : *Store Jar*
3266 Novelty : *Drum Preserve*
3267 Dovecote Range : *Tea Pot* : £40 - £60
3268 Novelty : *Hare Mug*
3269 Novelty : *Duck Mug*
3270 Novelty : *Frog Mug*
3271 Pig : *Water Jug, 2 sizes* : £45 - £75
3272 Novelty : *Orange Pepper & Salt*
3273 Hovis : *Toast Rack* : £15 - £30
3274 Novelty : *Tortoise Mug*
3275 Novelty : *Figure Cup*
3276 Novelty : *Whisky Dirk*
3277 Fruit : *Banana Tray* : £10 - £20
3278 Advertising Ware : *Brown & Poulson Cream* : £10 - £20
3279 Novelty : *Dolls Head & Hands*
3280 Novelty : *Fred Man Pepper, Salt & Mustard*

3281 Walking Ware Other Items : *Child of the Year Mug* : £35 - £70
3282 Novelty : *Wine Bottle, Beaujolais*
3283 Novelty : *Dust Bin*
3284 Novelty : *Large Flower Man*
3285 Novelty : *Egg Cup & Tray*
3286 Novelty : *Fred Pie Funnel*
3287 Novelty : *Bird Custard Jug*
3288 Money Box : *Fred* : £35 - £55
3289 Novelty : *Bilton Pepper & Salt*
3290 Walking Ware Running Jumping Standing : *Cup* : £45 - £70
3290 Walking Ware Running Jumping Standing : *Egg Cup* : £30 - £50
3290 Walking Ware Running Jumping Standing : *Milk* : £45 - £70
3290 Walking Ware Running Jumping Standing : *Sugar with lid* : £55 - £85
3290 Walking Ware Running Jumping Standing : *Tea Pot* : £90 - £160
3290 Walking Ware Caribbean Series : *Cup* : £50 - £75
3290 Walking Ware Caribbean Series : *Egg Cup* : £35 - £55
3290 Walking Ware Caribbean Series : *Milk* : £50 - £75
3290 Walking Ware Caribbean Series : *Sugar with lid* : £50 - £80
3290 Walking Ware Caribbean Series : *Tea Pot* : £100 - £160
3291 Novelty : *Ice Cream Wafer* : £10 - £20
3292 Novelty : *Milk Shake Preserve (October 1979)* : £10 - £20
3293 Novelty : *Dolls Head, no hands*
3294 Walking Ware Other Items : *Santa Cup* : £60 - £90

Carlton Ware Patterns and Shapes

3295 Novelty : *Dragon Tea Pot* : £15 - £30
3296 Fruit : *Apple Tea Pot* : £40 - £60
3297 Fruit : *Pear Tea Pot* : £50 - £65
3298 Hovis : *Covered Butter (January 1980)* : £10 - £20
3299 Novelty : *Cat Cheese*
3300 Novelty : *Plant Pots*
3301 Walking Ware Other Items : *Birthday Cream* : £35 - £55
3302 Advertising Ware : *Water Jug, 100 Pipers*
3303 Novelty : *She Mug*
3304 Walking Ware Other Items : *Valentine/Hearts Cup* : £45 - £75
3305 Advertising Ware : *Glen Water Jug*
3306 Hovis : *Plate (January 1980)* : £10 - £20
3307 Novelty : *Bow Tie* : £10 - £20
3308 Walking Ware Other Items : *Easter Egg Cup* : £45 - £70
3309 Walking Ware Other Items : *Birthday Cup* : £35 - £55
3310 Novelty : *Culter handle*
3311 Novelty : *Round Sided Ice Jug*
3312 Fruit : *Orange Preserve* : £20 - £40
3313 Novelty : *Mustard Bottle*
3314 Novelty : *Cooks Tea Pot, etc*
3315 Novelty : *Tap Tea Pot* : £15 - £30
3316 Novelty : *Beans on Toast Toast Rack & Egg Cup* : £15 - £30
3317 Novelty : *Pie & Pea Plaque*
3318 Novelty : *Lady Book Ends* : £20 - £40
3319 Novelty : *Plug Ash Tray* : £10 - £20
3320 Novelty : *Nut & Bolt Vase* : £10 - £20
3321 Novelty : *Nail & Screw Pepper & Salt* : £10 - £20

3322 Novelty : *Legs Toast Rack, on Lettuce Rack* : £10 - £20
3323 Novelty : *Chocolate Box*
3324 Novelty : *Bean Cheese, Mug & Preserve*
3325 Novelty : *Michelle Vase, 3 sizes*
3326 Novelty : *Potts Family, Face Range, Egg Cup, Dish & Beaker* : £10 - £20
3327 Novelty : *Sweet Pea Desk Set*
3328 Novelty : *Lamb Mint Sauce Boat & Stand*
3329 Novelty : *Lamb Store Jar*
3330 Guinness : *Tankard Egg Cup*
3331 Novelty : *P K Franks Pepper, Salt, Egg Cup & Mug*
3332 Walking Ware Other Items : *Charles & Di Cup* : £45 - £70 each
3333 Advertising Ware : *Ash Tray & Ice Jug* : £10 - £20
3334 Novelty : *Asparagus Tray*
3335 Advertising Ware : *Mini Whisky Flask*
3336 Dove or Pillar Range : *Pepper, Salt, Ash Tray, Egg Cup, Sugar*
3337 Novelty : *Tea Rose*
3338 Circus : *Clown Sugar/Preserve* : £100 - £200
3339 Novelty : *Strong Man*
3340 Fruit : *Apple Sugar, Cream, Cup and Saucer* : £20 - £30, £20 - £30, £25 - £40
3341 Circus : *Women Wrestlers Butter* : £400 - £600
3342 Circus : *Clown Cream on Duck* : £100 - £200
3343 Circus : *Clown Cream on Pantomime Horse* : £100 - £200
3344 Novelty : *Sweet Pea Bath Salt Jar*
3345 Walking Ware Other Items : *Wellington Cup* : £50 - £80
3346 Walking Ware Other Items : *Maid or Waitress Cup* : £80 - £110

Carlton Ware Patterns and Shapes

3347 Novelty : *Alice through the Looking Glass Book Ends (February 1982)* : £20 - £40
3348 Novelty : *Early Bird Egg Pepper & Salt* : £10 - £15
3349 Advertising Ware : *Cadburys Mug*
3350 Walking Ware Other Items : *Adam Cup* : £75 - £110
3351 Circus : *Clown Tea Pot* : £100 - £200
3352 Novelty : *Early Bird Egg Cup* : £5 - £10
3353 Novelty : *Early Bird Beaker* : £5 - £10
3354 Novelty : *Early Bird Toast rack* : £10 - £15
3355 Circus : *Double Egg Cup* : £50 - £100
3356 Walking Ware Other Items : *Eve Cup* : £75 - £110
3357 Novelty : *Playing Card Man Toast Rack* : £10 - £20
3358 Novelty : *Lady with Mirror Plaque* : £5 - £10
3359 Haig : *Square Ash Tray* : £5 - £10
3360 Novelty : *Lady Mirror* : £5 - £10
3361 Advertising Ware : *Toby Plaque*
3362 Novelty : *Tooth Cup*
3363 Novelty : *Wisdom Tooth Cup*
3364 Novelty : *Toothbrush Holder*
3365 Advertising Ware : *World Cup Ball*
3366 Advertising Ware : *Rugby Ball*
3367 Novelty : *Alice Mirror* : £5 - £10
3368 Novelty : *Bath Towel Soap*
3369 Novelty : *Half Pint Beer Tankard*
3370 Novelty : *Cushion Spoon Rest*
3371 Novelty : *Sandcastle Tooth Brush Holder*
3372 Novelty : *Hamburger*
3373 Walking Ware Big Feet : *Bookend* : £50 - £90
3373 Walking Ware Big Feet : *Candlestick* : £55 - £90
3373 Walking Ware Big Feet : *Clock* : £70 - £110
3373 Walking Ware Big Feet : *Cup* : £30 - £55
3373 Walking Ware Big Feet : *Egg Cup* : £25 - £45
3373 Walking Ware Big Feet : *Cream* : £35 - £60

3373 Walking Ware Big Feet : *Napkin Ring* : £25 - £40
3373 Walking Ware Big Feet : *Nut Bowl or Soap Dish* : £40 - £70
3373 Walking Ware Big Feet : *Sugar with lid* : £45 - £70
3373 Walking Ware Big Feet : *Tea Pot* : £80 - £150
3373 Walking Ware Big Feet : *Toast Rack* : £80 - £140
3373 Walking Ware Big Feet : *Toothbrush Mug* : £30 - £55
3374 Novelty : *Shark Tidy Safe*
3375 Novelty : *Pelican Tidy Safe*
3376 Novelty : *Venice range of Table Ware*
3377 Money Box : *Rumbelows* : £35 - £55
3378 Novelty : *Pelican Spoon Rest*
3379 Novelty : *Sheep Toast Rack*
3380 Novelty : *Lip Egg Cup*
3381 Novelty : *Egg Cup*
3382 Money Box : *Rumbelows* : £35 - £55
3383 Advertising Ware : *Tetley Tea Carrier Bag*
3384 Advertising Ware : *J & B Ash Bowl* : £5 - £10
3385 Money Box : *Access* : £35 - £55
3386 Novelty : *Corset Mug*
3387 Gourmet : *Wedge Cheese*
3388 Gourmet : *Napkin Ring*
3389 Novelty : *Napoleon Clock*
3390 Novelty : *Napoleon Low Clock*
3391 Novelty : *Ridgeway Clock*
3392 Novelty : *Talles Candle Stick*
3393 Novelty : *Chambury Clock*
3394 Novelty : *Can Can Mug*
3395 Novelty : *School House Clock*
3396 Gourmet : *Gravy Boat*
3397 Novelty : *Queen of Hearts Preserve* : £15 - £30
3398 Novelty : *Mad Hatter Egg Cup* : £10 - £20

Carlton Ware Patterns and Shapes

3399 Gourmet : *Cream*
3400 Novelty : *Caterpillar Sugar*
3401 Novelty : *Mouse Egg Cup*
3402 Novelty : *Cat Butter Dish* : £10 - £20
3403 Novelty : *Card Pepper & Salt* : £10 - £20
3404 Novelty : *Shell Jar*
3405 Novelty : *Cat & Mouse Toast Rack* : £10 - £20
3406 Boots : *Cheese & Stand*
3407 Boots : *Pepper & Salt*
3408 Boots : *Toast Rack*
3409 Guinness : *One Pint Tankard* : £45 - £80
3410 Boots : *Butter*
3411 Boots : *Preserve*
3412 Novelty : *Small Bath*
3413 Novelty : *Large Bath*
3414 Novelty : *Tally Clock*
3415 Novelty : *Tally Clock*
3416 Novelty : *Tally Clock*
3417 Novelty : *Hexagonal Napkin Ring*
3418 Boots : *Egg Cup*
3419 Boots : *Toast Rack*
3420 Advertising Ware : *Small Cadbury Mug*
3421 Novelty : *Large Duck Egg Cup*
3422 Novelty : *Small Duck Egg Cup*
3423 Novelty : *Cherub Dish with Figure*
3424 Advertising Ware : *Singapore Airlines Whiskey*
3425 Novelty : *Cherub Round Tray*
3426 Novelty : *Cherub Barrel*
3427 Novelty : *Cherub Posy Holder*
3428 Boots : *Salad Bowl, large*
3429 Novelty : *Cherub*
3430 Boots : *Mustard, small*
3431 Boots : *Salad Bowl, small*

3432 Boots : *Crescent Tray*
3433 Boots : *Cream*
3434 Boots : *Serving Tray*
3435 Boots : *Gateaux Plate, 12ins*
3436 Boots : *Sauce Boat & Stand*
3437 Boots : *Mayonnaise & Stand*
3438 Lucerne : *Sewing Tray*
3439 Lucerne : *Sauce Boat & Stand*
3440 Novelty : *Shoe Book Ends*
3441 Novelty : *Heart Powder Box*
3442 Novelty : *Rolls Royce Range Tea Pot, Sugar, Cream*
3443 Lucerne : *Tea Pot, Sugar, Cream, etc*
3444 Novelty : *Queen Anne Tea Pot*
3445 Advertising Ware : *Castlemaine Ash Tray* : £5 - £10
3446 Advertising Ware : *Bisto Gravy Boat & Stand* : £10 - £20
3447 Advertising Ware : *Whiskey Flask*
3448 Advertising Ware : *Thompson Man Cruet*
3449 Hovis : *Mug* : £10 - £15
3450 Utility Ware : *Baking Tray, small*
3451 Utility Ware : *Baking Tray, large*
3452 Utility Ware : *Goblin Tea Pot*
3453 Utility Ware : *Percolator & Stand, 10 parts*
3454 Utility Ware : *Sugar, Cream, Cup, etc*
3455 Utility Ware : *Vegetable Dish, large*
3456 Utility Ware : *Vegetable Dish, small*
3457 Advertising Ware : *Singapore Airlines Tail Fin*
3458 Trinket Range : *Jug, Preserve, Plant Holder, etc*
3459 Novelty : *Handles for Beakers, Puffin, Pelican, Flamingo, Toucan, Parrot*
3460 Novelty : *Jack Tray*
3461 Cook Range : *Cooking Items*
3462 Novelty : *Sheep range (Vicar, Bikini Girl, etc)*

Carlton Ware Patterns and Shapes

3463 Various Patterns : *Percolator with Cover*
3464 Various Patterns : *Percolator with long Spout & Cover*
3465 Novelty : *Rugby Bar*
3466 Novelty : *Pickwick Plate*
3467 No details :
3468 Cook Range : *Soup*
3469 Cook Range : *Flan, 10ins & 8ins*
3470 Various Patterns : *Percolator*
3471 Guinness : *Egg Cup, Store Jar, Pepper, Salt, Sugar, Shaving Mug, etc* : £50 - £80
3472 Various Patterns : *Plants Pots, 2 sizes*
3473 Boots : *Cheese*
3474 Novelty : *Fryer Tuck Plate*
3475 Various Patterns : *Dish*
3476 Advertising Ware : *BHS Casserole*
3477 Advertising Ware : *Harrods Van, large & small* : £10 - £20
3478 Novelty : *Pirate Plate*
3479 Advertising Ware : *BHS Beaker*
3480 Advertising Ware : *Bovril Mug*
3481 Advertising Ware : *Russell Hobbs Percolator*
3482 Advertising Ware : *Sainsbury Toast Rack*
3483 Advertising Ware : *Sainsbury Cruet*
3484 Advertising Ware : *Sainsbury Preserve*
3485 Advertising Ware : *Sainsbury Egg Cup*
3486 Advertising Ware : *Sainsbury Cheese & Cover*
3487 Advertising Ware : *Sainsbury Butter & Cover*
3488 Hovis : *Egg Cup* : £5 - £10
3489 Robertsons Golly : *Singer* : £30 - £50
3490 Robertsons Golly : *Flute* : £30 - £50
3491 Robertsons Golly : *Accordion* : £30 - £50
3492 Robertsons Golly : *Double Base* : £30 - £50

3493 Robertsons Golly : *Guitar* : £30 - £50
3494 Robertsons Golly : *Drums* : £30 - £50
3495 Robertsons Golly : *Saxophone* : £30 - £50
3496 Robertsons Golly : *Trumpet* : £30 - £50
3497 Novelty : *TV Mug*
3498 Hovis : *Covered Sugar* : £10 - £20
3499 Hovis : *Cream* : £10 - £20

Shapes 3500 - 3999

3500 Hovis : *Tea Pot* : £25 - £40
3501 Hovis : *Salt & Pepper* : £10 - £20
3502 Robertsons Golly : *Band Stand* : £30 - £50
3503 Poppy & Daisy (New Interior) : *Vase, as 2057* : £60 - £160
3504 Various Patterns : *Corporate Ash Tray, large*
3505 Various Patterns : *Corporate Ash Tray, small*
3506 Various Patterns : *Whistle Whiskey Container*
3507 Poppy & Daisy (New Interior) : *Bowl, as 2010* : £60 - £90
3508 Advertising Ware : *Whitbread Tankard*
3509 Various Patterns : *Corporate Tankard*
3510 Advertising Ware : *Flowers Ash Bowl* : £5 - £10
3511 Novelty : *Face Tea Pot* : £10 - £20
3512 Novelty : *Maid Tea Pot* : £10 - £20
3513 Novelty : *Orange Mug* : £10 - £20
3514 Coronation Street : *Stan Ogden* : £30 - £50
3515 Coronation Street : *Albert Tatlock* : £30 - £50
3516 Coronation Street : *Ena Sharples* : £30 - £50
3517 Coronation Street : *Hilda Ogden* : £30 - £50
3518 Coronation Street : *Mike Baldwin* : £30 - £50
3519 Coronation Street : *Bett Lynch* : £30 - £50
3520 Various Patterns : *Corporate Tankard, cancelled*
3521 Hovis : *Storage Jar or Biscuit Barrel* : £20 - £30
3522 Novelty : *Hippopotamus Tea Pot* : £10 - £20
3523 Novelty : *Hippopotamus Handled Mug* : £10 - £20
3524 Novelty : *Rabbit Egg Cup* : £10 - £20
3525 Novelty : *Hippopotamus Egg Cup* : £10 - £20

3526 Novelty : *Seal Egg Cup* : £10 - £20
3527 Novelty : *Calf Egg Cup* : £10 - £20
3528 Novelty : *Ram Egg Cup* : £10 - £20
3529 Novelty : *Hippopotamus Preserve* : £10 - £20
3530 Novelty : *Cat Tea Pot* : £40 - £60
3531 Novelty : *Spitting Image Egg Cups* : £20 - £30
3531 Novelty : *Spitting Image Tea Pots* : £50 - £80
3532 Novelty : *Round Bath, 2 sizes*
3533 Various Patterns : *ITCT Toast Rack*
3534 Various Patterns : *Trophy Special Ash Bowl*
3535 Various Patterns : *Rectangular Ash Bowl*
3536 Novelty : *Pig Book Ends* : £10 - £20
3537 Novelty : *Mini Tea Pots*
3538 Novelty : *Elephant (Jumbo) Range: Cruet, Toast Rack, Tea Pot, etc* : £10 - £20 each
3539 Advertising Ware : *Long John Whiskey Bottle*
3540 Novelty : *Clock Tea Pot*
3541 Various Patterns : *Scandinavian A B Range*
3542 Various Patterns : *Handled Tankard*
3543 Novelty : *Alligator Range: Teapot, Sugar, Cream, Eggcup, Toast Rack, Butter Dish, Preserve, Salt and Pepper* : £10 - £20 each
3544 Novelty : *Clock Tea Pot*
3547 Novelty : *Tea Pots, Bi-plane, Red Baron, Lucy May, Blue Max, etc* : £60 - £120

List of shape numbers by shape name

Acorn: 1048
Advertising Ware: 1127, 1128, 1257, 1258, 1281, 1329, 1462, 1463, 2166, 2315, 2323, 2347, 2352, 2356, 2410, 2412, 2413, 2420, 2459, 2460, 2472, 2477, 2478, 2550, 2557, 2570, 2583, 2587, 2600, 2606, 2614, 2673, 2693, 2702, 2706, 2723, 2727, 2735, 2736, 2739, 2740, 2741, 2755, 2862, 2869, 2870, 2900, 2906, 2908, 2925, 3040, 3043, 3047, 3134, 3146, 3278, 3302, 3305, 3333, 3335, 3349, 3361, 3365, 3366, 3383, 3384, 3420, 3424, 3445, 3446, 3447, 3448, 3457, 3476, 3477, 3479, 3480, 3481, 3482, 3483, 3484, 3485, 3486, 3487, 3508, 3510, 3539
Aladdins Lamp: 2525
Anemone: 925, 928, 932, 933, 935, 945, 946, 970, 975, 976, 978, 979, 983, 997, 1014, 1015, 1026, 1027, 1028, 1029, 1030, 1031, 1032, 1033, 1041, 1042, 1067, 1068, 1069, 1096, 1097, 1174, 1184, 1753, 1761, 1762
Animals: 1423, 1424, 1425, 1426, 1427, 1430, 1437, 1438, 1440, 1441, 1442, 1445, 1446, 1447, 1448, 1449, 1450, 1451, 1466, 1467, 1468, 1469, 1470, 1471, 1475, 1480, 1481, 1506, 1507, 1508, 1509
Apple Blossom: 1614, 1617, 1618, 1621, 1638, 1648, 1649, 1650, 1651, 1652, 1653, 1654, 1655, 1663, 1664, 1665, 1668, 1669, 1670, 1671, 1680, 1686, 1687, 1688, 1689, 1696, 1697, 1700, 1701, 1704, 1707, 1710, 1714, 1720, 1723, 1728, 1729, 1756, 1799, 2008
Apple Blossom - AW: 3175, 3176, 3178, 3179, 3180, 3182, 3183, 3185, 3186, 3188, 3189, 3192
Arum Lily: 1740, 1855

Athena: 2794, 2795, 2796, 2800, 2801, 2802, 2803, 2805, 2806, 2807, 2808, 2809, 2810, 2811, 2812, 2836, 2837
Bamboo: 2798, 2799
Basket: 1764, 1775, 1803, 1810, 1876, 1907, 1908, 1909, 1910, 1911, 1912, 1913, 1922, 1944
Bathroom: 2939, 2940, 2941, 2942, 2943, 2945, 2947, 2948, 2949
Bee: 1527
Begonia: 1768
Bell: 1715
Bell Handle: 2175, 2177, 2178, 2179, 2180, 2181, 2182, 2183
Bird: 2851, 2855, 2859, 2860, 2865, 2866
Blackberry/Raspberry: 1266, 1473, 1477, 1515, 1516, 1545, 1546, 1547, 1548, 1559, 1560, 1564, 1565, 1570, 1580, 1581, 1584, 1586, 1593, 1598, 1599, 1602, 1662
Bluebell: 1099
Boots: 3406, 3407, 3408, 3410, 3411, 3418, 3419, 3428, 3430, 3431, 3432, 3433, 3434, 3435, 3436, 3437, 3473
Buttercup: 1395, 1402, 1478, 1479, 1482, 1483, 1486, 1501, 1510, 1511, 1512, 1513, 1514, 1522, 1523, 1524, 1525, 1526, 1528, 1529, 1530, 1531, 1532, 1533, 1534, 1558, 1574, 1583, 1585, 1587, 1595, 1597, 1613, 1661, 1709
Campion: 1771, 1873
Card Series: 2146, 2215, 2256, 2266
Carlton Village: 2645, 2646, 2647, 2648, 2649, 2650, 2651, 2652, 2653
Cat: 1132, 1158, 1159, 1160, 1206
Cherry: 1991, 2109, 2126, 2127, 2128, 2129, 2130, 2133, 2134, 2135, 2136, 2137, 2153, 2155, 2158
Chestnut: 1946, 1954, 1955, 1956

Carlton Ware Patterns and Shapes

Circus: 3338, 3341, 3342, 3343, 3351, 3355
Clematis: 1953, 1957, 1958, 1959, 1960, 1961, 1962, 1963, 1964, 2275
Clover/Shamrock: 1754, 1869, 1874
Cone: 1639
Convolvulus: 2480, 2485, 2488, 2489, 2490, 2491, 2494, 2495, 2496, 2497, 2498, 2499, 2500, 2501, 2504, 2507, 2508, 2509, 2510, 2511, 2512, 2513, 2518, 2519, 2520, 2521, 2523, 2524, 2537, 2609
Cook Range: 3461, 3468, 3469
Coral: 2305, 2337, 2339, 2342, 2344
Coronation Street: 3514, 3515, 3516, 3517, 3518, 3519
Cottage: 1725, 1745, 1848
Crab: 1270
Crab & Lobster: 1280, 1334, 1335, 1338, 1339, 1348, 1350, 1354, 1364
Crinoline: 1087
Crinoline Lady: 1705
Crocus: 1552, 1553, 1747, 1759, 1760, 1765, 1766, 1808, 1809, 1832
Curled Lettuce: 1367, 1372, 1374, 1375, 1380, 1382, 1383, 1385, 1386, 1389, 1390, 1391, 1392, 1412, 1542
Daffodil: 1732, 1780
Daisy: 1472, 1476, 1947, 1951
Delphinium: 2000, 2013, 2014, 2015, 2016, 2017, 2018, 2019
Denim: 3243, 3244, 3245, 3246, 3247, 3248, 3249, 3250
Dimple: 1133, 1134
Dogshead: 1866, 1914, 1915, 1916, 1917, 1918
Dolls Head: 1274, 1276, 1279, 1288, 1312, 1331, 1344, 1349, 1368
Dove or Pillar Range: 3336
Dovecote Range: 1263, 3262, 3267

Embossed: 3114, 3119, 3120
Embossed Birds: 2031
Embossed Flower: 1993, 2024, 2194, 2517
Embossed Flowers: 2035
Embossed Fruit: 2951
Embossed Salad: 3218, 3221
Engine Turned: 1487, 1488, 1489, 1490, 1491, 1492, 1493, 1494, 1495, 1496, 1497, 1498, 1499, 1500, 1502, 1561, 1562, 1573, 1590
Face: 3121
Fish: 1370
Fish Band: 1020, 1021, 1022, 1023, 1024, 1025
Floral Spray: 2639, 2641, 2642, 2644, 2654, 2655, 2656, 2657, 2658, 2659, 2664, 2665, 2666, 2667, 2668, 2669, 2670, 2671, 2672, 2674, 2675, 2676, 2677, 2678, 2679, 2680, 2681, 2682, 2683, 2684, 2685, 2686, 2687, 2688
Flow Blue - AW: 3177, 3181, 3184, 3187, 3190, 3191, 3193, 3200, 3202, 3203, 3204, 3205, 3206, 3216, 3224, 3233
Flower: 1544
Fluted: 2193, 2206, 2207, 2273, 2312
Forget-me-not: 1769
Foxglove: 1870, 1875, 1879, 1881, 1882, 1883, 1884, 1885, 1886, 1887, 1888, 1895, 1896, 1897, 1898, 1903, 1904
Fruit: 331, 1226, 1550, 1556, 1739, 2431, 2514, 2526, 2527, 2528, 2529, 2530, 2591, 2630, 2635, 2661, 2662, 2769, 2771, 2772, 2773, 2774, 2775, 2776, 2777, 2778, 2779, 2780, 2781, 2782, 2783, 2784, 3063, 3064, 3065, 3066, 3067, 3277, 3296, 3297, 3312, 3340
Fruit Basket: 245, 711, 760, 761, 830, 876, 995
Gazelle: 1217, 1223
Gladioli: 1744

Carlton Ware Patterns and Shapes

Gourmet: 3160, 3161, 3162, 3163, 3164, 3165, 3167, 3168, 3169, 3207, 3208, 3209, 3210, 3211, 3212, 3213, 3214, 3215, 3387, 3388, 3396, 3399

Grape: 2195, 2197, 2203, 2208, 2211, 2214, 2217, 2220, 2221, 2224, 2225, 2226, 2227, 2228, 2253, 2254, 2268, 2269, 2272, 2295, 2296, 2297, 2299, 2301, 2303, 2304

Green Apple Range: 3255

Guinness: 1255, 1282, 1464, 1485, 1681, 2060, 2222, 2298, 2308, 2317, 2319, 2320, 2322, 2325, 2331, 2360, 2365, 2375, 2378, 2398, 2399, 2401, 2421, 2463, 2556, 2566, 2584, 2602, 2619, 2627, 2632, 2637, 2643, 2663, 2689, 2690, 2703, 2704, 2705, 2709, 2720, 2722, 2728, 2750, 2751, 2752, 2756, 2757, 2758, 2759, 2760, 2765, 2767, 2768, 2770, 2793, 3330, 3409, 3471

Gum Nut: 949, 950, 952, 1009, 1010, 1011, 1035, 1036, 1037, 1038, 1040, 1043, 1044, 1045, 1063, 1064, 1066, 1082, 1084, 1086, 1089, 1100, 1101, 1126

Haig: 1271, 1406, 2433, 2434, 2437, 2505, 2506, 2660, 2879, 2886, 2924, 2933, 3253, 3254, 3359

Hazel Nut: 2277, 2306, 2307, 2309, 2310, 2311, 2313, 2316, 2318, 2321, 2324, 2326, 2327, 2330, 2357, 2358

Honeysuckle: 2628, 2629, 2633, 2634

Hovis: 3273, 3298, 3306, 3449, 3488, 3498, 3499, 3500, 3501, 3521

Hydrangea: 2086, 2154, 2161, 2165, 2167, 2169, 2170, 2171, 2172, 2173, 2174, 2176, 2209, 2210, 2219, 2261, 2264

Incised: 1290, 1291, 1292, 1293, 1294, 1295, 1296, 1297, 1298, 1299, 1300, 1301, 1302, 1303, 1304, 1305, 1306, 1307, 1308, 1309, 1310, 1320, 1321, 1322, 1323, 1324, 1325, 1326, 1853, 1856, 1871, 1889, 1890, 1891, 1892, 1893, 1894, 1923, 1924, 1925, 1926, 1927, 1928, 1929,

1930, 1931, 1932, 1933, 1934, 1935, 1936, 1937, 1938, 1939, 1940, 1941, 1942
Jaffa: 1065, 1088
Lampbase: 3094, 3095, 3096, 3097, 3098
Langouste: 2470, 2471, 2473, 2474, 2475, 2476, 2481, 2492, 2493, 2546
Late Buttercup or Buttercup Garland: 2030, 2046, 2047, 2055, 2061, 2062, 2063, 2064, 2065, 2066, 2068, 2069, 2074
Leaf: 1537, 1538, 1539, 1772, 2156, 2336, 2346, 2359, 2361, 2363, 2366, 2367, 2368, 2369, 2370, 2371, 2372, 2373, 2374, 2376, 2377, 2381, 2382, 2383, 2385, 2386, 2387, 2388, 2389, 2390, 2417
Lemon: 1170
Lily: 1868
Linen & Other: 2442, 2443, 2444, 2445, 2446, 2447, 2448, 2449, 2450
Lobster: 1267, 1269, 1272, 1273, 1277, 1278, 2125, 2185, 2186, 2218, 2230, 2231, 2232, 2242, 2243
Lucerne: 3438, 3439, 3443
Magnolia: 2515, 2531, 2558, 2559, 2560, 2561, 2562, 2563, 2564, 2571, 2592, 2593, 2594, 2595, 2596, 2597, 2598, 2599, 2601, 2604, 2605, 2607, 2610, 2611, 2612, 2613, 2615, 2616, 2617, 2618, 2620, 2621, 2622, 2623, 2624, 2625, 2626
Margarite: 1867
Military Figures: 2822, 2824, 2830, 2835, 2861
Moderne: 1245, 1246
Money Box: 3056, 3149, 3150, 3159, 3174, 3288, 3377, 3382, 3385
Money Box - Bug Eyes: 3128, 3129, 3130, 3131
Money Box - Flat Back: 2922, 2923, 2944, 2946, 2950, 3080, 3086, 3104, 3141, 3142

Carlton Ware Patterns and Shapes

Mugs & Jugs, Musical: 1213, 1260, 1284, 1285, 1289, 1330, 1543, 1549, 1685, 1972
Narcissus: 1767
New Buttercup and Somerset: 3009, 3016, 3021, 3024, 3025, 3026, 3027, 3028, 3029, 3030, 3031, 3032, 3033, 3035, 3036, 3037, 3038
New Daisy: 2043, 2044, 2045, 2056, 2402
Novelty: 1002, 1004, 1005, 1006, 1007, 1008, 1012, 1138, 1197, 1313, 1314, 1315, 1316, 1355, 1624, 1625, 1698, 1699, 1702, 1703, 1711, 1716, 1770, 2400, 2418, 2440, 2441, 2479, 2484, 2486, 2503, 2534, 2535, 2536, 2569, 2572, 2636, 2761, 2762, 2763, 2764, 2766, 2789, 2790, 2792, 2845, 2848, 2858, 2863, 3002, 3006, 3007, 3008, 3014, 3018, 3087, 3088, 3089, 3090, 3092, 3093, 3099, 3106, 3115, 3122, 3123, 3124, 3125, 3126, 3144, 3145, 3147, 3148, 3151, 3152, 3153, 3154, 3155, 3156, 3157, 3158, 3166, 3170, 3171, 3172, 3173, 3217, 3220, 3225, 3226, 3234, 3235, 3236, 3237, 3238, 3239, 3241, 3242, 3251, 3252, 3256, 3257, 3258, 3259, 3260, 3261, 3263, 3264, 3265, 3266, 3268, 3269, 3270, 3272, 3274, 3275, 3276, 3279, 3280, 3282, 3283, 3284, 3285, 3286, 3287, 3289, 3291, 3292, 3293, 3295, 3299, 3300, 3303, 3307, 3310, 3311, 3313, 3314, 3315, 3316, 3317, 3318, 3319, 3320, 3321, 3322, 3323, 3324, 3325, 3326, 3327, 3328, 3329, 3331, 3334, 3337, 3339, 3344, 3347, 3348, 3352, 3353, 3354, 3357, 3358, 3360, 3362, 3363, 3364, 3367, 3368, 3369, 3370, 3371, 3372, 3374, 3375, 3376, 3378, 3379, 3380, 3381, 3386, 3389, 3390, 3391, 3392, 3393, 3394, 3395, 3397, 3398, 3400, 3401, 3402, 3403, 3404, 3405, 3412, 3413, 3414, 3415, 3416, 3417, 3421, 3422, 3423, 3425, 3426, 3427, 3429, 3440, 3441, 3442, 3444, 3459, 3460, 3462, 3465, 3466, 3474, 3478, 3497, 3511, 3512, 3513, 3522, 3523, 3524, 3525, 3526, 3527,

3528, 3529, 3530, 3531, 3531, 3532, 3536, 3537, 3538, 3540, 3543, 3544, 3547
Oak Tree: 1098, 1143, 1144, 1145, 1146, 1147, 1148, 1149, 1155, 1162, 1163, 1164, 1165, 1166, 1167, 1168, 1169, 1175, 1183, 1185, 1186, 1187, 1188, 1189, 1190, 1191, 1192, 1193, 1194, 1208, 1214
Old Salad: 620
Old Water Lily: 1540, 1541
Orbit: 2639, 2641, 2642, 2644, 2654, 2655, 2656, 2657, 2658, 2659, 2664, 2665, 2666, 2667, 2668, 2669, 2670, 2671, 2672, 2674, 2675, 2676, 2677, 2678, 2679, 2680, 2681, 2682, 2683, 2684, 2685, 2686, 2687, 2688
Orchid: 2533, 2574, 2575, 2576, 2577, 2578, 2579, 2580, 2582, 2585, 2586
Ornament: 1003, 1016, 1017, 1018, 1019, 1046, 1047, 1049, 1050, 1051, 1052, 1056, 1061, 1083, 1085, 1090, 1091, 1092, 1093, 1102, 1130, 1202, 1203, 1204, 1261, 1517, 1518, 1519, 1520, 1521, 1535, 1536, 1726, 1731, 1802, 1812, 1813, 1814, 1815, 1816, 1817, 1818, 1819, 1821, 1822, 1823, 1824, 1825, 1826, 1827, 1828, 1829, 1830, 1831, 1833, 1834, 1835, 1836, 1837, 1838, 1839, 1840, 1841, 1842, 1843, 1844, 1845, 1846, 1847, 1849, 1850, 1851, 1852, 1854, 1857, 1858, 1859, 1860, 1861, 1862, 1863, 1864, 1865, 2082, 2083, 2255, 2539, 2540, 2541, 2542, 2543, 3132
Ornament Stand: 1899, 1900, 1901, 1902
Oslo: 2880, 2883, 2890, 2892, 2893, 2895, 2896, 2897, 2898, 2903, 2905, 2911, 2912, 2919, 2921
Oven Ware: 1094
Pear: 1039, 1474
Persian: 2815, 2816, 2817, 2818, 2819, 2820, 2821, 2823, 2825, 2826, 2827, 2828, 2829, 2831, 2832, 2833, 2834

Carlton Ware Patterns and Shapes

Perth: 3039, 3041, 3048, 3051, 3052, 3053, 3054
Pig: 3271
Pinstripe: 2419, 2428, 2429, 2430, 2435, 2439, 2451, 2452, 2453, 2454, 2455, 2456, 2457, 2458, 2461, 2462, 2464, 2465, 2466, 2467
Plain: 1557
Poppy: 1746, 1872, 2257, 2263, 2276, 2278, 2281, 2284, 2285, 2287, 2288, 2289, 2290, 2291, 2292, 2293, 2294
Poppy & Daisy (New Interior): 3503, 3507
Poppy and Daisy: 2010, 2033, 2034, 2042, 2051, 2053, 2054, 2057, 2079
Primula: 1975, 1982, 2005, 2012, 2036, 2038, 2039, 2040, 2041, 2048, 2049, 2052
Pyrethrum: 1751, 1757
Rabbit: 1137
Red Currant: 1603, 1605, 1606, 1607, 1637, 1656, 1657, 1658, 1659, 1660, 1679, 1708, 1730
Ribbed: 2244, 2245, 2265
Rings: 1356, 1357, 1358, 1359, 1360, 1361
Robertsons Golly: 3489, 3490, 3491, 3492, 3493, 3494, 3495, 3496, 3502
Rock Garden: 1237, 1238, 1239, 1240, 1241, 1243, 1244, 1247, 1248, 1249, 1250, 1251, 1252, 1253, 1254, 1262, 1264, 1265, 1287, 1336, 1337, 1353
Rope: 1616, 1640, 1641, 1642, 1643, 1644, 1645, 1646, 1647, 2058
Rope Pattern: 2097, 2100, 2101, 2102, 2103, 2104, 2105, 2106, 2107, 2110, 2111, 2112
Royalty: 1328, 1332, 1414, 1432, 1434, 1435
Salad Range: 3232
Salad Ware: 2092, 2093, 2094, 2095, 2096, 2099, 2131
Scroll: 2258
Shelf: 2538, 2544, 2545

Shell: 1973, 1976, 1978, 1979, 1980, 1981, 1992, 1994, 1996, 1997, 1998, 1999, 2087, 2145, 2196
Skye: 2804, 2813, 2814, 2846, 2847, 2849, 2850, 2852, 2853, 2854, 2856, 2857, 2888, 2889
Spectrum: 3103, 3105, 3108, 3109, 3113
Spiral: 2235, 2236, 2237, 2238, 2239, 2240, 2279, 2280, 2282, 2283, 2286
Stone Ware: 1070, 1071, 1072, 1073, 1074, 1075, 1076, 1077, 1078, 1079, 1080, 1081, 1103, 1104, 1105, 1106, 1107, 1108, 1109, 1110, 1111, 1112, 1113, 1114, 1115, 1116, 1117, 1118, 1119, 1120, 1121, 1122, 1123, 1124, 1140, 1161, 1171, 1172, 1177, 1178, 1179, 1180, 1181, 1182, 1205, 1211, 1212, 1567
Strawberry: 1396
Sunflower: 2954, 2973, 2974, 2975, 2976, 2977, 2978, 2979, 2980, 2981, 2982, 2983, 2984, 2986, 2988, 2990, 2991, 2992, 2994, 2995, 2997, 2998, 3000
Swirl: 1974
Tangier: 3057, 3059, 3060, 3062, 3068, 3070, 3071, 3072, 3076, 3077, 3078, 3079
Tapestry & Daisy Chain: 2700, 2707, 2710, 2711, 2712, 2713, 2714, 2715, 2716, 2717, 2718, 2719, 2721, 2724, 2725, 2726, 2729, 2730, 2731, 2732, 2733, 2734, 2737, 2738, 2742, 2743, 2744, 2745, 2746, 2747, 2748, 2749, 2754
Thistle: 1576, 1577, 1578, 1579
Toby Jug: 3061, 3230, 3231
Tomato: 1748
Trinket Range: 3458
Trinket Set: 2588, 2589, 2590, 2603
Tulip: 1403, 1404, 1416, 1417, 1418, 1419, 1420, 1421, 1422, 1439, 1453, 1457, 1459, 1461, 1736, 1811, 2483
Utility Ware: 3450, 3451, 3452, 3453, 3454, 3455, 3456

Vine or Canterbury: 2872, 2878, 2881, 2882, 2884, 2885, 2887, 2891, 2894, 2899, 2901, 2902, 2904, 2907, 2909, 2910, 2917, 2920
Walking Ware Big Feet: 3373
Walking Ware Caribbean Series: 3290
Walking Ware First Range: 3143, 3194, 3195, 3196, 3197, 3198, 3199, 3228, 3229
Walking Ware Other Items: 3219, 3227, 3240, 3281, 3294, 3301, 3304, 3308, 3309, 3332, 3345, 3346, 3350, 3356
Walking Ware Running Jumping Standing: 3290
Wallflower: 1752, 1758, 1763, 1995, 2020, 2021, 2022, 2023, 2025, 2026, 2027, 2028, 2029, 2032
Warwick: 2867, 2873, 2874, 2875, 2876, 2877
Water Lily: 1588, 1718, 1738, 1741, 1750, 1773, 1774, 1776, 1777, 1778, 1779, 1781, 1782, 1783, 1784, 1786, 1787, 1788, 1789, 1798, 1801, 1804, 1805, 1806, 1820, 1952
Wedding Cake: 1717, 1742, 1743, 1785, 1790, 1791, 1793, 1794, 1795, 1796, 1797, 1800, 1905, 1906, 1948, 1949
Wellington: 2954, 2973, 2974, 2975, 2976, 2977, 2978, 2979, 2980, 2981, 2982, 2983, 2984, 2986, 2988, 2990, 2991, 2992, 2994, 2995, 2997, 2998, 3000
Wild Rose: 1551, 1554, 1555, 1724, 2108, 2114, 2115, 2116, 2117, 2118, 2119, 2120, 2121, 2122, 2123, 2124, 2132
Windswept: 2394, 2395, 2396, 2403, 2404, 2405, 2406, 2407, 2408, 2409, 2411, 2414, 2415, 2416, 2422, 2423, 2424, 2425, 2426, 2438
Wood: 2468, 2469, 2482, 2487

Printed in Great Britain
by Amazon